D1134644

Atlas of
Adult Autopsy Pathology

Atlas of
Adult Autopsy Pathology

Julian Burton, MBChB(Hons), MEd, FHEA
Lead Coronial Pathologist
The Medico-Legal Centre
Sheffield
South Yorkshire
United Kingdom

Sarah Saunders, BSc(Hons), MBChB, MD, DMJ (Path), PGCert Clin.Ed, FHEA
Speciality Registrar
Department of Cellular Pathology
Royal Devon & Exeter Hospital
Devon
United Kingdom

Stuart Hamilton, MBChB, BMSc(Hons), FRCPath, MFFLM
Home Office Registered Forensic Pathologist
East Midlands Forensic Pathology Unit
Leicester
United Kingdom

CRC Press
Taylor & Francis Group
Boca Raton   London   New York

CRC Press is an imprint of the
Taylor & Francis Group, an **informa** business

CRC Press
Taylor & Francis Group
6000 Broken Sound Parkway NW, Suite 300
Boca Raton, FL 33487-2742

© 2015 by Taylor & Francis Group, LLC
CRC Press is an imprint of Taylor & Francis Group, an Informa business

No claim to original U.S. Government works

Printed and bound in India by Replika Press Pvt. Ltd.

Printed on acid-free paper
Version Date: 20150519

International Standard Book Number-13: 978-1-4441-3752-1 (Pack - Book and Ebook)

Visit the Taylor & Francis Web site at
http://www.taylorandfrancis.com

and the CRC Press Web site at
http://www.crcpress.com

Contents

Acknowledgments

We would like to thank the following people who helped us during the preparation of this book and to whom we are indebted:

- Dr. C. A. Schandl and Dr. C. J. Salgado who kindly provided images for Chapter 1.

- Dr. S. K. Suvarna who kindly provided some images needed for Chapters 3, 4, and 13.

- American Medical Systems who kindly provided an image for Chapter 14.

- Drs. C. Mason, C. Keen, A. Jeffrey, and J. Denson who allowed us to browse through their archived image collections to source missing images.

- CRC Press and the Editors of *Forensic Neuropathology, Practical Cardiovascular Pathology 2e* and *Knight's Forensic Pathology 3e* for kindly allowing us to use some images from their textbooks.

- The anatomical pathology technicians at The Medico-Legal Centre in Sheffield for their help, support, and patience.

- Kay Conerly, Jennifer Blaise, and Charlene Counsellor at CRC Press for keeping us motivated, focused and on track throughout the production of this book.

- Caroline Makepeace of Hodder Arnold who played an important role in the initial development of the project proposal.

- Most importantly, we thank the patients whose autopsy examinations made this atlas possible. The book adheres to current GMC guidelines related to images acquired at autopsy examination.

Introduction

The last 15 years have witnessed significant changes to adult autopsy practice. First, there has been the virtual extinction of the hospital or consented autopsy, performed with the permission of the deceased's relatives usually at the request of the deceased's clinician. In many centres such consented autopsies now account for far less than 5 per cent of the autopsy workload. Consequently the vast majority of autopsies are now performed on the instruction of a medico-legal authority, and most of these relate to sudden and unexpected deaths in the community. Many medico-legal authorities are unwilling to permit or pay for histological examinations if the autopsy allows the pathologist to determine the cause of death on the balance of probability based on macroscopic findings. There is often no remit within medico-legal autopsies to retain tissue from interesting but seemingly coincidental pathology that is unrelated to the cause of death.

Today, the majority of autopsies around the globe are performed by histopathologists (surgical pathologists) without a special interest in autopsy practice. Many histopathologists now face increasing demands on their time from the samples taken from the living. Amongst other reasons these time pressures have resulted in some histopathologists withdrawing from autopsy work. Hospital laboratories have become less willing to subsidize the work of the medico-legal authority and are less willing to absorb the cost of histopathology relating to medico-legal autopsies.

Finally, the quality of autopsy work has come under increasing scrutiny from both the general public and national bodies with oversight of autopsy practice. The standard of autopsy practice is frequently criticized. Nonetheless the standard expected of pathologists engaged in autopsy practice has definitely increased and this area of practice has become more litigious. The days when pathologists could consider medico-legal autopsies to be an easy source of extra income have passed.

Together these changes conspire to produce some significant challenges for those hoping to develop or maintain competence in autopsy practice. Those learning to perform autopsies will generally develop competence in the basic autopsy techniques of external examination, evisceration and dissection within 20–30 examinations. Achieving proficiency and an ability to perform less common autopsy techniques is undoubtedly more difficult. The greatest challenge is learning to identify and interpret pathological findings as they are discovered at autopsy, relate them to the clinical history and formulate a cause of death. Although much of the pathology encountered at autopsy is discussed in undergraduate medical curricula the decline in the hospital autopsy means that pathologists learning to practice struggle to encounter all of the common pathologies prior to the completion of training, let alone the less common but important diseases. In our experience it is not unusual to encounter pathologists nearing the end of training who have yet to see a range of commonly identified pathologies in their autopsy practice. This is exacerbated by the restrictions pertaining to medico-legal autopsies which impede or make impossible the practice of being able to sample abnormalities and compare the macroscopic appearances with the microscopic findings. It was the reality of these limitations, as well as our observation that there were few books available that helped to navigate trainees who may struggle to identify pathologies seen at autopsy, that led us to create this atlas.

Some pathologies, but not all, might be seen by a pathologist in their surgical pathology practice and/or training, but many trainees struggle to make connections between the pathology they see in that arena which may not look the same to them at autopsy. Unlike other atlases, this isn't just an image collection; this atlas also provides advice on how to interpret the macroscopic findings and suggests when further investigations will be useful. At present, we suspect that pathologists generally gain the information in this atlas through experience.

By its nature, histopathology training teaches people to interpret the microscopic appearances of tissues and to make diagnoses based largely on these within the context of a clinical history. Although they draw on a similar basic knowledge set, autopsies require a uniquely different skill set. Histopathology certainly plays a vital role in the post mortem diagnosis of some fatal conditions but those performing autopsies must place greater reliance on the evidence gained by naked-eye examination; this atlas is designed to help build confidence in that visualization skill set.

How to Use This Book

The atlas is organized to reflect the sequence in which an autopsy is performed, that is: external examination, internal examination, and then histology. When deciding what images to include and exclude, we used the following litmus tests:

- Is this a commonly encountered pathology?
- Is this a pathology that is rare but important?
- Is this a pathology that trainees often struggle to identify?
- Is this a pathology that we have encountered within 3 years of autopsy practice?

Pathologies that did not meet any of the above criteria were not included in the book.

There are two ways in which you might choose to use this atlas. You might wish to read it as a textbook, starting at the beginning and working your way through to the end. Indeed, we recommend this approach for junior pathologists in training who are about to embark on their autopsy training, or who have performed only a small number of autopsies. While nothing can replace the experience of seeing and touching pathology in the postmortem room, we hope that this will help you to become familiar with some of the common pathologies that you will encounter.

This atlas does not aim to discuss the approach to every autopsy scenario as this has been discussed elsewhere in detail.[1] However, many autopsy findings should prompt further investigations, and where this is the case we have indicated it in the text. More advanced autopsy practitioners are recommended to regard this atlas as a reference text, and we recommend that it be kept close by the postmortem room. In this way it can be used as a reference to familiarize oneself with pathologies that one expects to encounter having read the available clinical history. It will also then be possible to readily step out of the postmortem room and review the book should you find something unexpected that you have not encountered before!

However you choose to use this book, we hope that you will find it helpful in developing your autopsy skills.

Reference

1. Burton JL, Rutty GN (Eds). 2010. The Hospital Autopsy: a manual of fundamental autopsy practice. 3rd ed. Hodder Arnold: London.

Further Reading

NCEPOD. The Coroner's Autopsy: do we deserve better? National Confidential Enquiry into Patient Outcome and Death, London, 2006. Available online at: http://www.ncepod.org.uk/2006.htm.

Chapter 1

External Examination
Natural Disease and Common Artifacts

Introduction

Before undertaking the evisceration and internal examination it is essential that the pathologist perform a systematic and thorough external examination. It is a common misconception that the external examination is less important than the internal examination. As a result the examination is often poorly conducted and documented.[1] The external examination yields not only important information about the natural diseases the deceased suffered from in life, but also information on the time, place, and manner of death, as well as contributing toward the identification of the deceased.[2]

The first and most important part of the external examination is to confirm the identity of the deceased. Local practice varies; however, this is typically done by checking identification bands around the wrists or ankles of the body. The pathologist must not begin the autopsy until satisfied that an adequate identification has been made. It is the pathologist's responsibility to ensure that the correct body is examined by autopsy, and it should be remembered that performing an autopsy examination on the wrong body is unlawful in many jurisdictions. It is good practice to record how identification was established in the autopsy report; for example: "The body was identified by means of an identification band around the right wrist stating the correct mortuary number, name, and date of birth."

The Royal College of Pathologists' guidelines on autopsy practice state that, as a minimum, the sex, ethnicity, apparent age, weight, crown-heel length, body mass index, and injuries specifically to the eyes, genitalia, and anus must be reported in every case.[3] General features such as the style, length, and color of the head hair, general cleanliness of the body, and the presence or absence of natural teeth should be noted. The eyes should be inspected to look for the presence of petechial hemorrhages and natural disease. The color of the irides can change after death. Blue and gray eyes may turn brown. The external examination should include both the front and back of the body, without exception, even in decomposed bodies.

If present, a description of the clothing should be made, noting features such as staining or tearing of the material. Any jewelry should be described.

The presence, location, and type of any body modifications should be recorded. Body modifications include tattoos and piercings, along with branding and scarification.[4] These can be important in aiding identification in cases where the identity of the deceased has not yet been established. The site, size, type, and depiction of the tattoo should be noted. Although some tattoos are said to have specific connotations in certain cultures and subcultures, the increase in the prevalence of tattoos in the general population means that interpretation should be approached with caution.

As with a clinical examination in living patients, the external examination can provide clues to the presence of systemic diseases. A thorough examination of the hands, skin, and joints should be performed. In all cases the presence or absence of anemia, jaundice, and cyanosis, as well as edema, lymphadenopathy, abnormal skin pigmentation, and lesions, should be recorded.[1] The hands, in particular the nails, can give indications of natural disease, for example, clubbing, leukonychia, koilonychia, pitting, and splinter hemorrhages.

It is imperative to identify suspicious injuries that may result from criminal activity early, in order to stop the autopsy and refer to senior colleagues or a forensic pathologist. This is to minimize the loss of important trace evidence or further disturbance of pathological features and also to prevent the pathologist from working beyond his or her medicolegal expertise. Documentation of injuries and marks of medical intervention is critical; this is discussed in Chapter 2.

Pathologists need to be able to identify normal postmortem changes and artifacts generated by cardiopulmonary resuscitation and postmortem handling of the body. This is important to prevent incorrect interpretations of these changes. The author has seen early *tache noir* formation in a young child that was interpreted as conjunctival hemorrhage leading to an unnecessary investigation into potential child abuse.

This chapter presents common findings on external examination and how to identify post-mortem changes and artifacts.

Body Modification

◀ **Figure 1.1a** Professional tattoos

Tattooing is the creation of permanent pigmentation by the insertion of non-native pigments into the dermis of the skin. Modern professional tattoos are made by using an electric tattoo machine, which is composed of a group of needles mounted onto an oscillating unit. This repeatedly punctures the skin and injects the ink particles into the dermis. Designs of tattoos are as varied as the people who have them. Tattoos may be found on any part of the body including the scalp, inner surface of the lips, and the genitals.

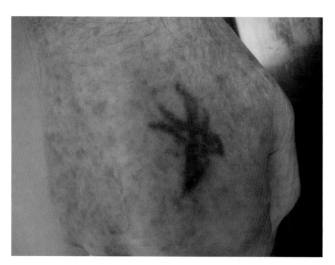

◀ **Figure 1.1b** Professional tattoos

The site, size, type, and depiction of the tattoo should be noted. Tattoos can be extremely important for identification. Not all designs are unique because they can be taken from a tattooist's "art book." However, some individuals design their own tattoos or have unique "one off" designs. Photographs of such tattoos can be shown to relatives to aid identification if viewing of the body is not practicable.[4]

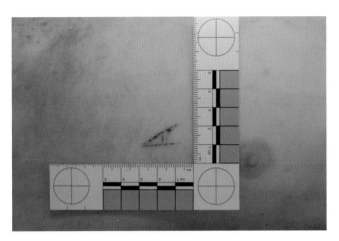

◀ **Figure 1.2** Homemade tattoos

Homemade tattoos are created using a more crude method of pigment insertion than professional tattoos. This is typically done with a sharp instrument, such as a needle, knife, or pen with writing ink, charcoal, or ash forming simple designs or words. These usually involve only one color of ink. They are often created in institutions such as prison, performed by the individual or by another inmate or gang member. Homemade tattoos raise the possibility of suboptimal hygiene and should alert the pathologist to a possibly increased risk of bloodborne infections.[5] (Image courtesy of Dr. A. Jeffrey.)

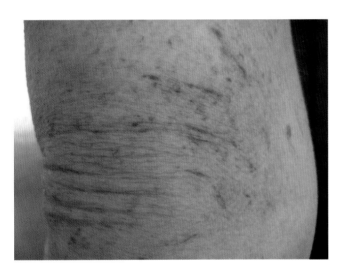

◀ **Figure 1.3** Occupational tattoos

Nonintentional tattoos may occur as a result of lifestyle or occupation. Coal miners comprise one group of individuals who commonly had occupational tattoos. The carbon dust tattooing on the face, hands, and bony prominences of coal miners used to be a common occurrence, but it is a vanishing observation. The presence of such dust tattooing may indicate an increased risk of associated industrial disease.

3

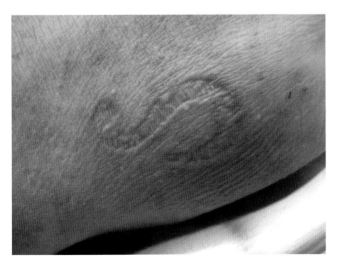

◀ **Figure 1.4** Branding

Human branding is a process in which a mark, usually a symbol or pattern, is burned into the skin with the intention to cause scarring. This is performed using a very hot or very cold branding iron dipped in liquid nitrogen. In the past the technique was used as a form of punishment or as a mark of ownership for slaves or oppressed persons. The practice is having a resurgence, especially in US students as a "rite of passage" to college fraternities or sororities, but it is still relatively uncommon in the United Kingdom.[5]

Genitalia

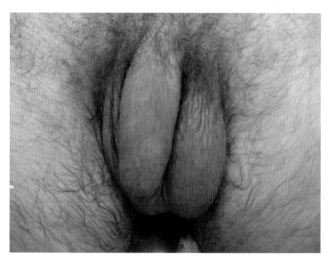

◀ **Figure 1.5** Normal male external genitalia
The appearance of the normal male external genitalia varies greatly among individuals. The genitals are composed of the penis and scrotum. The penis has a shaft with the glans penis at the end and the opening to the urethra, termed the meatus. The penis may have a foreskin, or this may have been removed (circumcision).

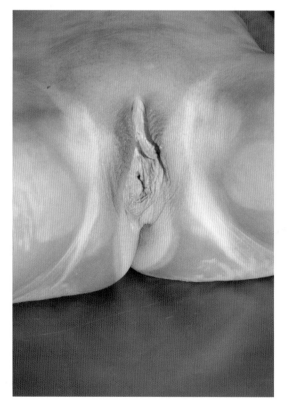

◀ **Figure 1.6a** Normal female genitalia
The appearance of the normal female external genitalia varies greatly among individuals. It is important for pathologists to be able recognize what is normal so that abnormal features such as trauma can be readily determined.

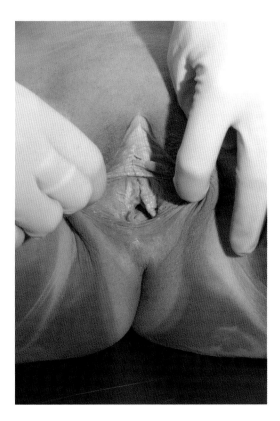

◀ **Figure 1.6b** Normal female genitalia
The female genitals are composed of the clitoris, the outer labia majora (singular, labium majus), and the inner labia minora (singular, labium minus). Lying in between the labia minora are the openings to the vagina and the urethra. Posterior to these structures are the perineum and anus.

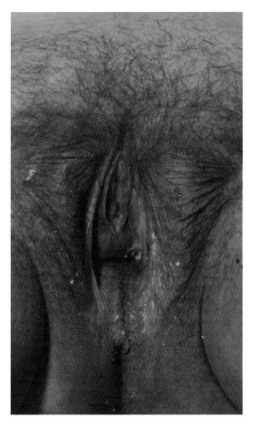

◀ **Figure 1.7** Transsexual genitalia: male to female
Gender reassignment surgery for male to female involves the skin being stripped from the penis and inverted to form a vagina. The muscles of the perineum are separated to allow the inversion of the new vagina. The glans is separated and fashioned into the clitoris and the urethra is shortened. The scrotum is split and the testicles removed. The residual skin is then used to form the labia. The body may show signs of further surgery such as breast implants and surgery to modify the profile of the prominence of the thyroid cartilage (Adam's apple) or jawline.

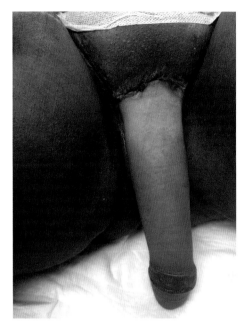

◀ **Figure 1.8** Transsexual genitalia: female to male
Gender reassignment surgery for female to male is a more complex surgical procedure and can be very varied in its appearance.

Prior to surgery androgenic hormones are given to enlarge the clitoris. During the surgery a penis is constructed using tissue graft, commonly from the arm, thigh, or abdomen. The urethra is then rerouted through the newly constructed penis. The labia majora are sutured to form a scrotum with prosthetic testicles. In more advanced procedures erectile devices can be implanted to produce erections. The body may show signs of other surgery such as bilateral mastectomy, hysterectomy, and removal of the ovaries.

This example demonstrates a radial forearm phalloplasty four months post surgery. Note that the surgery results in scars along the inguinal creases, scrotum, and shaft of the penis. (Image courtesy of Dr. C. J. Salgado.)

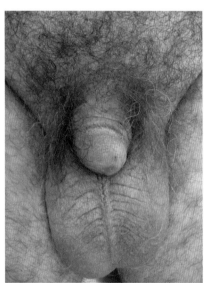

◀ **Figure 1.9** Circumcision: male
Male circumcision is the removal of some or all of the foreskin. This can be done for religious reasons, perceived hygiene reasons, or for medical reasons. Faith groups, namely Islam and Judaism undertake the practice on young infants, traditionally 7–8 days old. Medical indications for circumcision include phimosis (tight inelastic foreskin) and balanitis (inflammation of the glans penis and/or foreskin). Circumcision can lead to increased thickening of the skin covering the glans penis (keratinization). The presence or absence of the foreskin can be used to assist in the identification of the deceased.

Eyes

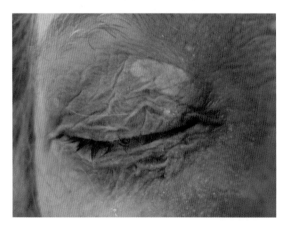

◀ **Figure 1.10** Xanthelasma
Xanthelasma are well-defined yellow plaques seen over the upper or lower eyelids. They are areas of lipid-containing macrophages in the skin. Approximately 50% of individuals with xanthelasmata have elevated plasma lipid levels. These plaques may be associated with familial hyperlipidemia. The presence of the lesions should prompt further assessment for atherosclerotic disease.

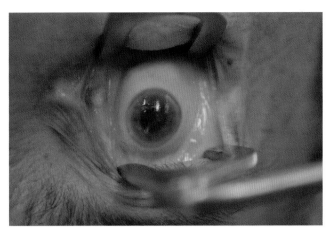

◀ **Figure 1.11** Arcus senilis

Arcus senilis (or corneal arcus) is a white or gray opaque ring around the iris. It is often present in older persons, and when present in individuals more than 65 years old it has no clinical significance. In younger adults arcus senilis is associated with hypercholesterolemia. A unilateral arcus can be a sign of decreased blood flow resulting from carotid artery disease or ocular hypotony.

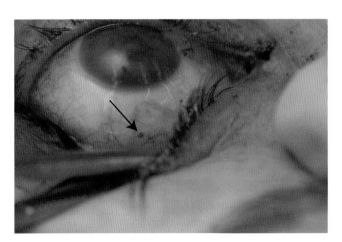

◀ **Figure 1.12a** Petechial hemorrhages

Petechial hemorrhages (also known as petechiae) are pinpoint hemorrhages in the skin, sclera, and conjunctivae or under serous membranes such as the pleura or pericardium. By definition they are less than 2 mm in diameter, and they occur as a result of venous engorgement usually from mechanical obstruction of venous return to the heart.

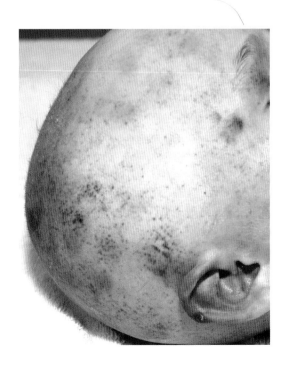

◀ **Figure 1.12b** Petechial hemorrhages

Conjunctival petechial hemorrhages should alert the pathologist to a possible asphyxial mechanism of death, especially manual strangulation, crush, or positional asphyxia. However, they can be seen in natural mechanisms such as acute cardiac death. For this reason the mouth and the eyes should be examined in every case, and the presence of these hemorrhages interpreted in the context of other pathological findings.

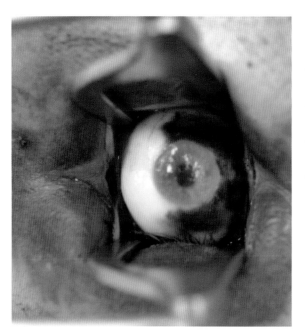

◀ **Figure 1.13** Scleral hemorrhages

Scleral hemorrhages (or subconjunctival hemorrhages) are areas of bleeding underneath the conjunctiva. These are larger than petechial hemorrhages. This condition can be related to increased blood pressure, trauma, or a base of skull fracture. Their presence should alert the pathologist to a possible asphyxial or traumatic mechanism of death. The presence of scleral hemorrhages should prompt a layered dissection of the neck and referral of the autopsy to a forensic pathologist if this reveals bruising.

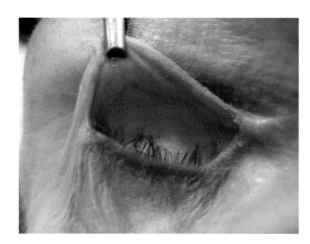

◀ **Figure 1.14** Anemia

Anemia is said to be present when the hemoglobin level is more than two standard deviations below the mean hemoglobin for that sex and age. Anemia will be apparent only if the hemoglobin concentration of the blood is less than 9 g/L.[6,7] It is suggested by pallor of the conjunctivae and palmar creases, as in living patients. Its presence can indicate chronic disease or a significant internal or external hemorrhage.

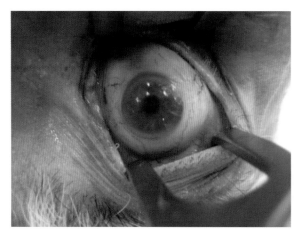

◀ **Figure 1.15** Jaundice

Jaundice, as a result of elevated bilirubin levels in the blood, can result from a range of pathological processes from acute short-lived illness (e.g., hepatitis A) to chronic disease (e.g., decompensated cirrhosis). Jaundice is classed as prehepatic, hepatic, or posthepatic. This distinction may be evident from the past medical history provided, but samples of liver may be required for histological examination to determine the cause of the jaundice.

Jaundice appears first in the conjunctiva. There may be other stigmata of chronic liver disease such as spider nevi, palmar erythema, or Dupuytren contracture.

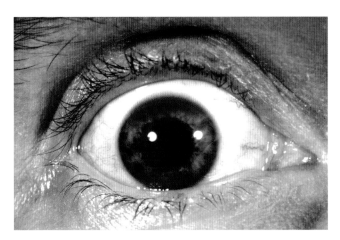

◀ **Figure 1.16** Kayser-Fleischer ring

Kayser-Fleischer rings are dark brown rings seen encircling the iris of the eye. They may be difficult to see in the early stages without slit-lamp examination. They occur as a result of copper deposition associated with Wilson disease. Wilson disease is a rare autosomal recessive disorder causing abnormal copper handling by the liver that results in the accumulation of copper in the body. The disease can lead to chronic liver disease and fulminant liver failure, along with neuropsychiatric disorders, cardiomyopathy, and renal diseases.

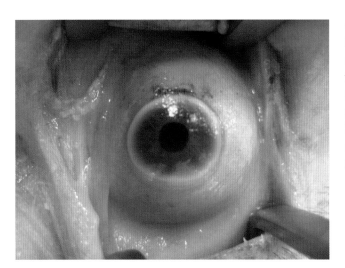

◀ **Figure 1.17** Blue sclera (osteogenesis imperfecta)

Osteogenesis imperfecta is an inherited disorder of collagen synthesis. Of the eight types described, types I and III are characterized in part by a blue-gray discoloration of the sclera. Patients typically also have a history of frequent pathological fractures and hearing loss. This patient, with an autosomal dominant form of osteogenesis imperfecta, also has a pronounced arcus senilis.

9

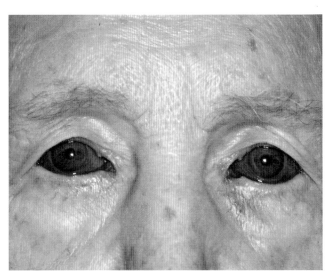

◀ **Figure 1.18** Argyrosis

Argyrosis is caused by exposure to compounds of silver and silver dust, resulting in a blue-gray discoloration of tissues. In generalized argyria the skin is affected, but the changes can be more localized, affecting the mucous membranes or, as in this photograph, the sclera.

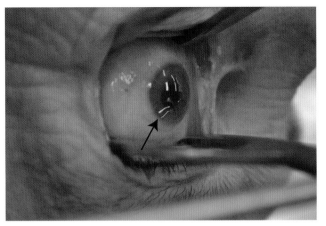

◀ **Figure 1.19** Contact lens
A contact lens is a corrective, cosmetic, or therapeutic lens usually placed on the cornea of the eye. Corrective contact lenses are designed to improve vision by correcting refraction errors. These are the most common lenses seen. Cosmetic lenses are used to alter the appearance of the eye, such as color or different pupil shape. Therapeutic lenses are used in the management of nonrefractive disorders of the eye such as corneal ulcers, erosions, and keratitis. They protect the injured or diseased cornea from the constant rubbing of blinking eyelids, thereby allowing the cornea to heal.

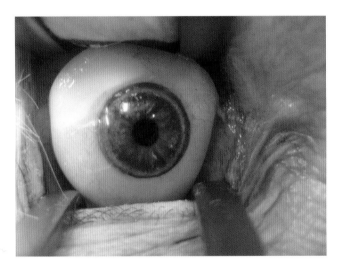

◀ **Figure 1.20** Glass eye
Glass eyes (or ocular prostheses) are medical devices used to replace an absent natural eye following its removal because of trauma or malignant disease. The prostheses fit over orbital implants and under the eyelids. The prostheses are typically made of medical-grade plastic, acrylic, or more rarely cryolite glass. A variant of the ocular prosthesis is a very thin, hard shell known as a scleral shell that can be worn over a damaged eye.

Head and Neck

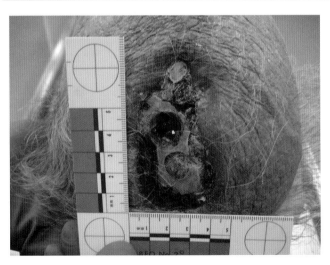

◀ **Figure 1.21** Squamous cell carcinoma of the scalp
The association between skin cancers and exposure to ultraviolet light is well known, and squamous cell carcinoma of the skin is commonly seen in sun-exposed skin, such as that of the scalp (as in this example), face, forearms, hands, and shins. In this example of a locally advanced squamous cell carcinoma of the scalp, the tumor is indurated, focally necrotic, and ulcerated. The tumor was invading into the calvarium. Metastases are rare.

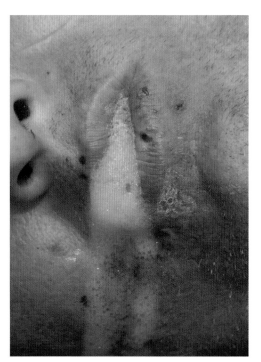

◀ Figure 1.22 Plume

A plume of foam, formed from a combination of pulmonary edema fluid and surfactant, at the mouth and/or nose may be seen in patients who have drowned. Such plumes are also sometimes seen in patients with severe acute left ventricular failure resulting from cardiac disease (described as pink tinged), head injury, or drug overdose. The plume dissipates rapidly and can often be absent at autopsy but may be seen by witnesses at the scene of death, such as in bodies pulled from water. See also Figure 4.10.

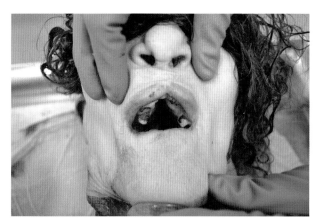

◀ Figure 1.23 Cleft lip and palate

These are common congenital abnormalities. They are rarely encountered at autopsy because most patients now undergo reconstructive plastic surgery. In this patient, note the left paramedian scar on the upper lip (to the right of the image) indicative of a repaired cleft lip. A defect in the midline of the hard palate is visible through the opened mouth. This patient also has marked dental caries.

11

Nails and Hands

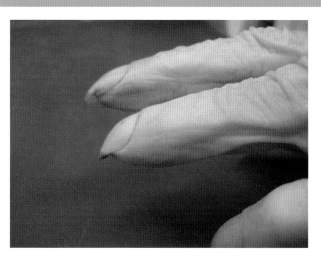

◀ Figure 1.24 Finger clubbing

Clubbing of the fingernails (also known as drumstick fingers) has a wide range of causes, including cyanotic heart disease, subacute bacterial endocarditis, suppurative lung diseases, pulmonary fibrosis, lung cancer, mesothelioma, chronic idiopathic inflammatory bowel disease, and cirrhosis. The presence of clubbing should prompt the pathologist to think about such differential diagnoses before the internal examination.

◄ Figure 1.25 Tar staining of the fingers

The smoking history of the deceased is not always known at the time of autopsy. In smokers, and particularly in those who roll their own cigarettes, there may be a focal brown discoloration of the skin of the fingers (typically the index and middle fingers) with or without associated discoloration of the fingernails. The discoloration results from deposition of tar (and not, as commonly thought, nicotine) on the skin.

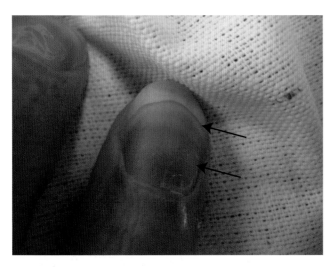

◄ Figure 1.26 Mees lines

Mees lines are single or multiple transverse white bands across the nail plate. They are classically seen in patients subjected to poisoning with arsenic, thallium, or other heavy metals. However, they can be a nonspecific reaction pattern in conditions such as Hodgkin disease, heart failure, leprosy, malaria, chemotherapy, and carbon monoxide poisoning.

◄ Figure 1.27 Osteoarthritis

Osteoarthritis is a common arthropathy in adults. It is characterized by progressive cartilage loss and hypertrophic changes to the surrounding bones, which lead to progressive degeneration of joints in the absence of inflammation. The hands, hips, and knees are most commonly affected. Bony swelling of the distal and proximal interphalangeal joints (Heberden and Bouchard nodes) and squaring of the thumb base can be easily seen in the hands.[6]

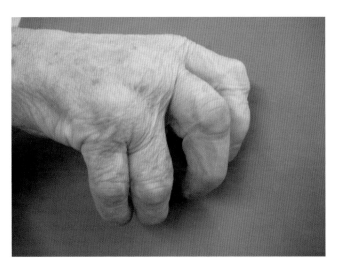

◀ Figure 1.28a Rheumatoid arthritis

Rheumatoid arthritis is a systematic autoimmune disease characterized by chronic, symmetrical, and erosive arthritis of the synovial joints. It is more frequent in women. The most common location for signs at autopsy is the hands. Features such as ulnar deviation of the hands and flexion-hyperextension (swan-neck) deformities of the fingers will be seen in varying degrees depending on the severity of the disease.[6]

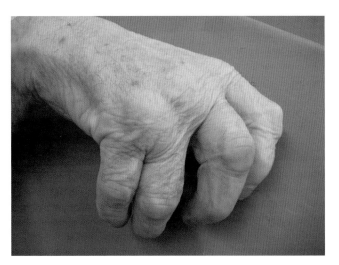

◀ Figure 1.28b Rheumatoid arthritis

13

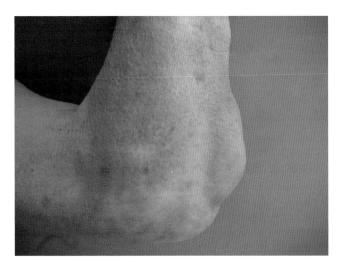

◀ Figure 1.29 Rheumatoid nodules

Rheumatoid nodules are firm, nontender nodules occurring in one fourth of patients with rheumatoid arthritis. The nodules appear in the soft tissue over bony prominences such as the elbow. They can also appear in visceral organs such as the heart and lungs. They range greatly in diameter from a few millimeters up to several centimeters. They can be movable or fixed when attached to underlying tendons or fascia. They have a firm, fibrous outer shell with central necrosis.

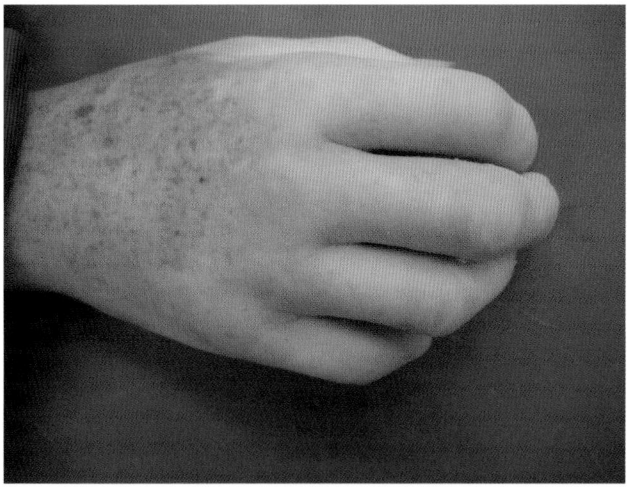

◀ **Figure 1.30** Sclerodactyly

Patients with certain autoimmune disorders, such as systemic sclerosis (scleroderma), and mixed connective tissue disorders may develop a thickening of the skin of the fingers and toes known as sclerodactyly. The fingers appear "sausage-like," and the skin has a waxy appearance and feels thickened.

Vascular Disease

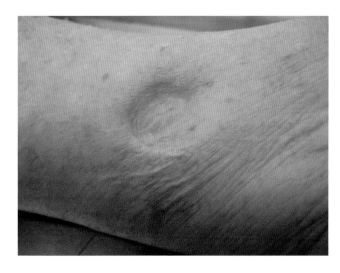

◀ **Figure 1.31** Pitting edema

When edema is present its location should be noted. Pitting edema is found in patients with right ventricular failure, protein-losing enteropathy, chronic liver disease, nephrotic syndrome, and kwashiorkor. The edema can be generalized or restricted to the legs or sacral region. As in clinical practice, this finding can be demonstrated by pressing the area with a thumb to see whether there is pitting.

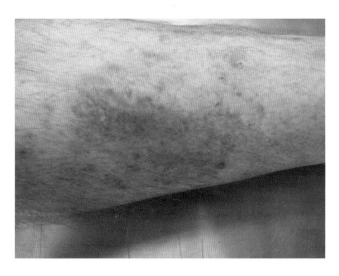

◀ **Figure 1.32a** Chronic venous insufficiency

Chronic venous insufficiency occurs as a result of an increase in venous pressure in the legs. This can be caused by incompetent valves in the deep or superficial veins or thrombosis in deep veins that leads to obstruction to venous flow (with or without valve damage). As a result there is leakage of blood constituents into the surrounding tissues that causes inflammation. There is also lymphedema, with chronic swelling of the legs and ankles, with discoloration and thickening of the skin (venous eczema). The condition can also lead to ulcers and cellulitis. Shown here are (a) a mild example and (b) a more severe case.

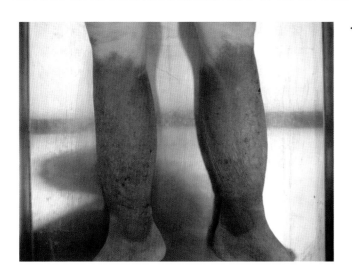

◀ **Figure 1.32b** Severe chronic venous insufficiency

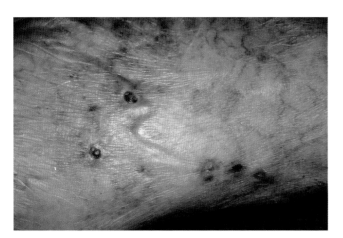

◀ **Figure 1.33** Venous ulcers

Venous ulcers are caused by incompetent valves in the veins of the lower leg, especially in the perforator veins. These incompetent valves cause blood to be diverted out into the superficial veins when the calf muscles are contracted. Dilation of theses superficial veins occurs (varicosities), and the raised venous pressure results in edema, venous eczema, and ulceration.

15

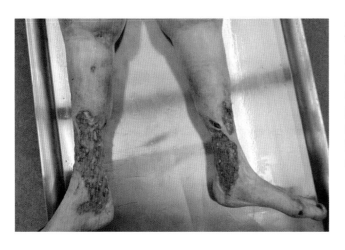

◀ **Figure 1.34** Infected venous ulcers

Venous ulcers are usually large, shallow, painless, and situated around the medial or lateral malleoli. They are associated with other signs of venous hypertension such as varicose veins, varicose eczema, and hemosiderin pigmentation. They can be very difficult to heal and require specialist nursing. In some cases, such as this image, they can become infected and produce a copious discharge and an offensive odor.

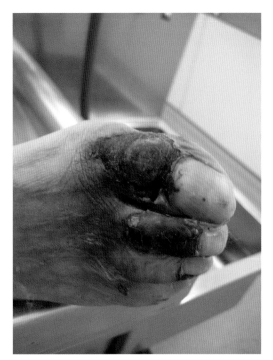

◀ **Figure 1.35** Gangrene

Necrosis of tissues secondary to an insufficient blood supply results in gangrene. In dry gangrene, as in this example from a diabetic patient, the affected tissues become blackened, dry, and firm, and there is little if any associated odor. Autoamputation may result. If such tissues become infected, wet gangrene supervenes; this is odoriferous, and the tissues are wet and slimy.

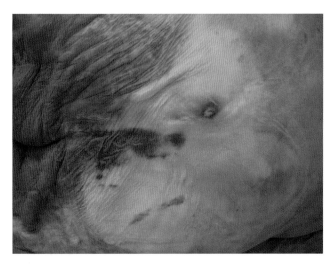

◀ **Figure 1.36a** Superficial pressure sore

A pressure sore (or decubitus ulcer) is localized injury to the skin and/or underlying tissue usually over a bony prominence, as a result of pressure or pressure in combination with shearing force and/or friction. There are many contributing factors such as malnutrition, increasing age, urinary or fecal incontinence, immobility, spinal injury, and poor nursing care, to name a few.

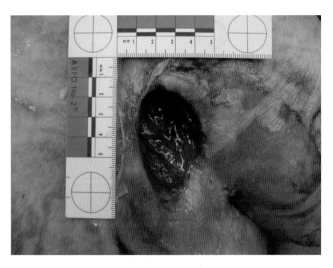

◀ **Figure 1.36b** Deep pressure sore

Pathologists are often asked to preform autopsies on such individuals to investigate claims of neglect by third parties. The location, size, and depth of the sores should be recorded. Photography should be considered. The presence of severe pressure sores should alert the pathologist to the possibility of overwhelming sepsis as the cause of death; therefore, microbiological sampling is also recommended.

Pressure sores (decubitus ulcers) are not trivial injuries, and they may result in septicemia and death. They are typically found over the sacrum, hips, and heels. Pressure sores are currently graded by European Pressure Ulcer Advisory Panel from grades I to IV, depending on the depth of the ulcer and the degree of underlying tissue destruction (Table 1.1).[8]

Table 1.1 Pressure sores: severity

EPUAP grade	Description
I	Nonblanching erythema of the skin.
II	Partial-thickness loss of the epidermis/dermis. The ulcer is superficial and may be mistaken for an abrasion.
III	Full-thickness skin loss with damage extending into the subcutaneous tissues. The ulcer does not extend to the underlying fascia and appears as a deep crater, with or without undermining of adjacent tissue.
IV	Full-thickness skin loss with extensive destruction and necrosis of underlying tissue. These are very deep ulcers and may reach underlying bone.

EPUAP, European Pressure Ulcer Advisory Panel.
Data from Beeckman D, Schoonhoven L, Fletcher J, Furtado K, Gunningberg L, Heyman H, Lindholm C, Paguay L, Verdú J, Defloor R. EPUAP classification system for pressure ulcers: European reliability study. *Journal of Advanced Nursing* 2007;**60**(6):682–691.

Miscellaneous Disorders

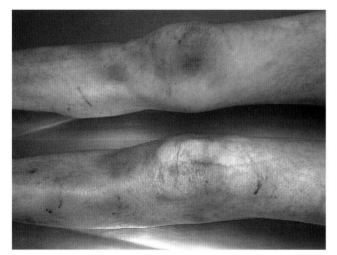

◀ **Figure 1.37** Hypothermic erythema
Hypothermic erythema (or frost erythema) is pink-brownish discoloration of the skin that is commonly distributed over the extensor surfaces of the large joints, such as knees and elbows. It has also been described on protruding areas of the face (e.g., ears and nose), over the shoulders, and even the male genitalia. Frost erythema can be very difficult to differentiate from lividity or bruising. It is not seen in immersion hypothermia.[9] Hypothermic erythema may result from refrigeration of the body in the mortuary.

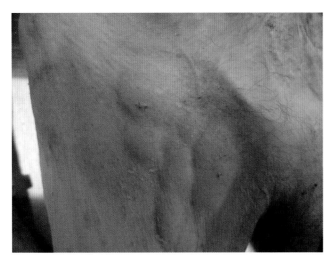

◀ **Figure 1.38** Lymphadenopathy
A search for lymphadenopathy in the neck, axillae, and groin should be part of every external examination. In patients with cachexia, as in this example, the lymphadenopathy may be visible. Enlarged lymph nodes may be the result of neoplasia, inflammatory processes, and infections (including human immunodeficiency virus/acquired immunodeficiency syndrome). This patient had stage 4 lymphoma.

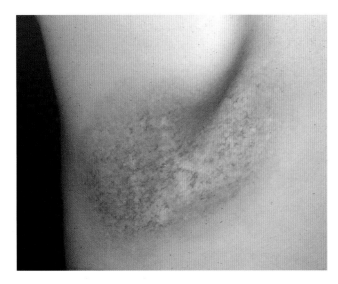

◀ **Figure 1.39** Cutaneous radiotherapy injury
Cutaneous radiotherapy injury (also known as radiodermatitis) results typically from external beam radiation. It manifests as burns approximately 10 days following treatment. Over time, as in this example, the affected skin becomes hyperpigmented, with telangiectasia and scarring. This injury may also rarely result from exposure to radiation during interventional procedures such as coronary angiography, embolization procedures, and indwelling catheter placements.

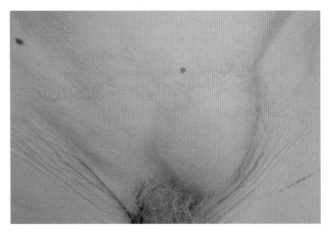

◀ **Figure 1.40** Inguinal hernia
Inguinal hernias are common autopsy findings. On evisceration, the contents of the hernia should be explored. The bowel proximal to the hernia should be examined for evidence of obstruction. Bowel within the hernia should be opened, to seek evidence of ischemia and infarction.

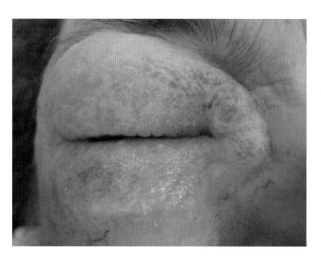

◀ **Figure 1.41** Surgical emphysema

Surgical emphysema, also known as subcutaneous emphysema, is the presence of gas or air in the subcutaneous tissues of the skin. It is typically found on the chest, but it may also be present on the neck and face. This example shows marked surgical emphysema in the eyelids following the insertion of a chest drain. Other causes include fractures of the larynx, tracheal perforation, pulmonary laceration, pneumothorax, pneumomediastinum, chest surgery, barotrauma, rib fractures, and gas gangrene. The skin is crepitant, and gas bubbles may be seen.

Perimortem and Postmortem Changes

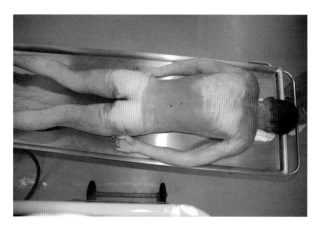

◀ **Figure 1.42a** Hypostasis

Hypostasis (otherwise known as lividity or livor mortis) develops in dependent areas of the body as the blood pools when the circulation ceases. Areas of the body in contact with firm surface remain pale. Any local pressure can exclude lividity such as pressure from rumpled bed linen, clothing creases, belts, and underwear.

After a variable time period (depending on the environment), the lividity becomes fixed and does not blanch or shift on repositioning of the body. Predicting the time of death based on the lividity is incredibly inaccurate; the variability is such that it is useless for any estimation.

19

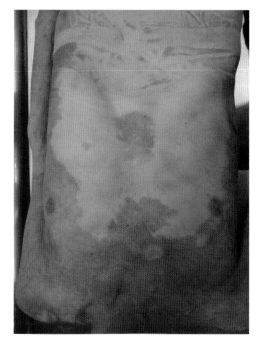

◀ **Figure 1.42b** Hypostasis

Hypostasis can help the pathologist to determine whether the body has been moved after death (after the lividity has fixed). Therefore, if a corpse is found with lividity inappropriate to the posture it is found in, this finding should prompt further investigation. Interpretation of injuries (especially bruising) within areas of lividity can be very difficult and should be done with caution. If there is any doubt about bruising, then an incision should be made into the skin to look for hemorrhage in the subcutaneous tissue.

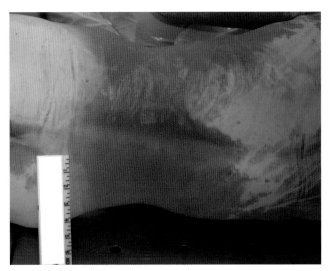

◀ **Figure 1.43** Carbon monoxide poisoning

Carbon monoxide poisoning can impart a "cherry-red" discoloration to the skin and mucous membranes, but its absence does not exclude poisoning. One of the best places to appreciate the color is in areas of postmortem lividity, or in the musculature during evisceration. The cherry-pink color is evident if the saturation of the blood exceeds 30%.

Carbon monoxide poisoning via car exhaust has become less of a suicide option since the introduction of catalytic converters. However, there has been an increase in newer methods of carbon monoxide poisoning such as burning charcoal or fossil fuels within a confined space. (Image courtesy of Dr. C. A. Schandl.)

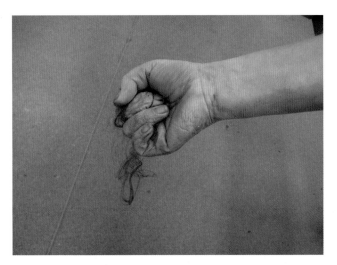

◀ **Figure 1.44** Cadaveric spasm

Cadaveric spasm is a rare condition in which the muscles remain contracted after death. The contraction is said to be instantaneous. It is thought to indicate that death occurred while the individual was experiencing a profound emotional state of fear or excitement. As in this example, this spasm most typically affects the hands (the deceased is clutching strands of their own hair), but it can affect the whole body. It cannot be simulated after death.

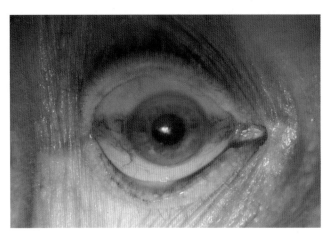

◀ **Figure 1.45** Tache noir

Tache noir is a postmortem artifact of the sclera associated with failure of the eye to close after death. Initially, it is seen as two yellow triangles on either side of the cornea. With time this changes to brown and eventually black. This discoloration is caused by desiccation of the cornea resulting from prolonged exposure to the air. This postmortem change should not be misinterpreted as hemorrhage associated with strangulation or abuse.

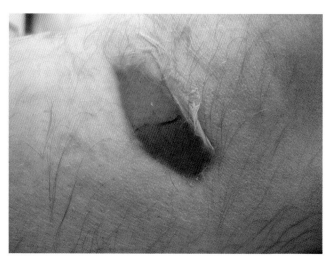

◄ Figure 1.46a Postmortem abrasions

Artifactual postmortem abrasions are very common and can occur for a variety of reasons such as body handling by funeral directors or mortuary staff and animal activity. After death the area of abrasion becomes stiff and leathery and takes on a brown, parchment-like color. This results from drying of the intracellular fluid exposed by an abrasion. It is almost impossible to tell whether these injuries occurred immediately before or after death, and they are best described as "perimortem" injuries.

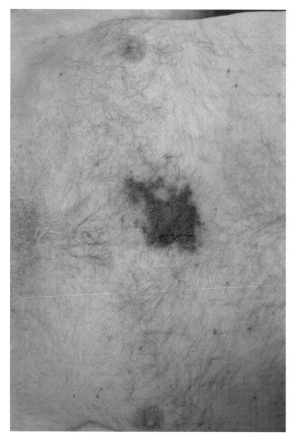

◄ Figure 1.46b Postmortem abrasions

One common site for such abrasions is in the center of the chest overlying the lower aspect of the sternum (xiphisternum). This is as a result of manual chest compressions during resuscitation.

21

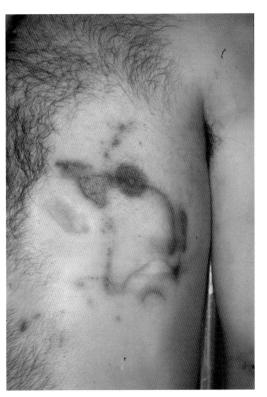

◀ **Figure 1.47a** Resuscitation artifacts

Some of the most common artifacts, both externally and internally, are those related to cardiopulmonary resuscitation. It is important for the pathologist to recognize these and not misinterpret them. Defibrillator "burns" can frequently be found on the anterior chest wall. Bruising can be seen on the chest wall and in the underlying subcutaneous tissues. There can be fracturing of the sternum and the ribs anteriorly.

Internally there may be lacerated lungs and punctured pericardium with underlying myocardial damage as a result of bony fractures. Less commonly, there can be rupture of the stomach, esophagus, lung, or intestine resulting from overinflation with subsequent compression. Vigorous cardiopulmonary resuscitation may lacerate the liver or spleen.

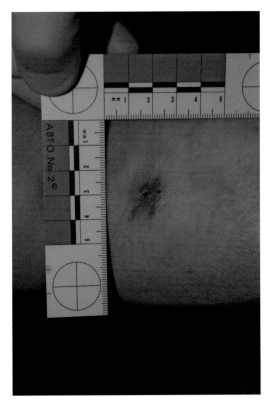

◀ **Figure 1.47b** Resuscitation artifacts

Abrasions can be seen on the face and neck along with finger and nail marks caused by application of masks for artificial resuscitation. There can be further damage to the lips, gums, teeth, and pharynx resulting from airway adjuncts such as endotracheal tubes.

There may be many venipuncture sites on the body. These can be impossible to differentiate from drug-related injection sites. They can be sited in the antecubital fossae and the groin, but also in the veins of the neck. Intracardiac injections can lead to puncture marks on the center of the chest.

References

1. Burton JL. The external examination: an often-neglected autopsy component. *Current Diagnostic Pathology* 2007;**13**(5):357–365.
2. Burton JL, Rutty GN, editors. *The hospital autopsy: a manual of fundamental autopsy practice.* 3rd ed. London: Hodder Arnold; 2010.
3. Royal College of Pathologists. *Guidelines on autopsy practice.* London: Royal College of Pathologists; 2002.
4. Knight B. *Knight's forensic pathology.* 3rd ed. London: Arnold; 2004.
5. Swift B. Body art and modification. In: Rutty GN, editor. *Essentials of autopsy practice: recent advances, topics and developments.* London: Springer; 2004:159–186.
6. Davey P. *Medicine at a glance.* 2nd ed. Malden, MA; Blackwell; 2006.
7. Finkbeiner WE. *Autopsy pathology: a manual and atlas.* 2nd ed. Philadelphia: Saunders; 2009.
8. Beeckman D, Schoonhoven L, Fletcher J, Furtado K, Gunningberg L, Heyman H, Lindholm C, Paguay L, Verdú J, Defloor R. EPUAP classification system for pressure ulcers: European reliability study. *Journal of Advanced Nursing* 2007;**60**(6):682–691.
9. Turk EE. Hypothermia. *Forensic Science, Medicine, and Pathology* 2010;**6**(2):106–115.

Chapter 2

External Examination
Trauma

Introduction

One of the most important aspects of the external examination is to identify injuries, both recent and old, on a body. The accurate documentation of injuries during the external examination is of critical importance. A fundamental first principle of autopsy practice is "do not undertake autopsies that you are not competent to perform." The search for injuries should be thorough. Pathologists must be aware that significant injuries such as strangulation and falls from a height can result in minimal external injuries that can be easily overlooked. Injuries are extremely common; indeed, it would be most unusual for an individual not to have had some form of injury during life. Injuries may be coincidental or related to the cause of death. Many individuals sustain injuries during a terminal collapse, especially to the face or scalp.[1]

The identification of injuries that raise suspicion of an unnatural or violent death should prompt the pathologist to stop and seek assistance from a more experienced colleague or forensic pathologist. It is imperative to stop at this stage to prevent loss of important trace evidence or further disturbance of pathological features. Forensic pathologists undertake meticulous documentation of injuries, with diagrammatic recording of injuries along with photographic documentation. Such fastidiousness may not be practical in everyday practice, but diagrams can help assist with report writing and explaining injuries to other parties, especially at inquest.

Injuries are traditionally divided into five groups: bruise, abrasion, laceration, incised wound, and burn. Gunshot wound is a specific form of laceration. The general pathologist may see many cases of suicidal gunshot wounds. These wounds are of contact or close discharge type, depending on the weapon, and ideally the putative weapon should be examined to ensure that it is physically possible for the deceased to have discharged it to cause the injuries present. Identification of a more distant range–type pattern or an unusual site of election should prompt discussion with a forensic pathologist. The interpretation of gunshot wounds in terms of entry and exit wounds and range of discharge is highly specialized and should be left to forensic pathologists and ballistics experts.

When describing an injury it is imperative that the correct terminology is used. The terminology assists in the identification of the mechanism of causation. For example, the term "laceration" indicates the application of blunt force. The incorrect description and naming of injuries are common by clinical physicians, especially in the emergency department setting. Such errors can be perceived by lawyers as lack of knowledge and can undermine any evidence provided. Therefore, it is imperative that pathologists use the correct terminology.

If in doubt about how best to describe a finding, then the nonspecific term "injury" is best used. The legal definition of the term "wound" refers to an injury that affects the full thickness of the skin (dermis and epidermis); therefore, the term would be incorrectly applied to bruises and abrasions.

For all injuries, the shape, color, dimension, and position on the body should be recorded. The position should be given relative to a fixed anatomical site such as the sternal notch or spinous processes. Structures such as nipples and navels can vary depending on an individual's age or body habitus, so they should not be used.[2]

Pathologists need to recognize the many mimics of bruising caused by natural disease or, in particular, postmortem lividity. The list of natural disease causes of mimics is long and varied including infections, dermatological conditions, and hematological disorders.

In addition to the documentation of the presence of medical devices, the marks of medical intervention should also be recorded such as chest drain insertion and venipuncture marks. This can be important to establish what degree of medical intervention was given and its efficacy.

This chapter presents an overview of common injuries seen during external examination.

Bruises

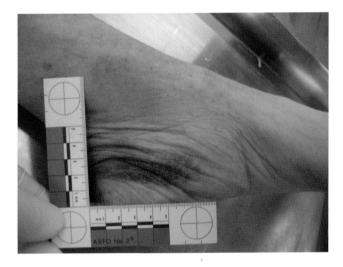

◀ **Figure 2.1a** Color progression of bruises
Bruises (or contusions) are areas of hemorrhage into the skin that result from rupture of small vessels within the tissue. The size, shape, and color of the bruise should be recorded, as well as its location. Bruises result from blunt trauma injury. Age, body habitus, and natural disease or drug therapy altering the coagulability of the blood affect ease of bruising and the appearance of the bruise.[3] Bruising occurs easily to areas where the skin is lax. Equally, significant internal injury may result in the absence of skin injury.

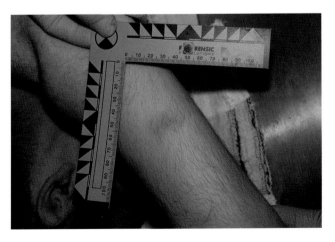

◀ **Figure 2.1b** Color progression of bruises
Bruises change color with time, the sequence being red, blue, green, yellow, and brown. The color of a bruise does not permit the accurate dating of the injury, and any pathologist would be unwise to comment on this beyond the broad categories of old or fresh injury. Langlois concluded that all one could say about a bruise is that if there was yellow coloration then that bruise is more than 18 hours old.[4] However, the absence of a yellow color does not mean that the bruise is less than 18 hours old.

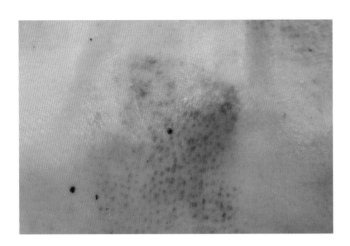

◀ **Figure 2.1c** Color progression of bruises
Bruises can take hours to days to appear in the skin and may become more obvious with time. This is as a result of the increased contrast as the settling lividity drains blood from the skin. In cases with a history of trauma but no bruising is seen, it may be helpful to revisit the external examination after 24 hours to see whether deep bruises have become more apparent with time.

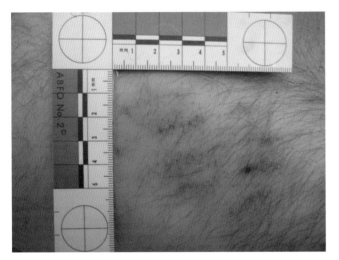

◀ **Figure 2.2a** Patterned bruising
Patterned intradermal bruising results from impact with a hard, patterned object with ridges or grooves. Skin is forced into the grooves and the vessels rupture, whereas the skin over the ridges is compressed but the vessels remain intact. This situation leads to accumulation of blood that demonstrates the pattern of the causal surface, such as tire or shoe treads, car bumpers, or gun muzzles.

27

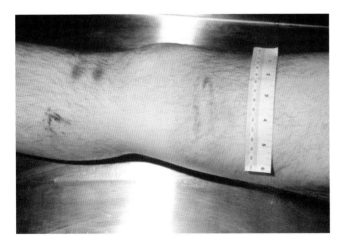

◀ **Figure 2.2b** Patterned bruising

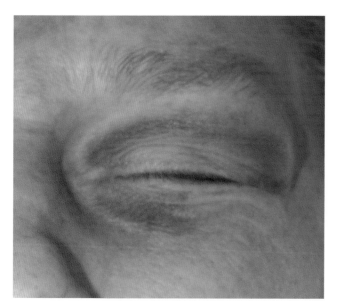

◀ **Figure 2.3** Periorbital hematoma
Periorbital hematomas (or black eyes) are often thought to suggest the use of considerable force in their production. Black eyes can result from orbital or base of skull fractures, but also from the tracking of blood from injuries to the forehead, nose, and orbit, as well as, of course, direct trauma to the orbit. The periorbital tissues are lax, especially in older persons, and permit considerable extravasation of blood from relatively trivial injury.

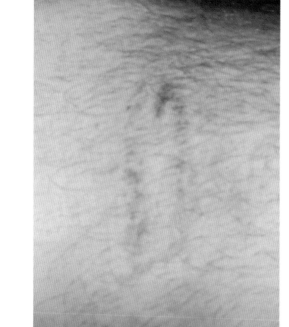

◀ **Figure 2.4** Tram-line bruising
Tram-line bruises are seen as a number of parallel linear bruises with a space between them. These bruises are caused by blunt force with a cylindrical or rectangular object, such as a pole, plank of wood, or metal bar. The mechanism is that the weapon sinks into the skin on impact, so that the edges drag the skin downward and the traction tears the blood vessels at the edges. The central areas of compression cause minimal damage.

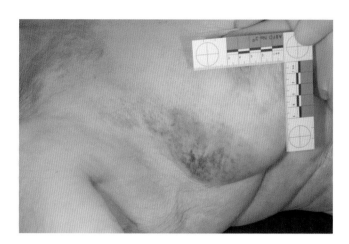

◀ **Figure 2.5** Seat belt bruising

One of the most useful pieces of information a pathologist can provide regarding vehicle occupants in a road traffic death is whether the deceased was wearing a seat belt at the time of impact. Seat belt bruises are seen as linear areas of bruising extending from the front of the shoulders diagonally across the chest and horizontally across the abdomen. The identification and location of seat belt bruising can help locate the individual in the car (e.g., driver side or passenger side). The absence of bruising does not exclude the wearing of a seat belt. Multiple or thick layers of clothing and seat belt pads can prevent bruising from occurring.

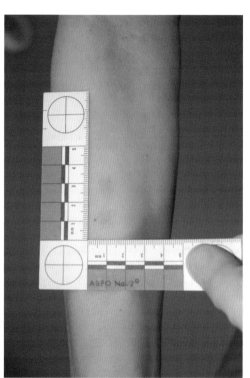

◀ **Figure 2.6** Fingertip bruising

Discoid bruises approximately 1 cm in diameter, especially when in clusters, are suggestive of fingertip bruises left by gripping or possibly pinching. This bruising can result from forceful restraint or general perimortem handling. If these bruises are found on the limbs and face of a child, they could indicate abuse. They can be seen on the thighs of rape victims and on the neck in strangulation.

29

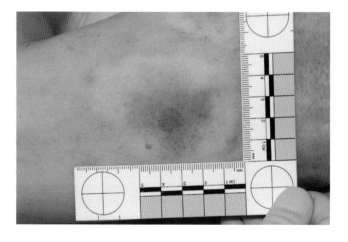

◀ **Figure 2.7a** Mimics of bruising *Pseudomonas vasculitis*

Pathologists need to be aware that not all areas of skin discolorations are bruises. Many natural disease processes cause changes in the skin that mimic bruises. Hypostasis, skin pigmentation, necrotizing fasciitis, and decomposition can mimic or mask bruising. Postmortem lividity especially can be difficult to distinguish from bruising, and where there is doubt about a potentially significant injury, the area of skin may be incised to assess for deep bruising and, if necessary, sampled for microscopic examination. Shown here are (a) an area of discoloration caused by *Pseudomonas* vasculitis and (b) ecthyma gangrenosum, both of which were initially interpreted as bruising.

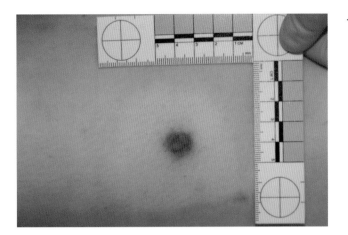

◀ **Figure 2.7b** Mimics of bruising—ecthyma gangrenosum

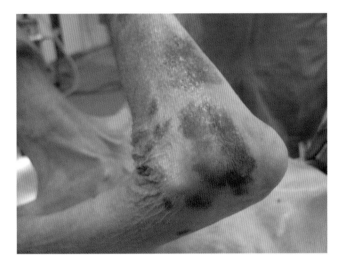

◀ **Figure 2.8** Senile purpura

Senile purpura (solar or actinic purpura) is a condition characterized by dark purplish-red bruises commonly seen on the forearms and back of the hands of older persons. The purpuric areas are clearly delineated and are never associated with swelling. Older persons bleed more easily as part of the normal aging process. The blood vessels in the skin are more fragile as a result of years of accumulated sun exposure. There is loss of subcutaneous fat, which also reduces the natural cushioning that would normally prevent bruising. Even light contact may cause a bruise. In addition, many older persons take medications such as warfarin that can further increase susceptibility to bruising.

Abrasions

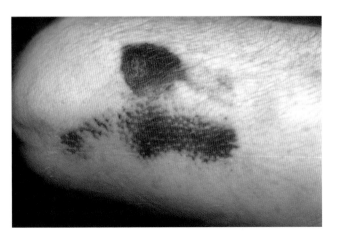

◀ **Figure 2.9** Abrasions

Abrasions (or grazes) are superficial injuries to the skin that involve the epidermis only and result from blunt trauma. This force can be either a directly vertical impact causing crushing of the epidermis (crush abrasion) or a tangential (glancing) impact that scrapes the epidermis in the direction of impact (brush abrasions and "scratches"). Abrasions can occur before or after death (see Chapter 1 for postmortem abrasions).

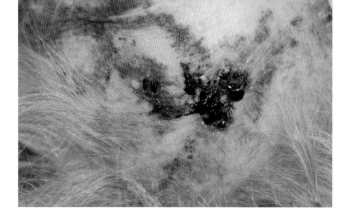

◀ **Figure 2.10** Scabbed abrasion
Abrasions typically cause little or no bleeding, but they exude a serous fluid. As the abrasion heals, this exudate dries to form a scab over the injury.

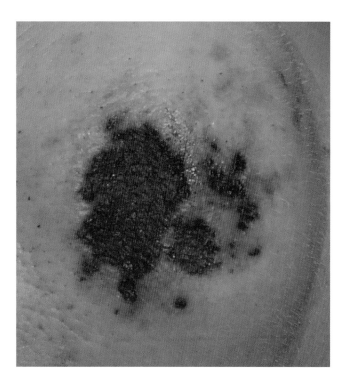

◀ **Figure 2.11** Abrasions: crush
Crush abrasions result from direct vertical impact to the epidermis causing crushing of the epidermis. The causative object may stamp its shape or surface pattern onto the skin, such as ropes when used as ligatures, fabric patterns, shoe treads, or fingernail marks on neck.

31

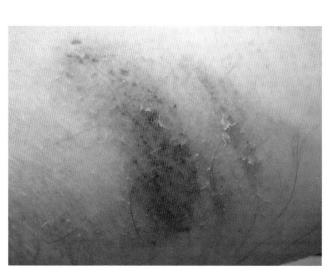

◀ **Figure 2.12a** Abrasions: brush
Brush abrasions result from tangential impact against the skin. This is either due to the object moving against the stationary body or the moving of the body against a rough stationary surface. The direction of impact can be assessed by the presence of terminal skin tags at the point distal to the impact (the finishing edge) and the presence of parallel furrows indicating the direction of travel. These injuries are commonly seen with road traffic collision (Figure 2.12b) when the body has slid along the road ("road rash").

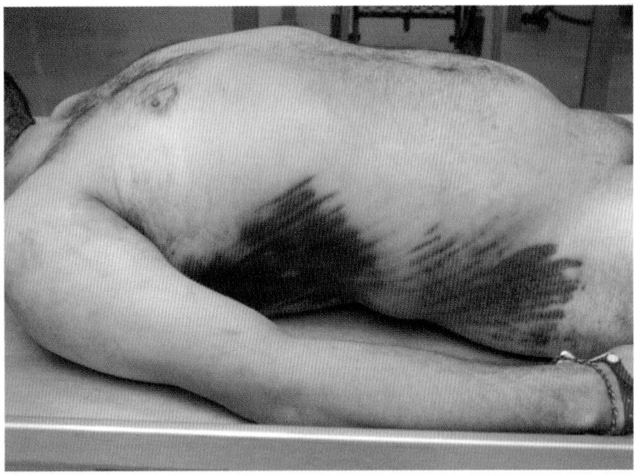

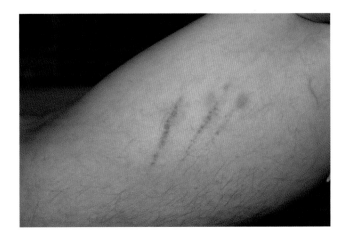

◀ **Figure 2.12b** Abrasions: brush

◀ **Figure 2.13** Linear abrasions caused by a dog
This individual has two approximately parallel linear interrupted abrasions on the thigh that were caused by a dog's claws. (Image courtesy of Dr. A. Jeffrey.)

Bites

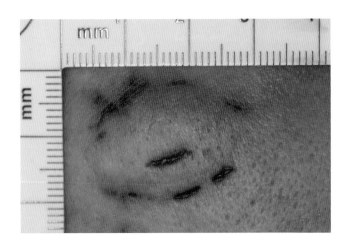

◀ **Figure 2.14a** Bite mark
One particular pattern of injury that pathologists should be able to recognize is the bite mark. This is often more easily said than done. Bite marks can be abrasions, bruises, or lacerations, or a combination of these. Bite marks can be of animal or human origin. The presence of human bites should raise suspicion. If there are concerns regarding a bite mark, then assistance from a forensic pathologist or odontologist should be sought. Interpretation of such injuries is highly specialized, and it may be possible to obtain trace DNA evidence from the surface of the wound. The three examples shown here are all human bite marks. ((a) and (c) courtesy of Dr. A. Jeffrey.)

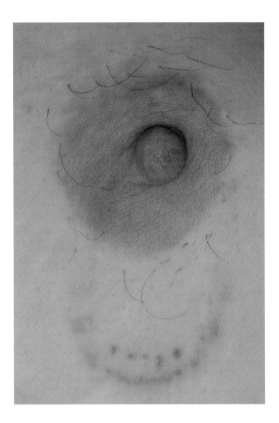

◀ **Figure 2.14b** Bite mark

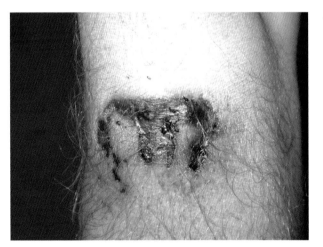

◀ **Figure 2.14c** Bite mark

◀ **Figure 2.15** Tongue biting
Bite marks on the tongue may be seen in individuals who have suffered a blow to the jaw or who have had an epileptic seizure. The tongue should be carefully examined for the presence of bite marks in all autopsies, but the absence of bite marks does not exclude death resulting from epilepsy.

Asphyxia

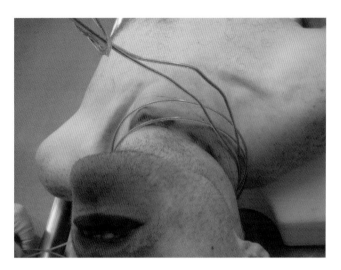

◀ **Figure 2.16a** Ligature marks

Suicidal hanging is a very common form of suicide. Hanging is a form of ligature strangulation in which the force applied to the neck results from the weight of the body. In these cases it is important that the ligature is left in place for autopsy. If the ligature has been removed at the scene (e.g., during resuscitation), it is imperative that the pathologist sees it before the autopsy. It is essential to ensure that the ligature marks on the body are consistent with the nature of the alleged ligature.

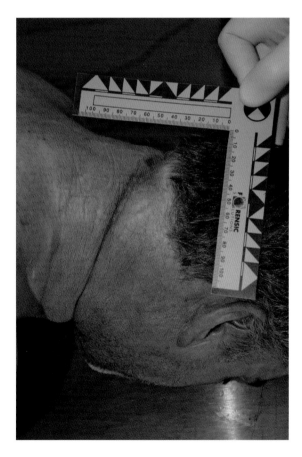

◀ **Figure 2.16b** Ligature marks

Suspension by a ligature produces a furrow in the neck that rises upward to a point of suspension, with an area of skin sparing that sometimes forms a "V" pattern. This is typically behind an ear or at the back of the neck. A hanging mark hardly ever completely encircles the neck unless a slipknot was used. If a low suspension point was used, such as a door handle, then a more horizontal ligature mark may be seen, but these need to be treated with considerable caution.

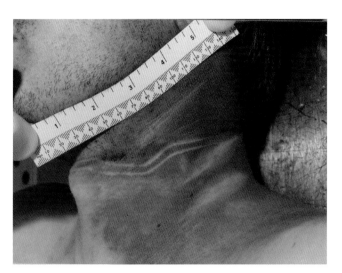

◀ **Figure 2.16c** Ligature marks

Ligature strangulation is an uncommon form of suicide, and such cases should be considered homicide until proven otherwise. The presence of small round bruises and small linear scratches around the ligature that may be caused by fingertips and fingernails are worrying features. Homicide by ligature strangulation may produce petechial hemorrhages to the face and eyes, as well as hemorrhage into the muscles of the neck. A homicidal ligature mark also tends to encircle the whole neck horizontally and not produce a point of suspension.

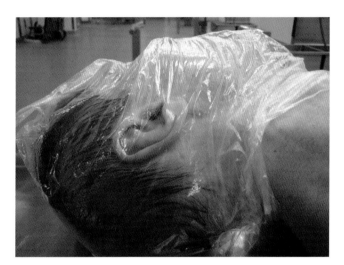

◀ **Figure 2.17** Plastic bag asphyxia

Placement of a plastic bag over the head or face can produce asphyxia by means of mechanical obstruction or occlusion of the external airways. This is known as smothering. Deaths in this manner are either homicide or suicide, although an accidental manner is possible, especially in children. Such cases may have no specific autopsy findings. Petechiae of the face, sclera, and conjunctivae are almost always absent. If the plastic bag has been removed from the body before autopsy, it can be impossible to determine the cause of death without the correct history.

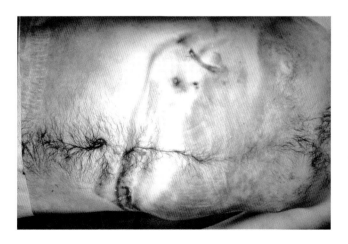

◀ **Figure 2.18** Crush asphyxia

The diagnosis of crush asphyxia typically relies on a history of chest or abdominal compression with the finding of skin petechiae and congestion. Circumstances leading to crush asphyxia include road traffic accidents, industrial and farming accidents, building collapses, and crowd-related crushing (e.g., in the 1989 Hillsborough Stadium disaster in Sheffield, United Kingdom). In younger individuals there may be little damage to the underlying rib cage or organs.

Lacerations, Incised Wounds, and Their Scars

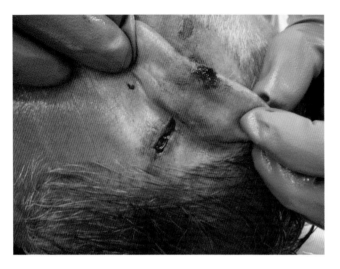

◀ Figure 2.19a Lacerations

Lacerations are full-thickness tears in the skin caused by blunt force trauma. They have irregular margins with associated bruising and crushing. Fibrous bridges and hair shafts may be present across the wound. These features, especially the presence of bridging, can help distinguish a laceration from an incised wound. Sometimes the differentiation can be difficult.

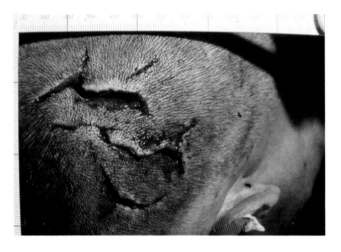

◀ Figure 2.19b Lacerations

Lacerations tend to occur over bony prominences, especially the scalp, face, and shin areas. They are rarely seen on the abdomen. It is possible to lacerate the skin over a soft area. This injury is most often caused by a lacerating agent with a projecting point or edge. Lacerations also occur if fractured bones protrude through the overlying skin (e.g., fractured limbs). Indeed, particularly sharp fractured bones may produce injuries that appear to be incised wounds.

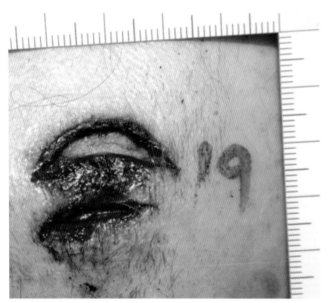

◀ Figure 2.19c Lacerations

Lacerations on the scalp can appear to have clean margins and can be easily mistaken for incised wounds. This is especially true if the lacerations were inflicted by a weapon. This figure shows several curvilinear lacerations (arc) to the scalp caused by the head of a hammer. Abrasion and bruising to the margin are visible; however, the wound appears to have a clean margin.

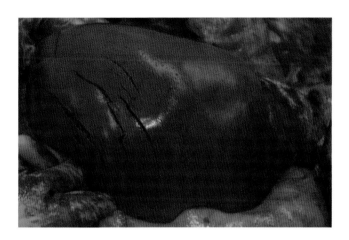

◀ Figure 2.19d Lacerations

Lacerations can be caused internally whenever there is a hard surface for the tissues to be crushed against (e.g., inside the lips). This injury can be seen on the surface of the lungs and the heart following cardiopulmonary resuscitation as a result of sternal and rib fractures.

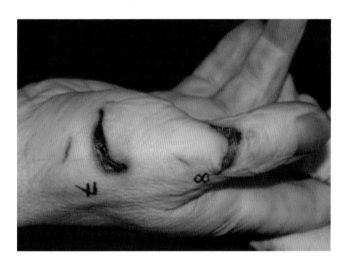

◀ Figure 2.20a Incised wound-cut

Incised wounds are caused by a sharp edge. The wounds have a clean division of the full thickness of the skin caused by a sharp-edged instrument such as a knife, glass or broken pottery. They have minimal damage to the surrounding tissue. They can be subdivided into "cut/slash" and "stab" wounds. A cut/slash is where the length of the injury on the surface is greater than its depth. A stab is where the depth is greater than the width.

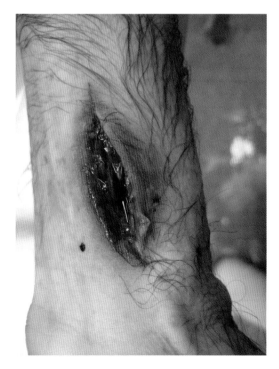

◀ Figure 2.20b Incised wound-cut

The characteristics of an incised wound relative to a laceration are the edges are clean cut and can be slightly everted. There are no tissue bridges or abrasions at the margins. The wound often gapes due to tension in the skin. A jagged edge can be seen if the cut has been made into loose or folded skin.

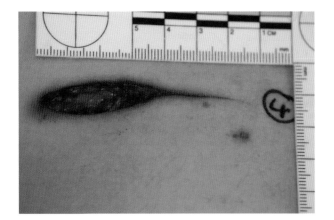

◀ **Figure 2.21a** Incised wounds—stabs
A stab wound is an incised wound that is deeper than it is long. The presence of a stab wound on the body should prompt the pathologist to stop and evaluate if there is a possibility of homicide and seek appropriate help if unsure. Stab wounds are most commonly inflicted with knifes, but scissors, screwdrivers, chisels, forks, and numerous other tools can be used. Pathologists should be very wary about commenting on type of weapon and the degree of force used as this very much lies within the expert opinion of a forensic pathologist.

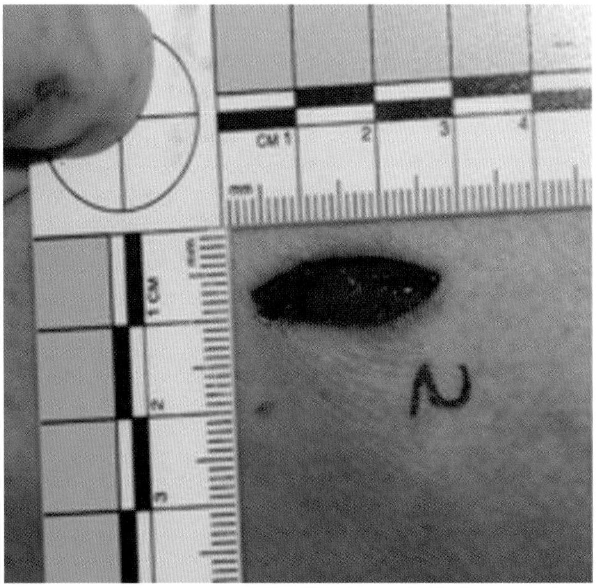

◀ **Figure 2.21b** Incised wounds—stabs
The length and width of the wound both gaping and with the wound edges opposed should be recorded, along with the orientation, and position on the body in relation to fixed bony land marks and the height above the heel. Comments should be made on the edges and margins of the wounds as this aids in possible identification of the type of weapon used. Shelving of the underlying subcutaneous tissues along with the direction of the wound track can provide information on direction. Damage to the underlying organs should also be recorded.

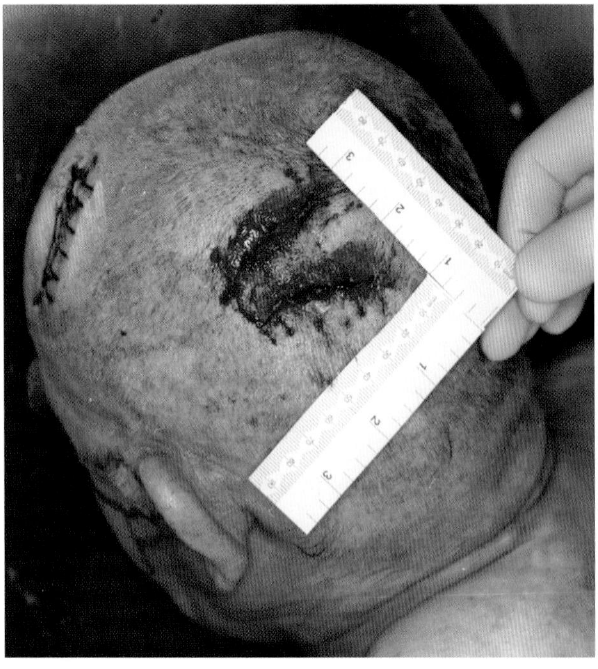

◀ **Figure 2.22a** Chop wound
Chop wounds are a variant of incised wounds. They have clean-cut edges but also an abraded margin that results from the friction of the wide blade on impact. This is commonly seen in ax wounds. ((b) Courtesy of Dr. A. Jeffrey.)

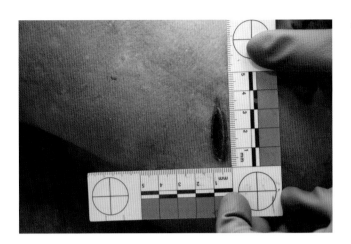

◀ **Figure 2.22b** Chop wound

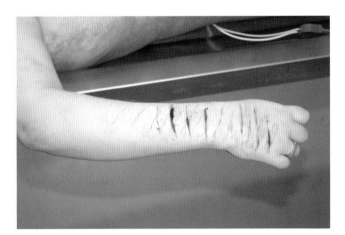

◀ **Figure 2.23** Deliberate self-harm—new
Self-inflicted injury can occur on any part of the body that an individual can reach with their own hands. Common sites of election include the wrists, neck, cubital fossae, chest, abdomen, and groin. Self-inflicted injuries classically are incised wounds or burns. They can be very severe. The author has seen one suicidal cut throat cut down to the cervical spine. There may be one or more shallow incised wounds associated with deeper incisions. These are termed "intention wounds." These injures often are not fatal, so if seen at autopsy such injuries may represent an initial failed attempt at suicide and another method or methods such as overdose may be present.

39

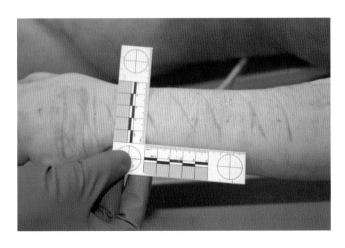

◀ **Figure 2.24** Deliberate self-harm—healed
Repeated self-harm can be an indication of chronic mental health problems or personality disorders, and is a common finding in young suicide victims. These injuries are classically seen as shallow cuts that occur as parallel groups of injuries, most commonly to the arms and thighs. They can be of varying stages of healing depending on the frequency of the self-harming behavior. Some of the injuries may show evidence of suturing if medical intervention was sought.

Medical and Surgical Intervention

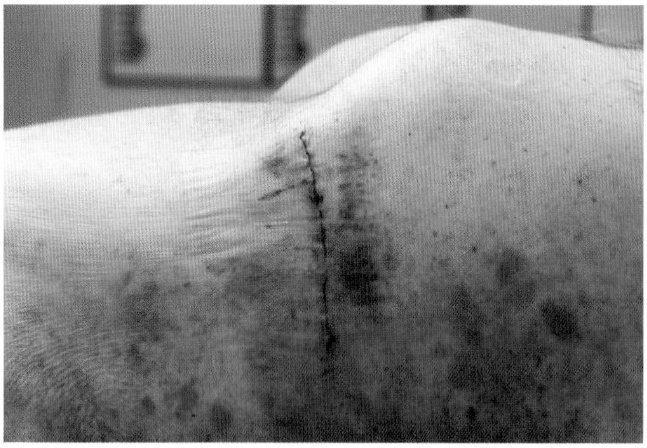

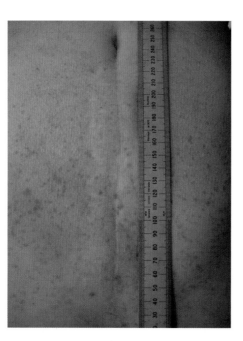

◀ Figure 2.25a Surgical scars

Scars are areas of fibrous tissue that replace normal tissue after injury. A scar results from the biological process of wound repair in the skin and other tissues of the body. Scars can result from injury or from surgical intervention (which may, itself, reasonably be described as "controlled trauma").

If scars are present, then the site relative to fixed bony landmarks, size, shape, and state of healing should be reported. The accurate dating of scars is impossible. Therefore, dating should be crudely grouped into young (pink and raised) or well-healed (white-silver and flat) scar. Evidence of infection, abnormal healing, or pigmentation can also be noted.

◀ Figure 2.25b Surgical scars

Surgical scars can be extremely important for confirming identity and can rapidly assist in this process by excluding possible candidates based on their surgical history. Scars can be easily seen even on extensively decomposed bodies.

Surgical scars are identified by their linear and neat appearance. They often have regular circular scarring on either side of the main scar from the sutures or staples used to close the wound. Some surgical scars can be common, such as cesarean section scars; however others such as from craniotomy are more unusual and can be strong identifying markers.

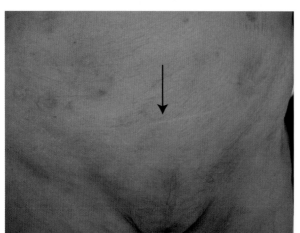

◀ Figure 2.25c Surgical scars

The presence of surgical scars can give a strong indication of an individual's medical history. For example, Pfannenstiel incisions, horizontal incisions just above the mons pubis, can indicate cesarean sections or other gynecological procedures in women. Vertical incisions on the chest in the midline can indicate previous cardiac surgery.

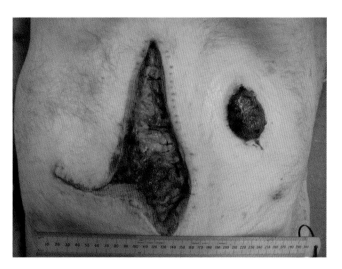

◀ **Figure 2.26** Dehisced surgical wound
If surgical wounds become infected they may break open (dehisce). This is most commonly seen in abdominal wounds and in persons with obesity or diabetes, but dehiscence may affect any surgical wound. Dehisced wounds may be treated with débridement and closure with deep buttress sutures or, as in this example, be left open and allowed to heal by secondary intention. This patient also has a colostomy.

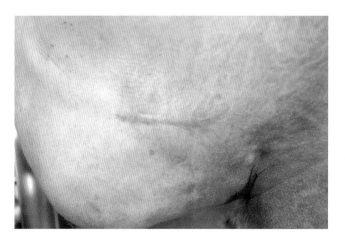

◀ **Figure 2.27** Keloid scar
A keloid scar is a type of abnormal scar formation that occurs at the site of a healed injury. It is an overgrowth of granulation tissue that forms firm fibrous nodules or lesions. It extends beyond the borders of the original wound. It does not normally regress spontaneously, and it will usually recur after excision. This type of scar contrasts with hypertrophic scars, which stay within the borders of the original wound. Keloid formation is more common in the skin of Afro-Caribbean persons between the ages of 10 and 30 years. The cause is unknown.

41

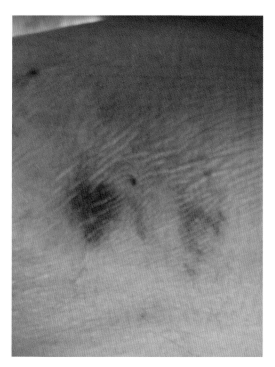

◀ **Figure 2.28a** Venipuncture marks
Venipuncture or needle marks on a body can represent recent medical intervention or possible intravenous drug use. When fresh, drug injection sites are indistinguishable from marks of diagnostic or therapeutic procedures. The most common medical needle marks seen at autopsy are those associated with resuscitation. These marks are commonly in the antecubital fossae, the backs of the hands, the groin, or, less frequently, the side of the neck. These needle marks are often larger as a result of the large cannulae used and may have surrounding bruising, or they may still be leaking at the time of the autopsy.

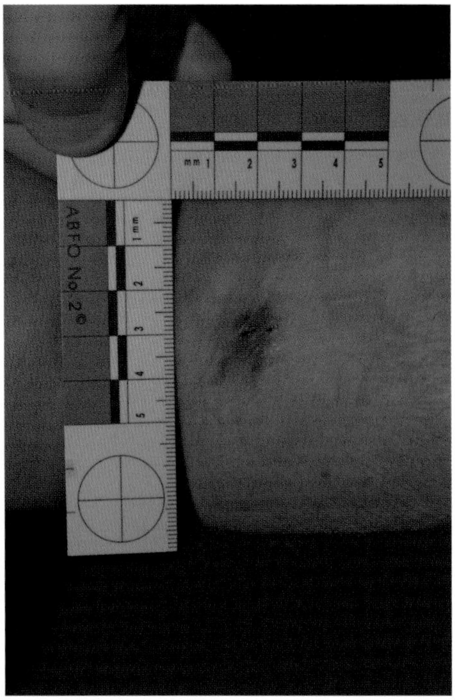

◀ **Figure 2.28b** Venipuncture marks

Repeated intravenous drug use over a long period of time leads to multiple needle marks on the body in varying states of healing. Commonly, the antecubital fossae and the forearms are used. With repeated use, the veins scar and can no longer be used. So-called tracks can be seen on the skin. The user will then move to other sites such as the groin, neck, and feet. Injection sites between the fingers and toes may be seen in individuals attempting to hide the stigmata of drug use. With very long-term use, more unusual sites may be used, or other individuals may be required to inject the drug in a site inaccessible to the user. Intravenous drug users are classified as high-risk autopsies, and the appropriate health and safety practices should be implemented.

Burns and Scalds

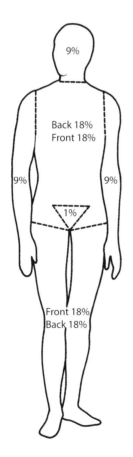

◀ **Figure 2.29** Burns—Rule of Nines

Burns result from heat, cold, chemicals, and electricity. The severity of the burn depends upon the nature of the causation and the duration of its application. For burns the depth (superficial or full thickness) and percentage of the body surface area affected (using the Rule of Nines) should be recorded. This is best done with diagrams, as in clinical practice. Any burns externally should prompt close examination of the mouth, pharynx, and airways for the presence of soot, desquamation, or swelling associated with the inhalation of hot gases. The Total Body Surface Area (TBSA) is an assessment measure of burns of the skin. In adults, the Rule of Nines is used to determine the total percentage of area burned for each major section of the body. (From Knight B. *Knight's forensic pathology*. 3rd ed. London: Arnold; 2004.)

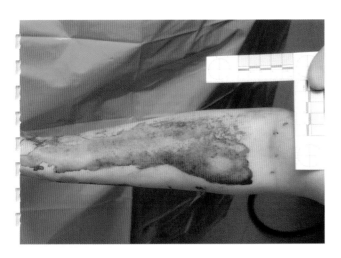

◀ **Figure 2.30a** Thermal burns—wet (scald)
Wet thermal burns (or scalds) result from tissue damage by hot liquids—water, steam, oils, or other substances. There is reddening, blistering, and loss of the epidermis. The edge of the scald is sharply demarcated. Water scalds are a common domestic accident, especially to children and the elderly. Scalds do not generally cause charring or singeing of hair, unlike dry heat. (Image courtesy of Dr. A. Jeffrey.)

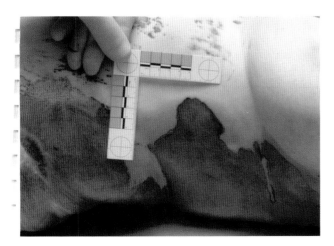

◀ **Figure 2.30b** Thermal burns—wet (scald)
If due to immersion in hot water then there will be a horizontal fluid level, but this can be made irregular due to splashing.[5] From the pattern of the scald it may be possible to determine the direction of the hot liquid across the skin by following the trickle lines. This can help reconstruct the final events and to consider if it fits with the history given. If an individual is, say, sat in a bath then there may be areas of sparing where the skin is in contact with the bathtub rather than the hot liquid. Death from scalds can be due to supervening infection in the long term, or fluid loss and electrolyte disturbance acutely.

43

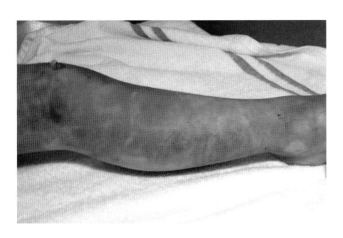

◀ **Figure 2.31a** Thermal burns—dry
Dry burns are the most common type of thermal injury. The extent of the tissue damage is related to the duration of heat application and the temperature. Superficial burns are confined to the epidermis and lead to redness and swelling of the skin with possible blister formation.

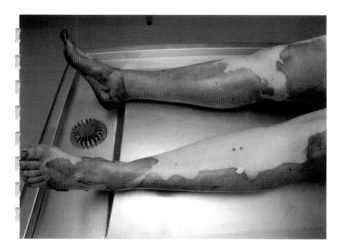

◀ Figure 2.31b Thermal burns—dry

More severe burns cause full thickness destruction of the skin with singeing of the head hair, eyelashes, eyebrows, and body hair. The skin becomes yellow-brown and leathery. Deeper burns will result in the skin becoming charred, carbonized, or completely destroyed. With more extensive burns there can be damage to fat, muscle, and bone.

It is possible to cause burns to the skin post-mortem. It is often impossible to determine if an injury is post or perimortem. The presence of reddening and blistering does not always indicate a vital reaction.

◀ Figure 2.31c Thermal burns—dry

There are many artefacts seen with burned bodies. Heat-induced skin splits may be misinterpreted as antemortem wounds. The absence of any hemorrhage and bruising in relation to the splits helps distinguish them from antemortem wounds and they are usually seen over extensor surfaces. Heat-induced fractures, commonly of the base of the skull and cranial vault, can be impossible to differentiate from antemortem fractures and can mimic blunt trauma. A heat hematoma occurs when heat is applied to the cranium and the blood boils out of the brain and collects in a thin layer between the dura and the skull. This can be mistaken for subdural hemorrhage by the inexperienced.

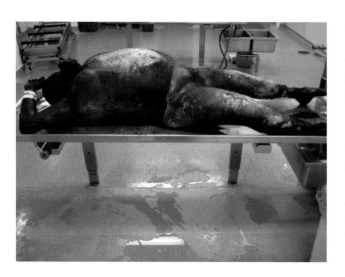

◀ Figure 2.32 Pugilistic pose

Muscular contraction occurs when the body is exposed to substantial heat. It is considered a postmortem occurrence. The muscle dehydrates and breaks down, essentially cooking. The elbows, knees, and wrists become strongly flexed because muscle contraction is stronger in the flexor groups. This contraction of the flexors leads to the so-called boxer's or pugilistic attitude. It is important to recognize this artifact because the position mimics defense against attack. Artifactual skin splitting commonly accompanies this degree of burning. These splits can mimic incised wounds.

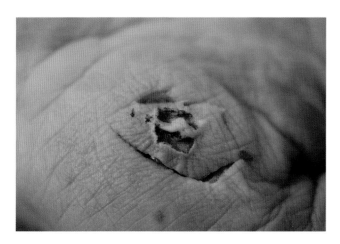

◀ Figure 2.33 Electrical burns

The passage of electricity through the body can cause damage to skin and internal organs, as well as death. Electrical burns can result from low- or high-voltage exposure. The current can be direct or alternating. Alternating current is more likely to cause arrhythmia than is direct current. High-voltage burns are typically associated with extensive injury. Low-voltage burns may leave no visible marks. The degree of injury is related to the duration.[5] Evidence of the point of entry may give rise to a specific type of pale burn with a punched-out center, raised "blistered" edges, and surrounding erythema, often called a "Joule burn" or, less commonly, a "spark burn." This pattern is seen with a small point of contact. With a wider contact there may be no marks. Rarely, there may be evidence of burning at the point of exit.

Death caused by electricity is most often the result of cardiac arrhythmia, diaphragm and intercostal muscle paralysis, or brain damage (inhibition of the respiratory center).

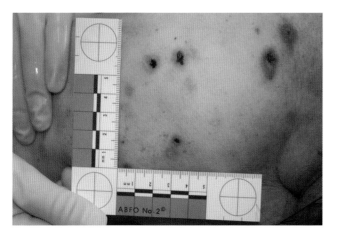

◀ Figure 2.34 Cigarette burns

It is unusual to see patterned burns at autopsy, but the pathologist should be vigilant for the presence of cigarette burns. Although such burns may be accidental, they raise the possibility of abuse or deliberate self-harm. The burns are typically full thickness, circular, or oval and may occur singly or, as in this example, in clusters. They are typically approximately 5 to 10 mm in diameter. The presence of cigarette burns should raise serious concern and prompt further consideration (including consideration of referring the death to a forensic pathologist).

45

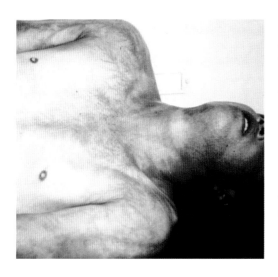

◀ Figure 2.35 Lightning

A lightning strike imparts an electrical burn at the point where the electricity hits the skin; this can sometimes create a fern leaf (arborescent) pattern resulting from the impulse through the small vessels of the skin (Lichtenberg figures). Alternatively, the contact may look like a severe flash burn of thermal type. The identification of such injuries may be difficult, and it is important to be guided by the history. There may be associated disruption of the clothing; this may mimic features of assault because the clothing can be severely torn. (From Knight B. *Knight's forensic pathology.* 3rd ed. London: Arnold; 2004.)

Gunshot Wounds

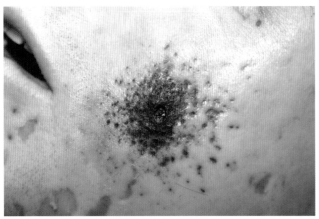

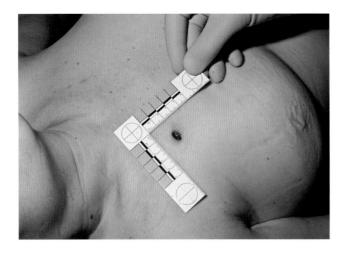

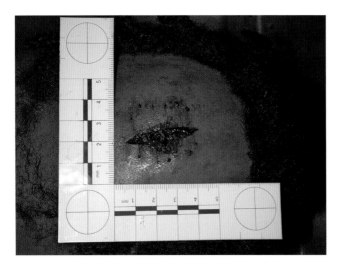

◀ **Figure 2.36a** Rifled entry wounds

The most common rifled weapon used in suicide is the handgun. Common sites of election include the head, chest, and abdomen. The temple, mouth, forehead, and under the chin are common sites on the head.

A contact entry wound from a rifled weapon is very variable in appearance because of the discharge of hot gases under the skin, and it is therefore difficult to interpret if the pathologist is inexperienced. These wounds may have a muzzle impression and can appear stellate if the discharge is over a bony prominence. They can resemble exit wounds. If a tight seal was formed, then there will be minimal burning and sooting.

◀ **Figure 2.36b** Rifled entry wounds

Rifled weapons discharge a single projectile. The appearance of the entrance wound depends on the distance at which the weapon was discharged. Single projectiles enter the skin and cause a well-defined wound unless the weapon was pushed tightly against the skin (contact wound). A close discharge is most often circular, and the edges are typically inverted. Soot deposition, powder stippling, and burning of the wound edge are also visible. Longer-distance entry wounds are almost circular or oval (depending on the angle of entry), with no burning, soiling, or bruising. The wound is clean and inverted. Classically, an entrance wound has an abrasion rim.

◀ **Figure 2.37** Rifled exit wounds

The exit wounds of rifled weapons tend to be larger than the entry wounds, the exception being if the entry wound was a contact wound because the gases under the skin expand the entry wound significantly. Exit wounds are typically clean and can appear as linear or stellate lacerations with an abraded and slightly everted margin. It is possible to mistake such injuries for ordinary lacerations. Exit wounds can show an atypical appearance if the exit skin is supported by tight clothing or a firm surface. The margins of these exit wounds can appear abraded. This is called a "shored exit wound." It is possible for the path of projectiles to deviate within the body, so the exit wound may not be directly opposite the entry wound. Therefore, it is important to identify the track that the projectile took through the body. If a general pathologist is at all unsure or lacking experience, then gunshot wounds are best left to forensic pathologists.

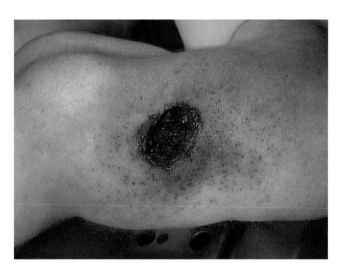

◀ **Figure 2.38a** Shotgun entry wounds
Common suicidal sites of election are under the chin, the center of the chest, or in the mouth. If the gun is placed in the mouth, radial splits can be seen to the lips because of gas expansion.

Shotguns discharge cartridges containing multiple metal pellets, and the patterns of injury are very different from those of rifled weapons. The appearance of the entrance wound depends on the distance at which the weapon was discharged, as well as the type of ammunition. A contact shotgun wound has a circular or oval appearance and shows some abrasion of the wound edge but minimal soot staining. There may be a muzzle impression.

Close discharge of a shotgun, as in this example, produces more irregular margins of the wound, with more sooting and burning of the wound margin. (Image courtesy of Dr. A. Jeffrey.)

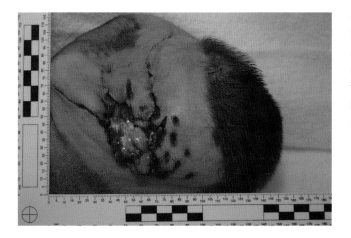

◀ **Figure 2.38b** Shotgun entry wounds
Longer-distance entry wounds show varying spread of shot, depending on the distance. Estimation of distance should be left to ballistics experts. It is essential to undertake postmortem imaging on gunshot and shotgun cases before the autopsy with either plain radiography or computed tomography.

47

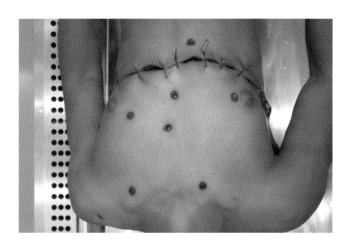

◀ **Figure 2.38c** Shotgun entry wounds—buckshot
This form of shot is much larger than birdshot. Buckshot is used for hunting larger game, such as deer (hence the derivation of the name). The most commonly produced buckshot shell is a 12-gauge, 00 buck shell that holds 9 pellets (each about 8 mm in diameter). The number of pellets can range from 8 to 18, depending on the make of cartridge. The pattern of injury is very distinct from that of birdshot and can be misinterpreted as each pellet wound being a separate rifled gunshot entry wound. Radiology, which should be considered mandatory in firearm injuries, assists in differentiation. In this example, the spread of the entry wounds indicates that the weapon was discharged from some distance, thus raising a concern of homicide.

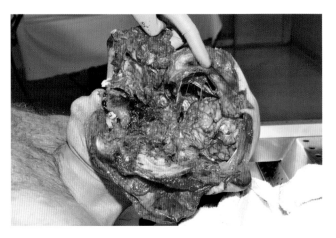

◀ **Figure 2.39a** Shotgun exit wounds
Shot from a shotgun penetrates poorly. The appearance of shotgun exit wounds varies depending on the part of the body injured and the size of the individual pellets. Typically, these wounds are jagged, irregular lacerations with everted edges and bone fragments under the skin.

In the head, neck, and limbs, shotgun exit wounds can be ragged and very large, with extensive tissue damage. In a suicide where the gun has been placed in the mouth, there will be significant disruption of the head, and brain may be expelled, the so-called "burst head" effect.

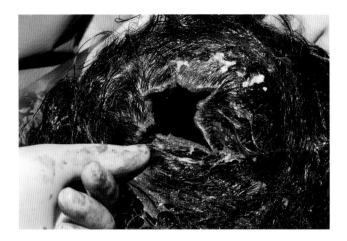

◀ **Figure 2.39b** Shotgun exit wounds
Initially, it may be difficult to distinguish the entrance and exit wounds, but by loosely reconstructing the skull and the wound edges, the injuries can be seen.

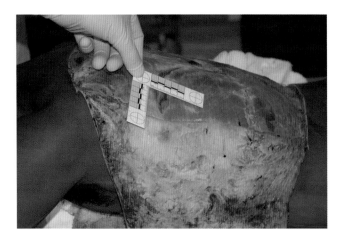

◀ **Figure 2.39c** Shotgun exit wounds
Exit wounds are uncommon in the trunk because the energy of each pellet is rapidly lost in the body. Bruising can be seen on the opposite side of the body, and pellets may be felt under the skin, a so-called "frustrated exit site."

Amputations

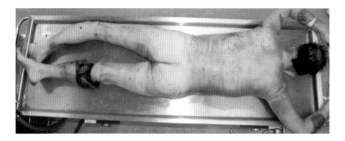

◀ **Figure 2.40a** Amputations

Traumatic amputation is the partial or total avulsion of a part of the body. These injuries are commonly seen in pedestrian-motor vehicle fatalities. When the vehicle strikes a standing pedestrian, the legs fracture at the level of impact and can amputate. It has been estimated that the speed has to be greater than 55 mph (89 km/hour) at the time of impact for amputation to occur.[6] There will be complex fracturing of the bone ends, with laceration of the skin and possible degloving of the soft tissue. There may also be soiling of the wound margins. Amputations can also occur in explosions and occupation accidents.

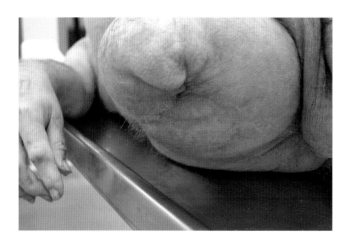

◀ **Figure 2.40b** Amputations

Limbs may also be amputated for medical reasons, such as peripheral vascular disease, diabetes, malignant disease, or gangrene. A surgical amputation is close to a joint and appears clean and neat. However, a traumatic amputation with subsequent plastic surgery may also appear neat. A medical amputation should prompt assessment for further disease, depending on the original etiology.

49

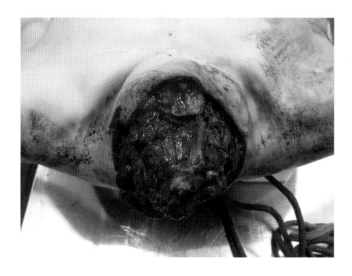

◀ **Figure 2.40c** Amputations

Decapitation may occur as a result of hanging when there is a long drop, such as when individuals hang themselves by jumping from a bridge. The ligature lacerates the neck structures, but there is typically no ligature mark.

References

1. Burton JL. The external examination: an often-neglected autopsy component. *Current Diagnostic Pathology* 2007;**13**(5):357–365.
2. Burton JL, Rutty GN, editors. *The hospital autopsy: a manual of fundamental autopsy practice*. 3rd ed. London: Arnold; 2010.
3. Vanezis P. Interpreting bruises at necropsy. *Journal of Clinical Pathology* 2001; **54**(5):348–355.
4. Langlois NE, Gresham GA. The ageing of bruises: a review and study of the colour changes with time. *Forensic Science International* 1991;**50**(2):227–238.
5. Knight B. *Knight's forensic pathology*. 3rd ed. London: Arnold; 2004.
6. Zivot U, Di Maio VJ. Motor vehicle-pedestrian accidents in adults: relationship between impact speed, injuries, and distance thrown. *American Journal of Forensic Medicine and Pathology* 1993;**14**(3):185–186.

Chapter 3
The Cardiovascular System

Introduction

Diseases of the cardiovascular system are common, and they are the most common cause of death in the Western world. Consequently, a careful and detailed examination of this organ system is an essential component of every autopsy examination.

Many pathologists find examination of the cardiovascular system to be one of the most difficult elements of the autopsy, and a systematic approach is crucial if significant disease is not to be missed. A fatal lesion in a coronary artery may be very small indeed. Before evisceration, consideration should be given to the possibility of cardiac air embolus, particularly in cases of neck injury or in deaths following neck surgery. Air emboli are most readily demonstrated radiographically, although they can be detected by careful dissection before evisceration.[1] The pericardium should be opened anteriorly; the appearance of the parietal and visceral layers and the presence, nature, and volume of any fluid present should be noted. The surfaces of the heart should be inspected before removing the heart from its vascular attachments.

The pulmonary trunk should be opened next, and the presence or absence of thromboemboli should be noted. Now the heart can be removed from its vascular attachments. The coronary arteries are examined by means of parallel transverse slices 2 to 3 mm apart, with observation of the presence or absence of atheromatous stenoses, calcification, thrombosis, dissection, stents, aneurysms, and grafts. The pathologist should comment on the degree of stenosis, which is most commonly assigned a percentage assessment of the degree of narrowing. Failure to examine the coronary arteries sufficiently closely is, in the author's experience, the most common reason for missing a cardiac cause of death at autopsy.

The ventricles of the heart are examined by means of two to three parallel 1-cm slices starting at the apex, with care taken not to reach the atrioventricular valves. The heart is then opened in the direction of blood flow, and the appearances of the valves, septa, and chambers are noted.

The aorta is most easily examined by opening it from the posterior aspect after removal of the diaphragm and extending the aortic incision into the common iliac arteries. The presence and extent of any atherosclerosis, aneurysm, or dissection are noted. The renal arteries should be opened longitudinally, with note taken of any atheromatous stenosis. The arteries arising from the aortic arch should be opened. Finally, the venae cavae and large veins should be examined.

Pericardium

Inflammation of the pericardium has a variety of causes and should prompt relevant investigation to exclude infective causes (Table 3.1). In many cases, the cause of pericarditis is unknown. In most cases, pericarditis is the result of the cause of death rather than the cause of death itself. The pericardium is typically inflamed, and there may be a fibrinous inflammatory exudate.

Table 3.1 Pericarditis: causes

Cause	Examples
Autoimmune disease	Ankylosing spondylitis Dermatomyositis Polyarteritis nodosa Sarcoidosis Systemic lupus erythematosus Rheumatoid arthritis Scleroderma
Bacterial infections	*Escherichia coli* *Salmonella typhimurium* *Staphylococcus aureus* *Streptococcus pneumoniae* *Mycobacterium tuberculosis* *Neisseria meningitidis*
Blunt chest trauma	—
Cancer	Breast cancer Lung cancer Lymphoma/leukemia Esophageal cancer Malignant melanoma Malignant mesothelioma Sarcoma
Cardiac surgery	Open heart surgery Radiofrequency ablation Cardiac catheterization
Chronic kidney disease	—
Drugs	Chemotherapeutic agents Hydralazine Isoniazid Penicillins Phenytoin Procainamide Tetracyclines Warfarin
Fungal infection	*Aspergillus* species *Candida albicans* *Coccidioides* species *Histoplasma capsulatum*
Genetic diseases	Familial Mediterranean fever
Hypothyroidism	—
Myocardial infarct	(Dressler syndrome)
Radiation therapy	Particularly in patients with lung cancer, breast cancer, or lymphoma
Viral infections	Adenoviruses Coxackieviruses Enteroviruses Epstein-Barr virus Hepatitis C virus Herpes simplex viruses Human immunodeficiency virus Influenza viruses Mumps virus

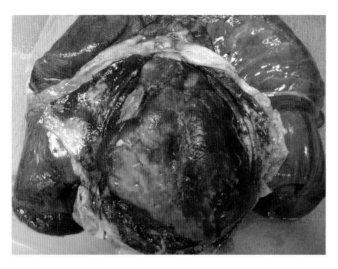

◀ **Figure 3.1a** Acute pericarditis
Acute pericarditis is typically a self-limiting illness, although the mortality rate for untreated tuberculous pericarditis is high. The acutely inflamed pericardium is erythematous, often with a fibrinous exudate. There may be a clear, turbid, or purulent pericardial effusion, which should be sampled for microbiological and virological testing. Shown here are (a) acute viral pericarditis and (b) pericarditis following a myocardial infarct.

◀ **Figure 3.1b** Acute pericarditis

53

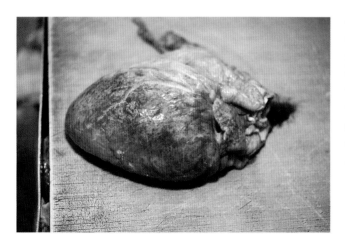

◀ **Figure 3.2** Chronic pericarditis
Chronic pericarditis is a rare complication of acute pericarditis, or it may be idiopathic. This example was a complication of chronic uremia. Over time, the chronically inflamed pericardium undergoes fibrous thickening, and focal or global calcification may supervene. The thickened or calcified pericardium constricts the heart, thus restricting venous filling during diastole and resulting in congestive cardiac failure.

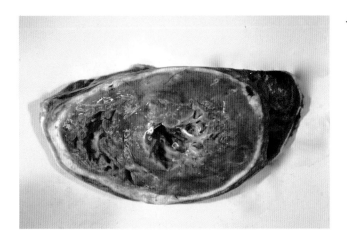

◀ **Figure 3.3a** Tumorous pericarditis
Tumorous pericarditis is most commonly seen as a result of direct invasion of the pericardium by an adjacent malignant tumor of the lung, esophagus, or pleura, although metastasis from a more distant site may also be seen. Primary malignant disease of the pericardium is rare. Histopathological examination confirms the diagnosis. (a) Involvement of the pericardium by a pleural malignant mesothelioma. (Image courtesy of Dr. S. K. Suvarna.) (b) Tumorous pericarditis in cross section.

◀ **Figure 3.3b** Tumorous pericarditis

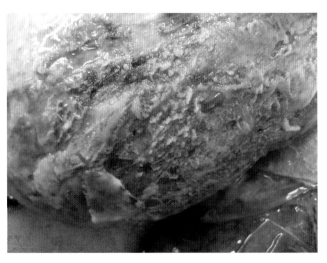

◀ **Figure 3.4** Pericardial adhesions
Fibrinous or fibrous adhesions are common complications of acute myocardial infarction and cardiac surgery, but they may complicate pericarditis of any cause. When fibrous, the adhesions commonly firmly bond the visceral and parietal layers of the pericardium together. They are typically most marked over the anterolateral surfaces of the heart and are therefore most easily divided by opening the pericardium posteriorly and then splitting the adhesions with blunt dissection using scissors. Care must be taken in patients who have undergone coronary artery bypass grafting not to sever the grafts. (Image courtesy of Dr. S. K. Suvarna.)

◀ Figure 3.5a Hemopericardium

Hemopericardium is readily recognized during evisceration and is commonly referred to as a "blue bag" because of the bluish appearance of blood beneath the visceral pericardium. It is most commonly the result of either a ruptured myocardial infarct or an aortic dissection. Other causes include chest trauma, ruptured coronary artery aneurysm, and anticoagulation therapy.[2]

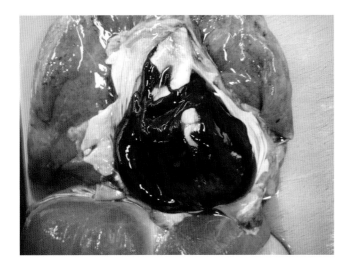

◀ Figure 3.5b Hemopericardium

A large volume (more than 250 mL) of blood in the pericardial sac causes tamponade of the heart, thus preventing venous filling during diastole and causing persistent electrical activity cardiac arrest.

55

Cardiac Trauma

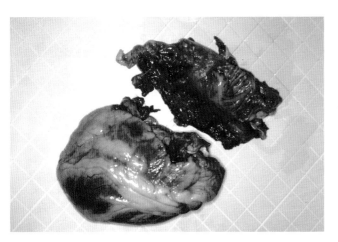

◀ Figure 3.6 Cardiac avulsion

Sudden deceleration, as may occur in falls from a height or in road traffic collisions, may result in fatal cardiac avulsion. The heart continues to move inside the chest after the chest wall has come to rest. In this example, the bulk of the ventricular tissues have been avulsed from the atria.

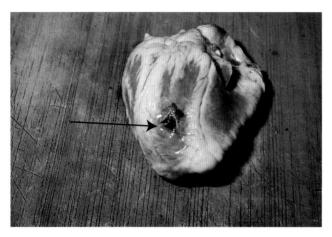

◀ **Figure 3.7** Gunshot wound to the heart
Gunshot wounds to organs should never come as a surprise—careful external examination, including of the back of the body, should reveal the entrance wound. This heart demonstrates a rifled gunshot entrance wound on the posterior surface of the left ventricle. Note the laceration, with associated superior subpericardial hemorrhage. There was a corresponding wound to the parietal pericardium. Such a wound should not be confused with a ruptured myocardial infarct.

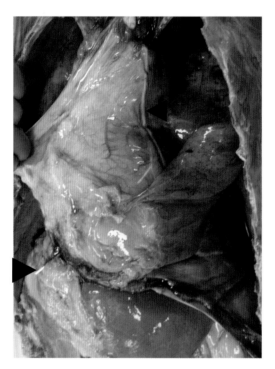

◀ **Figure 3.8a** Cardiac perforation during pericardiocentesis
Patients with a significant pericardial effusion may undergo drainage (pericardiocentesis) to prevent cardiac tamponade. This procedure may be complicated by cardiac perforation, with a resultant hemopericardium. A hemopericardium is visible through the unopened pericardium. The pericardiocentesis catheter can be seen entering the pericardium (bottom left) and within the pericardial sac (top right).

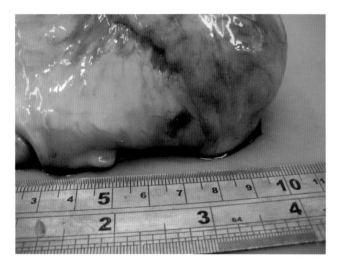

◀ **Figure 3.8b** Cardiac perforation during pericardiocentesis
On opening the pericardium and removing the blood, this 3-mm–diameter circular puncture wound was found in the apex of the right ventricle.

Coronary Arteries

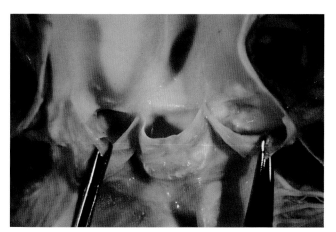

◀ **Figure 3.9** Anomalous coronary artery ostia
There are three cusps of the aortic valve: the noncoronary cusp, which contains no ostia; the right coronary cusp, which contains the ostia of the right coronary artery; and the left coronary cusp, which contains the ostia of the left coronary artery. The ostia of the left and right coronary arteries are located just above the aortic valve, as are the left and right sinuses of Valsalva. Anomalies of the coronary artery ostia are rare but well described, and they may be associated with a potentially fatal abnormal course of one or both coronary arteries. In this patient, both coronary arteries arise from the right anterior sinus.

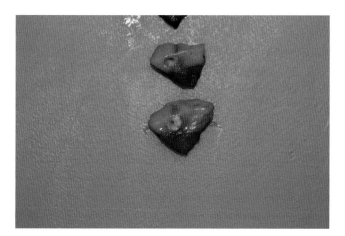

◀ **Figure 3.10a** Coronary artery atherosclerosis
Coronary artery atherosclerosis is thickening of the intima of the vessel wall secondary to deposition of lipid and fibrous tissue. This results in narrowing of the lumen, which can be concentric or eccentric. Atheromatous plaques may be complicated by calcification, rupture, hemorrhage, and thrombosis. The degree of coronary artery luminal stenosis can be estimated as a percentage or by a subjective scale of mild, moderate, or severe.

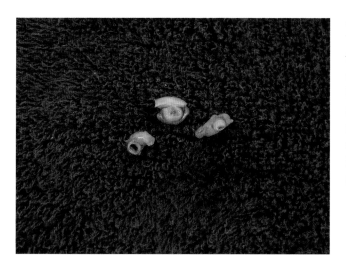

◀ **Figure 3.10b** Coronary artery atherosclerosis
The coronary arteries must be examined by careful serial transverse section at intervals of 2 to 3 mm. Severe stenosis is often focal and is easily missed. Sudden death is said to be confidently associated with more than 75% diameter stenosis. However, lesser degrees of stenosis may be acceptable for a diagnosis of cardiac death. The assessment of the degree of stenosis is highly subjective, but pathologists have been shown to be consistent at estimating severe stenosis (greater than 75%).

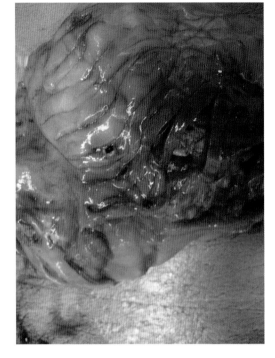

◀ **Figure 3.11a** Coronary artery thrombosis
Coronary artery thrombosis occurs as a result of ulceration or rupture of a coronary artery atheromatous plaque. The thrombus typically fills the arterial lumen, and it stands proud of the cut surface. Close inspection reveals it to have a matte granular surface, and lines of Zahn may be seen, allowing distinction from postmortem clot. Histopathological examination may be required to make this distinction. The myocardium supplied by the affected vessel or vessels must be examined carefully for the presence of an acute infarct. Such infarcts take at least 12 hours to become visible macroscopically.

◀ **Figure 3.11b** Coronary artery thrombosis

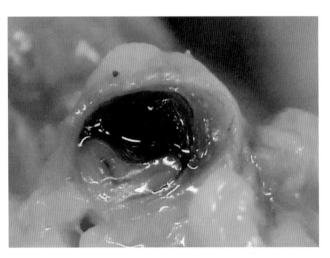

◀ **Figure 3.12** Coronary artery dissection
Spontaneous isolated coronary artery dissection is a rare event that can precipitate acute myocardial infarction and sudden death. The dissection starts as a subadventitial hematoma that enlarges and compresses the lumen. The pathological mechanism is not fully understood, but it is thought possibly to be related to female hormones. The condition has a higher incidence in women (80%), and is often seen in pregnancy. It is also possible for a thoracic aortic dissection to extend into the coronary arteries. Coronary artery dissection may also complicate percutaneous coronary instrumentation.[3] (From Sheppard MN. *Practical cardiovascular pathology.* 2nd ed. Boca Raton, FL: CRC Press; 2011.)

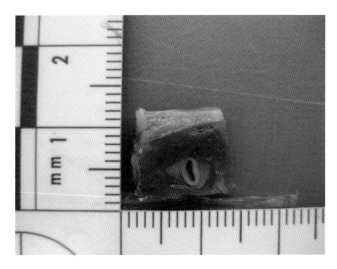

◄ Figure 3.13 Myocardial bridging
The coronary arteries normally run in the fat on the outside of the heart. Myocardial bridging occurs when one or more segments of one or more of these arteries takes an anomalous course and runs through the ventricular muscle. When this affects the left anterior descending coronary artery, when the artery lies 3 to 5 mm below the outer surface of the muscle layer of the heart, and when this occurs over a distance of at least 20 to 30 mm, it is associated with sudden cardiac death. The flow of blood through the coronary artery in systole and diastole is reduced (because the artery is compressed by the muscle), particularly in patients who have tachycardia. This reduces the supply of blood and oxygen to the heart muscle and predisposes to a sudden fatal cardiac arrhythmia.[4]

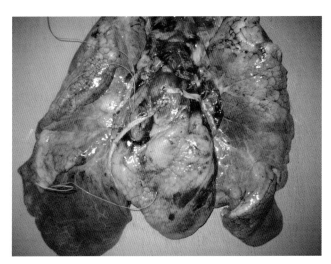

◄ Figure 3.14 Coronary artery bypass grafts
Coronary artery bypass graft surgery is a relatively common finding at autopsy, likely to instill terror in the trainee. Commonly, there is a graft from the left internal mammary artery to the left anterior descending coronary artery, in addition to saphenous vein grafts to one or more of the circumflex coronary artery, right coronary artery, or posterior descending coronary artery. The grafts should be opened longitudinally to determine their patency. The anastomosis sites must be examined carefully (with consideration to histopathological examination) for the presence or absence of thrombus, but the remainder of the natural coronary arteries should also be examined as usual.

59

Myocardial Disease

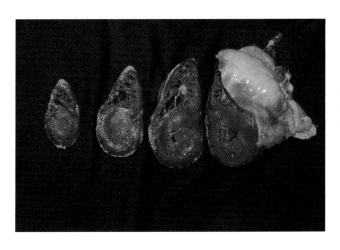

◄ Figure 3.15 Normal myocardium
Normal myocardium is a uniform dark brown. The atrial myocardium is normally 1 to 2 mm thick. The myocardium of the right ventricle is normally 3 to 5 mm thick at the outflow tract. The myocardium of the left ventricle is normally 12 to 15 mm thick at the outflow tract.

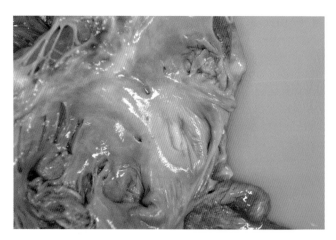

◄ **Figure 3.16** Normal fossa ovalis
In the fetal heart, the foramen ovale allows blood to enter the left atrium from the right atrium. The fossa ovalis is an oval depression in the inferior part of the interatrial septum. It represents the foramen ovale of the fetus. This normally closes within the first few months of life. Occasionally, fusion is incomplete, resulting in a patent foramen ovale (see Figure 3.17).

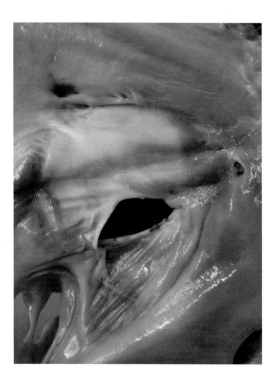

◄ **Figure 3.17** Patent foramen ovale
A patent foramen ovale is a common congenital heart defect and the most common cause of an atrioseptal defect in adults, but one that is often of no clinical significance. It is present in approximately 20% of the adult population. It is most easily detected at autopsy when opening the right atrium. The fossa ovalis should be examined with a probe. Patent foramina ovale are associated with paradoxical emboli, migraine, and decompression sickness. Larger atrial septal defects result in left-to-right shunting of blood that leads to pulmonary hypertension.

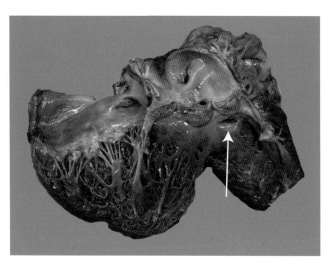

◄ **Figure 3.18** Ventricular septal defect
A ventricular septal defect (VSD) is a defect in the ventricular septum. Ninety percent of VSDs occur in the membranous septum, and the other 10% occur within the intraventricular septum. Large VSDs can produce left-to-right shunts that can lead to cardiac failure and pulmonary hypertension. VSDs are also associated with an increased risk of endocarditis. (Image courtesy of Dr. S. K. Suvarna.)

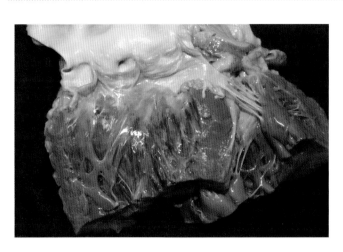

◄ Figure 3.19 Subendocardial hemorrhage

Subendocardial hemorrhages are commonly encountered at autopsy and are thought to be an agonal phenomenon. They are more commonly seen where there has been prolonged cardiopulmonary resuscitation with associated use of epinephrine.[5] Conditions associated with hypersecretion of epinephrine, including head injuries, abdominal injuries, and hypovolemic shock, may also result in subendocardial hemorrhage.

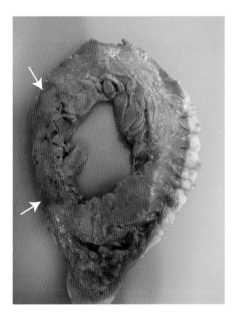

◄ Figure 3.20a Acute infarction

When death occurs within the first 6 to 12 hours following an acute infarct, the myocardium is typically both macroscopically and microscopically normal. As the interval between infarct and death increases, the infarcted myocardium becomes pale, and then tan-yellow with a rim of hyperemia (redness). This appearance is consistent with an infarct of 3 to 7 days' duration. The affected tissue is soft and friable, and there may be an associated mural thrombus.

61

◄ Figure 3.20b Acute infarction

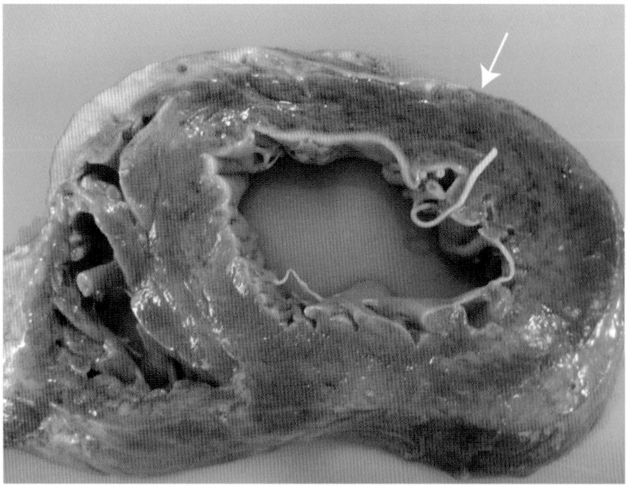

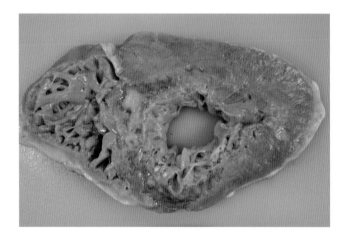

◀ **Figure 3.20c** Acute infarction

◀ **Figure 3.20d** Acute infarction

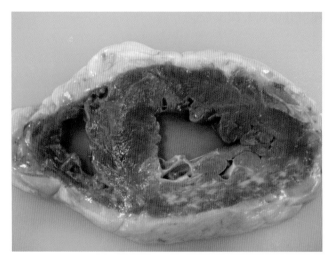

◀ **Figure 3.21** Myocardial fibrosis
Following infarction, the myocardium repairs itself with the deposition of collagen, typically 3 to 4 weeks after the insult. This forms dense collagenous scars that are seen as pale, irregular areas within the myocardium. These scars denote a previous myocardial infarct that occurred at least 6 weeks before death. The tissue is firmer to the touch, and the ventricular wall can be thinned as a result. Such a finding at autopsy is indicative of chronic ischemic damage.

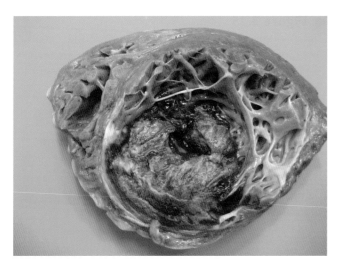

◄ Figure 3.22 Left ventricular aneurysm
Extensive transmural myocardial infarction of the left ventricle leads to replacement of the myocardium with fibrosis. The affected segment is noncontractile and appears white. Over time, the fibrotic wall becomes aneurismal and may calcify. Stasis of the blood occurs in the vicinity and leads to mural thrombus formation (as seen in this example).

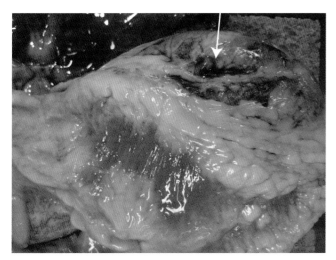

◄ Figure 3.23 Myocardial rupture secondary to infarct
Transmural myocardial infarct may be complicated by ventricular rupture. There may be no history of symptoms suggestive of a myocardial infarct. Such ruptures may affect the papillary muscles (resulting in acute valvular incompetence), the interventricular septum, or the free wall of the ventricle. Involvement of the free wall of the ventricle results in hemopericardium and cardiac tamponade. Following infarct, the necrotic myocardium is removed by phagocytes and is replaced by fibrosis. The myocardium is at its weakest approximately 4 to 5 days following the infarct, and this is when most postinfarct ruptures occur.[6]

63

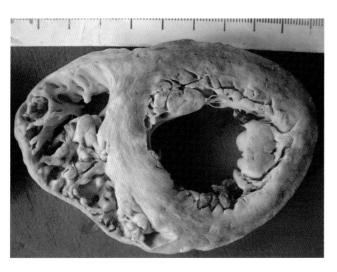

◄ Figure 3.24 Myocarditis: random scarring
Myocarditis is an uncommon autopsy finding. The heart often appears macroscopically normal[7] but the diagnosis should be suspected in cases where there is a history of cardiac failure and macroscopic examination reveals normal coronary arteries and valves. In up to two-thirds of patients the diagnosis has not been suspected in life.[8] Where macroscopic evidence is present it is generally very subtle. Close inspection of the myocardium may reveal pale yellow linear stripes (so-called tiger-striping). Small yellow abscesses may be seen on the epicardial surface. (Image courtesy of *Sheppard's Practical Cardiovascular Pathology, 2e,* Figure 6.12.)

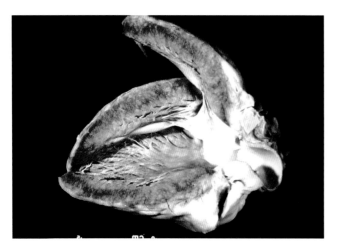

◀ **Figure 3.25** Giant cell myocarditis
Giant cell myocarditis is a rare cause of sudden death. The cause is unknown, but associations with thymoma and inflammatory bowel disease have been reported. The condition typically affects young, otherwise healthy adults. At autopsy the heart may appear macroscopically normal. In this example, a band of inflamed myocardium is evident in the left ventricle. Histopathological examination is recommended in any case of suspected myocarditis, and it confirms the diagnosis.

The normal left ventricular myocardium is 12 to 15 mm thick at the outflow tract. Hypertrophy of the ventricular myocardium is seen as a physiological response in athletes. Left ventricular hypertrophy is a cause of sudden death, and a search should be made for the underlying cause. Pathological causes are listed in Table 3.2.[9] Sarcomere disorders, mitochondrial myopathies, metabolic causes, syndromes, and left ventricular noncompaction are all rare.

Table 3.2 Left ventricular hypertrophy

Cause	Examples
Increased cardiac workload	Systemic hypertension Aortic stenosis Mitral regurgitation Obesity
Cardiac infiltration	Amyloidosis Hemochromatosis
Sarcomere disorders	Hypertrophic cardiomyopathy
Mitochondrial myopathies	Kearns-Sayre syndrome
Metabolic diseases	Fabry disease Pompe disease Danon disease PRKAG2-cardiomyopathy Primary carnitine deficiency
Syndromes	Noonan syndrome Friedreich ataxia
Unclassified	Left ventricular noncompaction

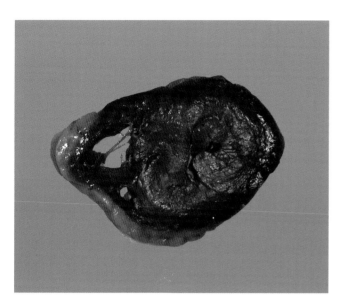

◄ Figure 3.26a Hypertrophic cardiomyopathy
Hypertrophic cardiomyopathy (HCM) is caused by a range of different gene mutations. The disease is characterized by left ventricular hypertrophy that is typically (but not always) asymmetrical, primarily affecting the intraventricular septum. The condition leads to reduced ventricular compliance with impaired left ventricular diastolic filling and outflow obstruction. Approximately 50% of cases are familial. The condition predisposes to arrhythmias and sudden cardiac death. (Image courtesy of Dr. S. K. Suvarna.)

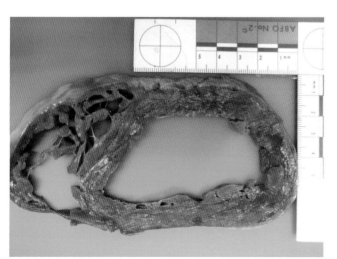

◄ Figure 3.26b Hypertrophic cardiomyopathy
In hypertrophic cardiomyopathy (HCM), the anterior cusp of the mitral valve moves forward to hit the expanded ventricular septum. This impaction leads to an area of endocardial thickening on the septum just below the aortic valve. This endocardial impact lesion is a definitive feature of obstructive HCM, but it is not always present. Where obstructive HCM is suspected, the myocardium should be sampled extensively for histopathological examination, and a sample of skeletal muscle or spleen should be retained to permit future genetic analysis. (Image courtesy of Dr. S. K. Suvarna.)

65

◄ Figure 3.27 Dilated cardiomyopathy
In dilated cardiomyopathy, the heart is enlarged and globoid. It is often described as "baggy" or "flabby." The ventricles show marked cavity dilatation with thinning of the wall around the whole circumference; this results in grossly impaired contractility of the heart and subsequent failure.

Many of these cases have no known etiology (idiopathic dilated cardiomyopathy), whereas others may be associated with chronic alcoholism (alcoholic cardiomyopathy). Other causes include myocarditis, hypertension, obesity, chronic ischemia, pregnancy, and genetic factors (familial dilated cardiomyopathy).

◀ **Figure 3.28** Hypertensive heart disease
Hypertensive heart disease (hypertensive cardiomyopathy) is the most common cause of left ventricular hypertrophy at autopsy. The myocardium of the left ventricle is concentrically hypertrophic (left ventricular outflow tract thickness >15 mm) in the absence of valvular heart disease or histological evidence of hypertrophic cardiomyopathy. Overall heart weight is also useful in the diagnosis of left ventricular hypertrophy. There may or may not be a history of systemic hypertension, and the kidneys may or may not reveal evidence of hypertensive damage.

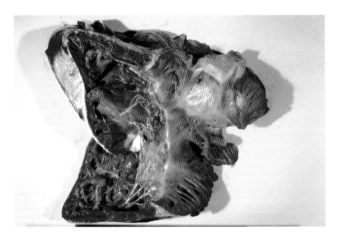

◀ **Figure 3.29** Right ventricular hypertrophy
The myocardium of the normal right ventricle is 2 to 5 mm thick, when measured at the outflow tract 1 cm below the pulmonary valve. Both pulmonary valve stenosis and pulmonary hypertension (as in this example) increase right ventricular afterload, with resultant right ventricular hypertrophy. Dissection of the heart using the Fulton method confirms right ventricular hypertrophy.

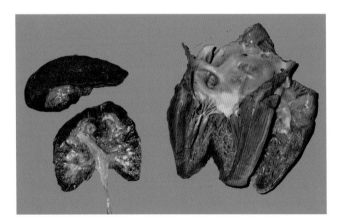

◀ **Figure 3.30** Cardiac amyloid
Amyloid heart disease can be classified as primary, secondary, familial, or senile. Primary amyloid heart disease is caused by overproduction of light-chain immunoglobulin, usually associated with multiple myeloma. Secondary amyloid heart disease is associated with chronic inflammatory conditions such as Crohn disease, rheumatoid arthritis, and tuberculosis. The presence of nearly normal left ventricular dimensions combined with increased myocardial wall thickness should arouse suspicion of infiltrative cardiomyopathy. The amyloid deposits can produce a finely granular endocardial surface to the chambers and the valves, giving a "sandy" texture when palpated. Histological sections stained with Congo red confirm the presence of amyloid. (Image courtesy of Dr. S. K. Suvarna.)

◀ **Figure 3.31a** Arrhythmogenic right ventricular cardiomyopathy

Arrhythmogenic right ventricular cardiomyopathy (ARVC) is a rare genetic nonischemic cardiomyopathy that involves primarily the right ventricle. Older texts may refer to it as arrhythmogenic left ventricular dysplasia (ARVD). It is characterized by hypokinetic areas of the right ventricle as a result of replacement of the myocardium with adipose and fibrous tissue. The right ventricle can be grossly dilated. The condition can lead to arrhythmias and sudden cardiac death. In approximately one third of cases, there is a left ventricular component. The autopsy finding can be very subtle, and hence the right ventricle should be extensively sampled after any sudden death in a young person. (Figure 3.31a courtesy of Dr. S. K. Suvarna.)

◀ **Figure 3.31b** Arrhythmogenic right ventricular cardiomyopathy

67

Cardiac Tumors

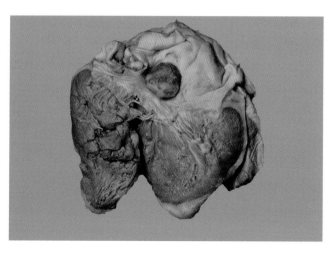

◀ **Figure 3.32** Atrial myxoma

Atrial myxoma is the most common primary cardiac neoplasm. These tumors are most frequently found as a polypoid mass attached to the atrial wall (90%), but they can also arise on the valve or ventricular wall. They can be associated with sudden death because the tumor can form a ball-like mass that can occlude the valve. It is also possible for tumor fragments to break off and embolize, leading to cerebral infarction. (Image courtesy of Dr. S. K. Suvarna.)

◀ **Figure 3.33** Fibroelastoma

Fibroelastomas are the second most common cardiac tumors after myxomas and are the most common tumor to arise from valves. They are typically found in the aortic valve and anterior mitral valve leaflet. The tumors are composed of branching avascular papillae, made up of collagen, that are covered by endothelium. Single or multiple lesions can develop. They can appear as myxoid masses at autopsy because of the fronds collapsing, but if the tumor is put in water, the fronds open up and the tumor resembles a sea anemone. These tumors are generally clinically insignificant and are often incidental findings at autopsy. As with atrial myomas, fibroelastomas have been reported in association with myocardial infarction and embolization causing stroke.[10] (Image courtesy of Dr. S. K. Suvarna.)

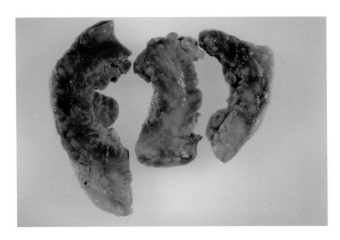

◀ **Figure 3.34** Cardiac lymphoma

Lymphomatous involvement of the heart is rare, and primary cardiac lymphoma is even rarer. Lymphoma most commonly affects the right atrium and ventricle, but the entire myocardium may be involved. Macroscopically, the tumor appears white and may be manifest as a discrete nodule or, as in this example, may be more diffuse. It should not be confused with myocardial fibrosis. Histopathological examination confirms the diagnosis. Death may result from sudden fatal cardiac arrhythmia.

Valvular Heart Disease

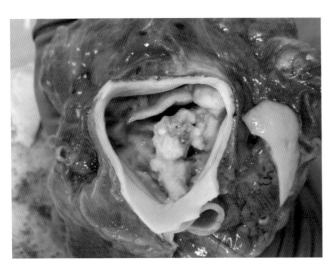

◀ **Figure 3.35a** Calcific aortic valve disease

The most common causes of a calcified aortic valve leading to stenosis are age-related change (senile aortic stenosis) and a bicuspid valve. In older adults, a normal tricuspid valve undergoes slow progressive degenerative calcification. Dense, white nodules of calcification can be seen on the valve cusps; this calcification leads to impaired function, subsequent left ventricular hypertrophy, and eventual cardiac failure. A valve diameter of 1 cm^2 or less can be associated with sudden left ventricular failure resulting from a massive increase in the pressure gradient. (Image courtesy of Dr. S. K. Suvarna.)

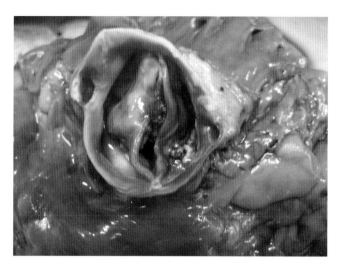

◀ **Figure 3.35b** Calcific aortic valve disease
Bicuspid valves are seen in approximately 1% to 2% of
the population, as a result of congenital fusion between
two of the cusps, thought to occur *in utero*. Bicuspid
valves are thought to be asymptomatic for the first 2 to
3 decades of life. (Image courtesy of Dr. S. K. Suvarna.)

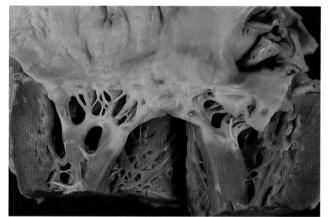

◀ **Figure 3.36** Rheumatic heart disease
Rheumatic heart disease is cardiac inflammation and
scarring triggered by an autoimmune reaction to
infection with group A streptococci. In the acute stage,
this condition consists of pancarditis. Small, uniformly
sized thrombotic "verrucous" vegetations can be seen
on the valves, although these do not produce valve
destruction. Although rheumatic fever was previously
the most common cause of heart valve replacement or
repair, this disease is currently relatively uncommon in
industrialized countries.

Chronic rheumatic fever leads to cusp fusion, valve
thickening, and calcification resulting in stenosis and/
or insufficiency. The mitral valve is most commonly
affected. The appearance of the mitral valve is likened
to a fish mouth. There is also diffuse scarring of the
aortic valve, with cusp fibrosis and thickening of the
leaflets. Shortened and thickened chordae tendineae
can also be seen. (From Sheppard MN. *Practical
cardiovascular pathology*. 2nd ed. Boca Raton, FL: CRC
Press; 2011.)

69

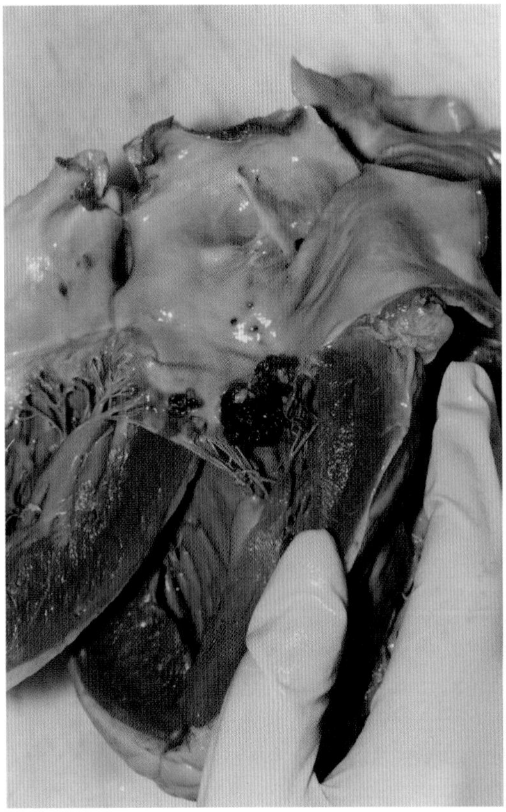

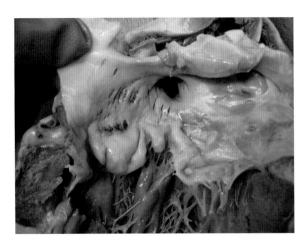

◀ **Figure 3.37a** Endocarditis: vegetations

Infective endocarditis is an infection of the endocardium of the heart, which produces cardiac effects such as valvular insufficiency and a wide variety of systemic effects including emboli.

At autopsy the valve demonstrates large, irregular, reddish-tan vegetations; these slowly destroy the valve cusps. The vegetations are composed of fibrin, platelets, mixed inflammatory cells, and bacterial colonies. Portions of the vegetation can break off and become septic emboli. The infection can spread from the valves into the underlying myocardium.

Multiple organisms can be associated, e.g., *Staphylococcus aureus*, *Streptococci sp.*, *Pseudomonas aeruginosa*, *Enterococci* as well as fungi. Virulent organisms, such as *S. aureus*, produce an "acute" bacterial endocarditis, while some organisms such as *Streptococcus viridans* produce a "subacute" bacterial endocarditis.

◀ **Figure 3.37b** Endocarditis: vegetations

A number of risk factors increase the chance of developing infective endocarditis: valvular heart disease, valve replacement, structural congenital heart disease including septal defects, hypertrophic cardiomyopathy, and intravenous drug abuse.

◀ **Figure 3.38** Floppy mitral valve

In this disease, the valve is degenerate, causing the affected part of the valve to prolapse into the left atrium when the left ventricle contracts. It is recognized that floppy mitral valve predisposes to the development of sudden fatal cardiac arrhythmias. Floppy mitral valve is a congenital heart disease. Although in many cases this is a sporadic change, this disease can occur in families as a result of an inherited autosomal dominant mutation. Because the disease may be asymptomatic but is a cause of sudden unexpected death, it is recommended that first-degree family members (parents, siblings, children) seek screening for this condition via their general practitioners.

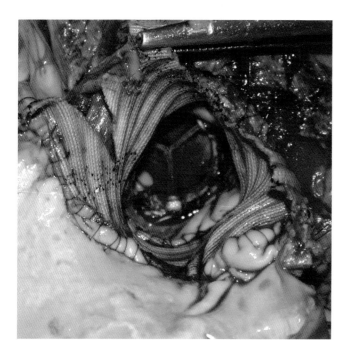

◀ **Figure 3.39a** Prosthetic valves

Many types of prosthetic valves are on the market. The main types are tissue valves and mechanical valves.

Tissue valves can be derived from either cadaveric human grafts or porcine xenografts. The valves consist of the donor valve grafted onto a metal stent. The main advantage of these bioprostheses is the lack of need for continued anticoagulation. However the valves have a limited life span of 5–10 years due to wear and calcification. (Image courtesy of Dr. S. K. Suvarna.)

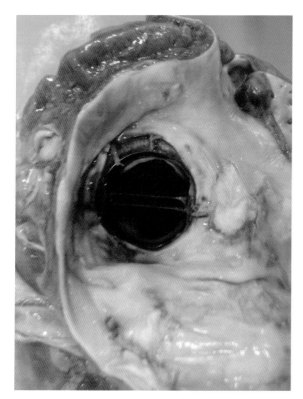

◀ **Figure 3.39b** Prosthetic valves

Mechanical valves have a longer life span but require life-long anticoagulation, due to the significant increased risk of thrombus formation. A variety of problems can complicate prosthetic heart valves, including thrombosis, infections, structural failure, and dehiscence leading to para-valvular leakage.

71

Peripheral Vascular Disease

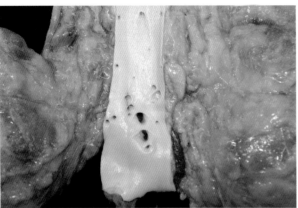

◀ **Figure 3.40** Normal arterial intima
The normal arterial intima is perfectly smooth and has a glossy off-white–pale cream color.

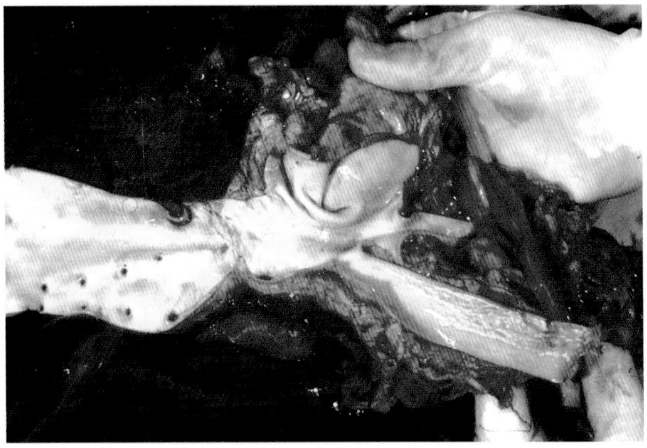

◀ **Figure 3.41** Coarctation of the aorta
Coarctation is a rare finding in the adult autopsy. It is caused by a congenital narrowing of the aorta, typically in the region of the site of insertion of the ductus arteriosus. The finding may be incidental to the cause of death, but severe coarctation may increase left ventricular afterload, resulting in left ventricular hypertrophy and sudden death. Coarctation also carries an increased risk of stroke, coronary artery atherosclerosis, and aortic dissection (all likely secondary to hypertension in the vasculature proximal to the coarctation).

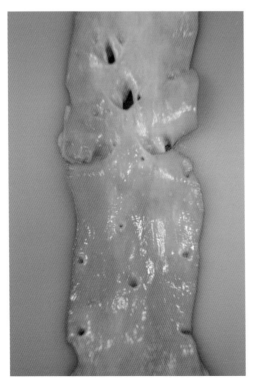

◀ **Figure 3.42a** Atheroma
Atheroma is a common finding at autopsy and is most commonly seen in the aorta. At autopsy, both the type of atheromatous lesion (fatty streak, fibrolipid plaque, complicated plaque) and the extent of the disease (mild, moderate, severe) should be noted.

Fatty streaks are the first macroscopically visible atherosclerotic lesions, developing by the age of 10 years. They are nonpalpable, irregular linear areas of yellow-white discoloration of the aortic intima. It is thought that they are the precursor lesions of fibrolipid plaques.

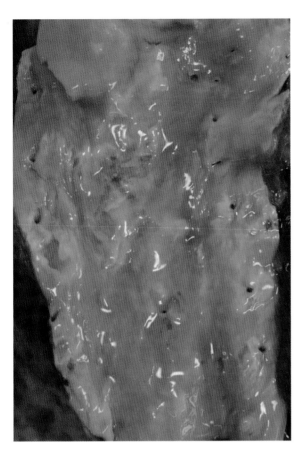

◀ **Figure 3.42b** Atheroma
Fibrolipid plaques are palpable lesions that are yellow or white. They are most commonly seen in the abdominal aorta below the level of the renal arteries and at the aortic ostia and bifurcation.

73

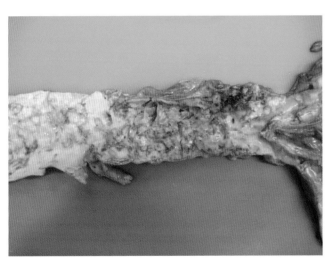

◀ **Figure 3.42c** Atheroma
Complicated atheroma is the most common form of atherosclerosis found in the adult autopsy population. Fibrolipid plaques are described as complicated if they are calcified, ulcerated, hemorrhagic, or associated with thrombus.

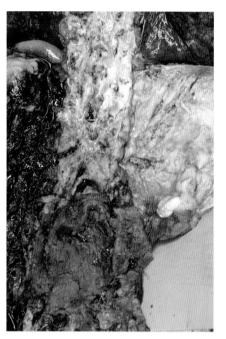

◀ **Figure 3.43a** Atheromatous abdominal aortic aneurysm

An aneurysm is an abnormally dilated artery. Aneurysms of the aorta are common autopsy findings, particularly in older persons, and they are most commonly the result of atherosclerosis. They are more common in smokers and in persons with systemic hypertension. The incidence rises with increasing age. Autopsy studies indicate that the prevalence of atheromatous abdominal aortic aneurysms is increasing,[11] most likely as the result of an aging population. Morphologically, aortic aneurysms may be fusiform or saccular. Both forms commonly contain laminated thrombus that is adherent to the intima. The location, diameter, and length of the aneurysm should be recorded in the autopsy report.

Fusiform aneurysms are spindle shaped and result from circumferential weakness in the wall of the aorta.

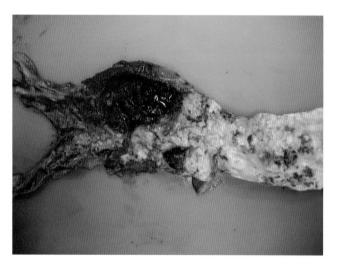

◀ **Figure 3.43b** Atheromatous abdominal aortic aneurysm

Saccular aneurysms are spherical, typically have a narrow neck, and result from a localized weakness in the wall of the aorta.

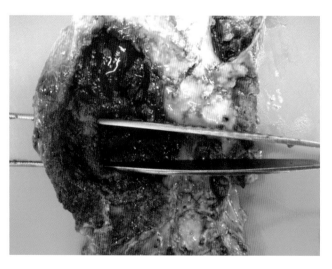

◀ **Figure 3.44** Ruptured abdominal aortic aneurysm

As abdominal aortic aneurysms increase in size, there is progressive thinning of the vessel wall, ultimately resulting in rupture, with consequent catastrophic hemorrhage into the retroperitoneal space. The hemorrhage is visible in the retroperitoneal tissues on opening the abdomen, and it may extend into the intestinal mesentery. Anterior rupture of large aneurysms may result in hemoperitoneum.

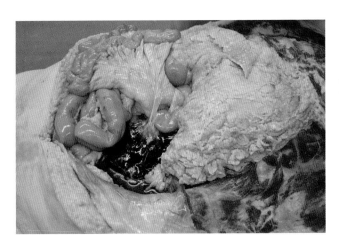

◄ Figure 3.45 Retroperitoneal hemorrhage resulting from a ruptured abdominal aortic aneurysm

A ruptured abdominal aortic aneurysm is typically first identified at autopsy on opening the abdominal cavity, before evisceration. Blood is readily seen in the retroperitoneal space, and this may extend into the root of the small intestinal mesentery. The volume of blood can be quite significant.

Aortic dissection occurs when blood penetrates the aortic intima and enters the medial layer, thus stripping (dissecting) the intima and inner media of the aorta away from the outer media and adventitia. It is typically seen in those with systemic hypertension, connective tissue diseases (including Marfan syndrome), Turner syndrome, bicuspid aortic valve, cardiac surgery, and blunt chest trauma. Dissection resulting from vasculitis (including tertiary syphilis) is rare. Two systems are in use to classify aortic dissections. In the Debakey system,[12] aortic dissections are classified according to the origin and extent of the dissection. In the Stanford classification,[13] dissections are classified according to whether or not the ascending aorta is involved (Table 3.3).

75

Table 3.3 Aortic dissection: classification

Description	Debakey	Stanford
Dissection begins in the ascending aorta and propagates to the aortic arch or beyond.	I	A
Dissection begins in and is confined to the ascending aorta.	II	
Dissection begins in the descending aorta and extends distally.	III	B

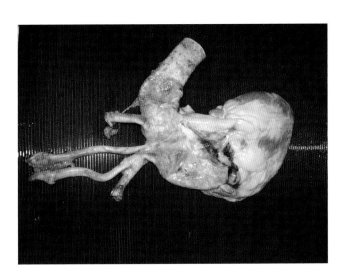

◄ Figure 3.46a Aortic dissection

Aortic dissection is readily recognized on opening the aorta at autopsy.

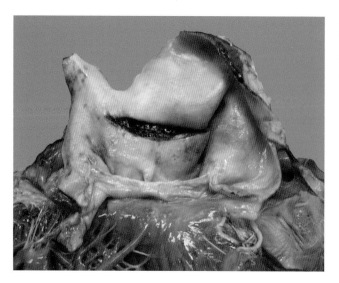

◀ **Figure 3.46b** Aortic dissection
The intima and inner media are separated from the outer media and adventitia by blood clot. (Image courtesy of Dr. S. K. Suvarna.)

◀ **Figure 3.46c** Aortic dissection
Close inspection of the intima along the full length of the aorta typically reveals the site of origin, thereby allowing classification. The dissection may rupture back into the aortic lumen, into the pericardium (causing hemopericardium), into either thoracic cavity (causing hemothorax), or into the retroperitoneal space.

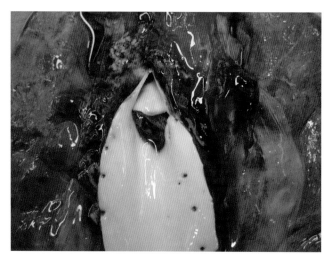

◀ **Figure 3.47a** Traumatic rupture of aorta
Partial or complete traumatic rupture/transection of the aorta is a common autopsy finding in those dying following a high-speed deceleration, such as is encountered in road traffic collisions and falls from a height.[14,15] The aorta typically transects at the junction of the arch and descending aorta, immediately distal to the origin of the left subclavian artery, with resultant catastrophic hemorrhage. Multiple tears are common.[16] Rupture may be partial (a) or complete (b). ((b) Courtesy of Dr. A. Jeffrey.)

◀ **Figure 3.47b** Traumatic rupture of aorta

◀ **Figure 3.48** Tram-line intimal tears
Sudden deceleration may cause parallel linear transverse intimal tears that resemble tram lines. As with traumatic rupture, these typically are seen in the proximal descending aorta. There may be an associated transection. They are also referred to as "ladder tears."

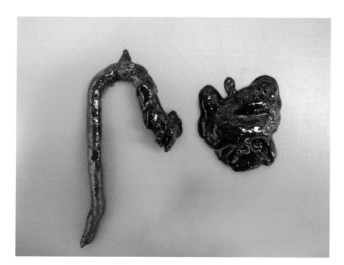

◀ **Figure 3.49** Thrombus versus clot
Although commonly regarded as synonyms, thrombus and clot are not the same. Thrombosis is the coagulation of blood within the cardiovascular system in life. Clot formation is the coagulation of blood in all other circumstances. At autopsy, thrombus and clot have different appearances.

Thrombus (on the left of the image) typically has a granular matte surface and a laminated structure (lines of Zahn). Unlike clot, thrombus cannot be easily rubbed into a sponge. When a vessel containing thrombus is cut transversely, the thrombus typically stands proud of the cut surface of the vessel, rather like toothpaste oozing from the tube.

Clots (on the right of the image) appear red or white, depending on whether their dominant constituent is cellular or acellular. Clots have a glossy surface, lack internal structure, and are soft. Red clots (sometimes referred to as "black currant jelly" clots) can be easily rubbed into a sponge. White clots (sometimes referred to as "chicken fat clots") are gelatinous and composed of blood plasma.

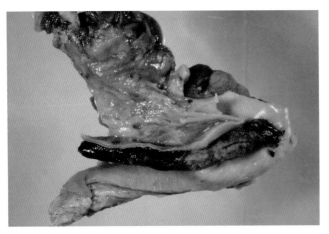

◀ **Figure 3.50** Thrombus in the carotid artery
The carotid artery may become occluded by thrombus as a complication of atherosclerosis, trauma, and endarterectomy. The carotid arteries should be opened and examined in every autopsy examination. Thrombotic occlusion of the carotid artery may itself be complicated by cerebral infarction.

◀ **Figure 3.51** Deep venous thrombosis
In a patient with a pulmonary thromboembolus, a search should be made for deep venous thrombosis. Venous thrombi most typically occur in the deep veins of the thighs or calves. Thrombi in the thighs may be demonstrated by firm caudal-to-cephalic pressure on the medial thighs while inspecting the cut end of the iliac vein in the pelvis, although this maneuver disrupts the interface between the thrombus and vessel wall and is inadvisable if it is necessary to attempt to date a thrombus (e.g., to identify whether it predates or postdates a surgical intervention). Thrombi in the deep veins of the calf are identified by making a deep vertical incision into the belly of the calf muscles and by then making serial transverse incisions into the muscles, down to bone. If no thrombus can be identified in the deep veins of the legs, then this may simply mean that the thrombus has migrated in its entirety and does not exclude the deep veins as the source of pulmonary thromboemboli.

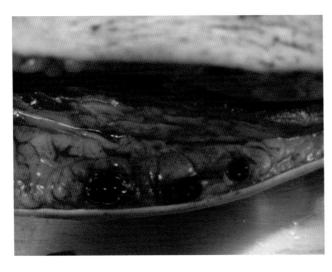

◀ **Figure 3.52** Varicose veins
Varicose veins are common but typically of no great pathological significance at autopsy unless they become injured and produce significant bleeding. They result from incompetence of venous valves and are more common in older persons and obese persons. They are more common in women than in men and are typically found on the calves or thighs. Seen in cross-section here, they are abnormally dilated veins containing blood clot.

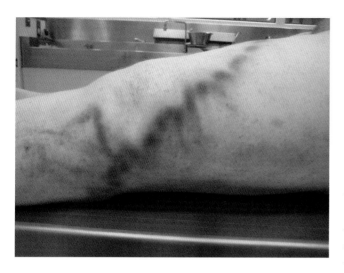

◀ Figure 3.53 Thrombophlebitis
Thrombophlebitis occurs when a superficial vein in the leg (typically a varicose vein) becomes inflamed. This disorder is more common in persons who are obese and in smokers. The blood within the inflamed vessel forms a thrombus. The affected vein is tender and hard, and there may be associated redness of the overlying skin, as shown in the image. Although it is painful, thrombophlebitis is typically a self-limited disease without serious complications. However, if the thrombus in the affected vein extends into the deep venous system of the leg, it may result in deep venous thrombosis, which can be complicated by pulmonary thromboembolism. This is a rare complication of thrombophlebitis.

References

1. Burton JL, Rutty GN. Dissection of the internal organs. In: Burton JL, Rutty DN, editors. *The hospital autopsy: a manual of fundamental autopsy practice.* 3rd ed. London: Hodder Arnold; 2010:136–158.
2. Levis JT, Degado MC. Hemopericardium and cardiac tamponade in a patient with an elevated international normalised ratio. *Western Journal of Emergency Medicine* 2009;**10**:115–119.
3. Hokken RB, Foley D, van Domburg R, Serruys PW. Left main coronary artery dissection during percutaneous coronary intervention treated by stenting. *Netherlands Heart Journal* 2002;**10**:395–398.
4. Alegria JR, Herrmann J, Holmes Jnr DR, Lerman A, Rihal CS. Myocardial bridging. *European Heart Journal* 2005;**26**:1159–1168.
5. Charaschaisri W, Jongprasartsuk K, Rungruanghiranya S, Kaufman L. Forensic aspect of cause of subendocardial hemorrhage in cardiopulmonary resuscitation cases: chest compression or adrenaline. *American Journal of Forensic Medicine and Pathology* 2011;**32**:58–60.
6. Mundth ED. Rupture of the heart complicating myocardial infarction. *Circulation* 1972;**46**:427–429.
7. Fabre A, Sheppard MN. Sudden adult death syndrome and other non-ischaemic causes of sudden cardiac death. *Heart* 2006;**92**:316–320.
8. Kytö V, Vuorinen T, Saukko P, Lautenschlager I, Lignitz E, Saraste A, Voipio-Pulkki LM. Cytomegalovirus infection of the heart is common in patients with fatal myocarditis. *Clinical Infectious Diseases* 2005;**40**:683–688.
9. Yousef Z, Elliott PM, Cecchi F, Escoubet B, Linhart A, Monserrat L, Namdar M, Weidemann F. Left ventricular hypertrophy in Fabry disease: a practical approach to diagnosis. *European Heart Journal* 2013;**34**(11):802–808.
10. Zurrú MC, Romano M, Patrucco L, Cristiano E, Milei J. Embolic stroke secondary to cardiac papillary fibroelastoma. *Neurologist* 2008;**14**:128–130.
11. Bengtsson H, Berggvist D, Sternby NH. Increasing prevalence of abdominal aortic aneurysms: a necropsy study. *European Journal of Surgery* 1992;**158**:19–23.

12. DeBakey ME, Henly WS, Cooley DA, Morris GC Jr, Crawford ES, Beall AC Jr. Surgical management of dissecting aneurysms of the aorta. *Journal of Thoracic and Cardiovascular Surgery* 1965;**49:**130–149.
13. Daily PO, Trueblood HW, Stinson EB, Wuerflein RD, Shumway NE. Management of acute aortic dissections. *Annals of Thoracic Surgery* 1970;**10:**237–247.
14. Burkhart HM, Gomez GA, Jacobson LE, Pless JE, Broadie TA. Fatal blunt aortic injuries: a review of 242 autopsy cases. *Journal of Trauma* 2001;**50:**113–115.
15. Teixeria PG, Inaba K, Barmparas G, Georgiou C, Toms C, Noguchi TT, Rogers C, Sathyavagiswaran L, Demetriades D. Blunt thoracic aortic injuries: an autopsy study. *Journal of Trauma* 2011;**70:**197–202.
16. Moar JJ. Traumatic rupture of the thoracic aorta: an autopsy and histopathological study. *South African Medical Journal* 1985;**67:**383–385.

Chapter 4
The Respiratory System

Introduction

Diseases of the respiratory system are very common and range from the trivial to the fatal. The respiratory system is the most commonly infected organ system of the body, presenting as it does a large surface area to the environment. It is a common site for primary and metastatic malignant disease. Inflammatory and occupational diseases are also common. A careful and thorough examination of the respiratory system is a vital component of any autopsy and frequently rewards the vigilant pathologist with a cause of death.

This chapter considers the macroscopic diseases most commonly encountered in the larynx, trachea and main bronchi, lungs, pleura, and diaphragm.

Larynx

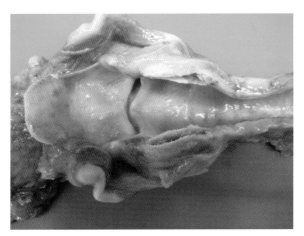

◀ **Figure 4.1** Normal larynx
The normal larynx is a cartilaginous box comprising the epiglottis, thyroid and cricoid cartilages, and the paired arytenoid, corniculate, and cuneiform cartilages. It extends from the tip of the epiglottis to the inferior border of the cricoid. The interior of the larynx is lined by respiratory epithelium, with the exception of the true vocal cords, which are lined by squamous epithelium. The lining mucosa is smooth and shiny.

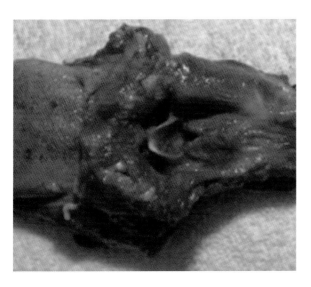

◀ **Figure 4.2** Edema (anaphylaxis)
Laryngeal edema is a rare autopsy finding. It may occur as a result of angioedema, anaphylaxis, or intubation. The absence of laryngeal edema does *not* exclude a diagnosis of anaphylaxis because the edema may resolve rapidly after death. The edematous larynx has a pale, swollen mucosa that partially or completely obstructs the airway. (Image courtesy of Dr. A. Jeffrey.)

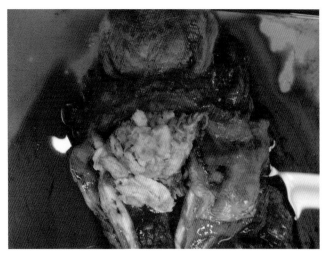

◀ **Figure 4.3** Obstruction resulting from food bolus
A history of sudden collapse and death while eating, with or without a history of choking, should raise concern that the patient died of airway obstruction by a food bolus (a so-called "café coronary"). The obstructing food bolus is best detected by dissecting the anterior neck structures and opening the larynx and trachea while *in situ*. The food bolus is typically found lodged in the glottis between the true vocal cords. Acute obstruction by a food bolus is most typically seen in persons with a neurological disease affecting swallowing, such as stroke, dementia, and Parkinson disease, but it is also seen in those wearing dentures and those intoxicated with alcohol.

◀ **Figure 4.4** Carcinoma of the larynx
Carcinoma of the larynx is typically squamous cell carcinoma, and it manifests either as a polypoid exophytic mass (as in this example) or as an ulcer. Fixation and decalcification of the larynx assist in histopathological sampling.

82

Trachea and Main Bronchi

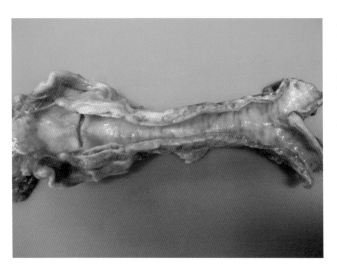

◀ **Figure 4.5** Normal trachea and main bronchi
The normal large airways are lined by a pale, cream-colored mucosa and are supported by hyaline cartilaginous rings, which in the trachea are C-shaped. The free ends of the C-shaped tracheal cartilages are bridged in the posterior wall of the trachea by the trachealis muscle.

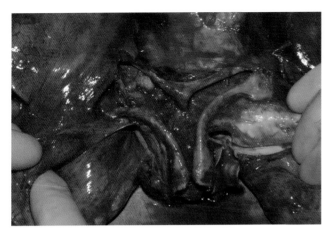

◀ **Figure 4.6** Food slurry resulting from postmortem shift
A thin slurry in the trachea and/or main bronchi is a very common autopsy finding because of the postmortem redistribution of gastric contents. It results from normal postmortem moving and handling of the body. The presence of such a slurry should not be overinterpreted as representing aspiration or airway obstruction.

◀ **Figure 4.7** Tracheobronchitis
Inflammation of the trachea and main bronchi is a common autopsy finding and may be caused by a viral upper respiratory tract infection, bacterial infection, or trauma. The mucosa of the large airways appears erythematous and inflamed. Swabs for virology and bacteriology may reveal the causative organism, and histopathological sampling with or without immunohistochemistry may also be of use.

83

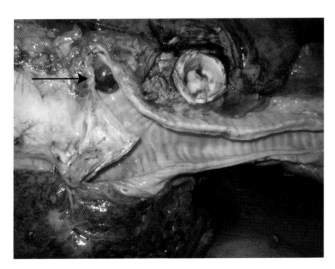

◀ **Figure 4.8** Inhaled foreign body
A wide variety of foreign bodies may be found in the large airways. Inhalation of foreign bodies may complicate alcohol intoxication, psychiatric disease, and neurological conditions such as dementia. There is typically, but not always, a history of choking or coughing followed by rapid collapse and death. In this example, the deceased had a history of dementia and inhaled a red grape that became impacted in the left main bronchus (top left of image). Inhaled foreign body is also common in children.

◀ **Figure 4.9** Inflammation resulting from an endotracheal tube

The placement of a cuffed endotracheal tube can give rise to localized inflammation, ulceration, and necrosis of the tracheal mucosa at the site of the cuff. This is a direct pressure effect, and it appears as a band of inflammation within the trachea. When the endotracheal tube has been removed before autopsy examination, review of the clinical history reveals the cause.

◀ **Figure 4.10** Plume (drowning or pulmonary edema)

Large amounts of fluid within the lungs may mix with the pulmonary surfactant to form a white foam that is found within the large airways. This finding is seen in patients with severe pulmonary edema and in wet drowning. When severe, the plume of foam may be evident at the nose and/or mouth (see Figure 1.22). It rapidly disappears in bodies that have been refrigerated and in bodies where there has been prolonged immersion. The presence or absence of a plume should be recorded by mortuary staff when bodies are admitted to the mortuary.

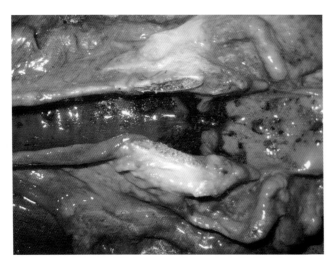

◀ **Figure 4.11a** Soot in the trachea or bronchi (fire death)

Soot may be found in the airways of those who have died in fires. The presence of soot in the mouth and above the level of the vocal cords is of little significance. Soot present below the level of the vocal cords (and in the esophagus and stomach) indicates that the individual was alive when the fire started. Soot is recognized as black particulate matter trapped within the mucus in the airways. The changes may be mild (a) or severe (b). Histological examination may also reveal soot within alveoli and alveolar macrophages.

◀ **Figure 4.11b** Soot in the trachea or bronchi (fire death)

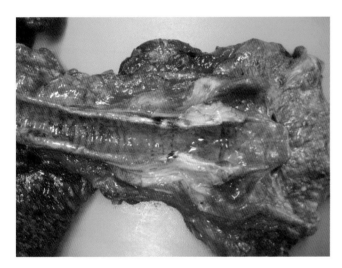

◀ **Figure 4.12** Burns in the trachea (fire death)
The inhalation of hot fire gases may burn the mucosa of the large airways (and may also precipitate pulmonary edema). In this example, from an individual who died in a house fire, there is little or no sooting of the airways, but there are focal gray burns to the tracheal and laryngeal mucosa. The former indicate that the deceased was alive when the fire started.

85

Lungs

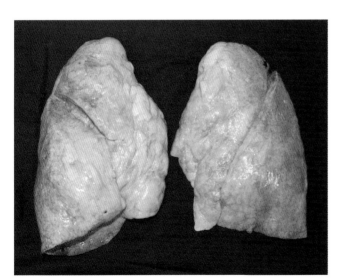

◀ **Figure 4.13** Normal lungs
The lungs are pink organs that fill the pleural cavities but that collapse slightly as the chest is opened. They are lined by a transparent, glistening visceral pleural membrane. Normal lungs weigh approximately 250 to 350 g each. The left lung has two lobes and the right lung has three lobes. When sliced, the lung parenchyma is seen to have a very fine, sponge-like appearance, from which little or no fluid can be expressed. Within this lies an arborizing pattern of airways and vessels that become progressively smaller as they approach the pleural surface.

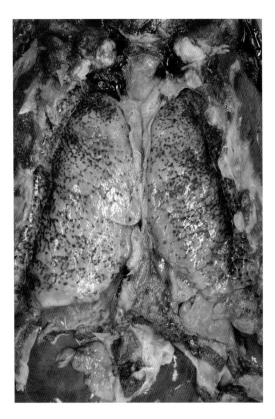

◀ **Figure 4.14** Pulmonary anthracosis
Anthracosis is a common autopsy finding, seen in smokers and city dwellers. It results from storage of inhaled carbon within pulmonary macrophages.

86

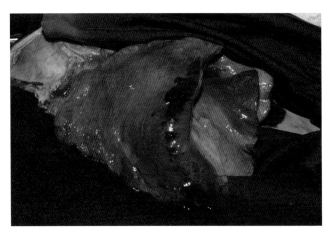

◀ **Figure 4.15** Pulmonary contusions
Blunt force trauma to the chest, as occurs in road traffic collisions, falls from a height, and blast injuries, can give rise to pulmonary contusions. The contused lung has a variably mottled appearance both externally and on slicing because of the presence of foci of intra-alveolar hemorrhage interspersed between areas of normal and atelectatic lung tissue.

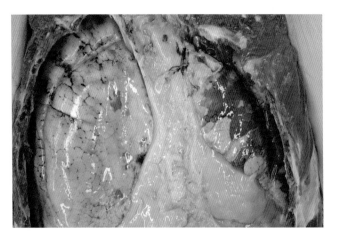

◀ **Figure 4.16** Inhalation of blood (harlequin pattern)
Blood may be inhaled into the lungs following head and neck trauma, upper gastrointestinal tract hemorrhage, or erosion of a pulmonary vessel by bronchial carcinoma. The presence of inhaled blood within the lungs gives their cut surface a "harlequin" pattern.

◀ Figure 4.17 Bronchopneumonia

In adults, bronchopneumonia is most common in the very old, in those with pre-existing lung disease, and in individuals with reduced mobility or reduced ability to take deep breaths. It typically affects the bases of the lungs (hypostatic pneumonia) and causes a mottled consolidation. A purulent exudate is present in the main bronchus and may also be expressed from the bronchi. It is widely recognized that naked-eye examination may miss bronchopneumonia or lead to overdiagnosis, and histopathological examination is recommended to make the diagnosis.[1] Microbiological sampling of the lungs is recommended to identify the causative microorganism.[2]

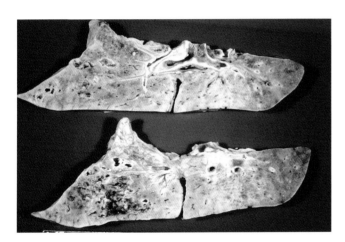

◀ Figure 4.18 Cavitating staphylococcal bronchopneumonia

In the majority of cases, bronchopneumonia is not complicated by necrosis or abscess formation. Infection by virulent pathogens may result in localized necrosis and cavitation of the lungs, as seen in this patient who died of staphylococcal bronchopneumonia.

87

◀ Figure 4.19 Lobar pneumonia

Lobar pneumonia typically affects previously fit adults of working age. Autopsy reveals confluent consolidation of part or all of a lobe of the lungs, and more than one lobe can be affected. The consolidated lung is firm, airless, and friable. Depending on the stage of the disease, the affected lung tissue may be red and resemble the liver (red hepatization) or gray (gray hepatization). The pleura overlying the affected lung is frequently inflamed. Microbiological sampling of the lungs is recommended to identify the causative microorganism.

◀ **Figure 4.20** Viral pneumonia
The cut surface of the lung is seen with florid congestion and consolidation changes in this case of influenza pneumonia. (Image courtesy of Dr. S. K. Suvarna.)

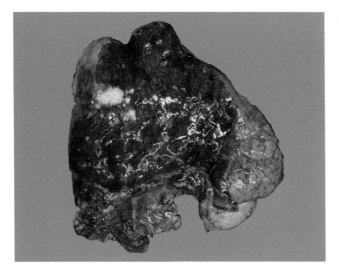

◀ **Figure 4.21a** Tuberculosis
Tuberculosis is caused by infection with the hazard group 3 pathogen *Mycobacterium tuberculosis.*

Tuberculosis manifests as a subpleural cavitating lesion with caseous yellow-white material in the midzone (primary Ghon focus) or apex (secondary Assmann focus) of the lung and enlargement of hilar lymph nodes. (The combination of Ghon focus and enlarged lymph nodes is the Ghon complex.) (Image courtesy of Dr. S. K. Suvarna.)

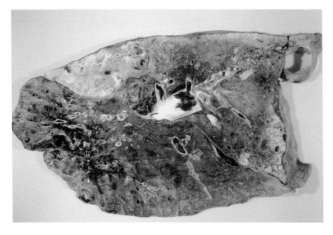

◀ **Figure 4.21b** Tuberculosis
The peripheral lung lesions calcify as they heal, leaving behind a resultant cavity.

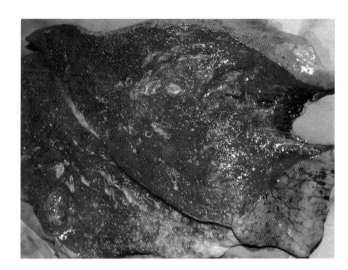

◀ **Figure 4.21c** Tuberculosis
Disseminated, or miliary, tuberculosis can be recognized as the presence of multiple yellow-white foci of caseous necrosis subpleurally and within the parenchyma of the lung. These foci are 1 to 2 mm in diameter and resemble millet seeds. Histopathological and microbiological examination confirms the diagnosis.

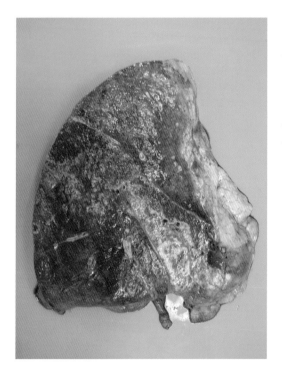

◀ **Figure 4.22a** Lung abscess
Lung abscesses result from parenchymal necrosis and the formation of pus-filled cavities. They may be single or multiple, and they arise as a complication of dental disease, aspiration pneumonia, necrotizing pneumonia, necrotic tumors, vasculitis, or septic emboli. Patients taking corticosteroids or other immunosuppressant therapies are at increased risk. Microbiological sampling and histopathological examination may reveal the causative organism.

89

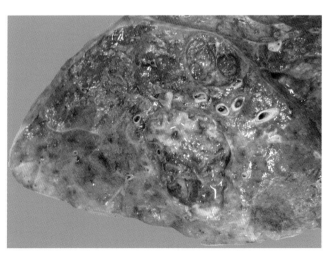

◀ **Figure 4.22b** Lung abscess
The cut surface of the lung shows several large spaces, one of which is clearly infected. There is residual purulent exudate on the wall of the cavity, in this example of a lung abscess. Much of the fluid drains from the cavity when it is opened. (Image courtesy of Dr. S. K. Suvarna.)

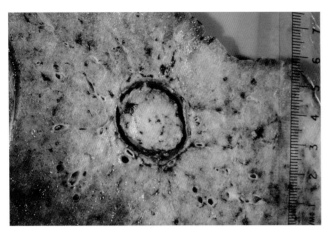

◀ **Figure 4.23a** Mycetoma
Patients with cavitating lung diseases, such as tuberculosis, are at risk of developing mycetomas.[3] These are balls of fungus, typically *Aspergillus,* that appear as gray-tan-brown friable masses with focal retraction away from the cavity wall. Histopathological and microbiological examination of the material confirms the diagnosis.

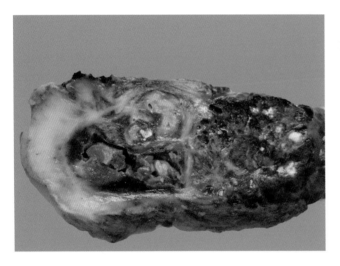

◀ **Figure 4.23b** Mycetoma
A surgical sample of lung tissue with an aspergilloma. There is a cavitated lesion in association with dense fibrosis. Granular midbrown-yellow material is present within this space, with histological examination confirming the characteristic branching fungal elements of *Aspergillus.* (Image courtesy of Dr. S. K. Suvarna.)

◀ **Figure 4.24a** Pulmonary edema and congestion
Pulmonary edema and congestion are extremely common autopsy findings, in part because of the pooling of fluid and blood in the lungs resulting from agonal cardiac failure and/or cardiopulmonary resuscitation and in part because cardiac, hepatic, and renal failure are common.

Edematous, congested lungs are abnormally heavy. Applying firm pressure to the visceral pleural surface with a thumb leaves an imprint, just as it does when applying pressure to the ankle when seeking the presence of peripheral edema.

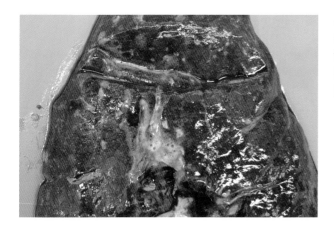

◀ **Figure 4.24b** Pulmonary edema and congestion
On slicing, the lungs are seen to be wet. Blood-stained frothy fluid oozes from the alveolar airspaces, and it can be freely expressed by applying gentle pressure to the lungs.

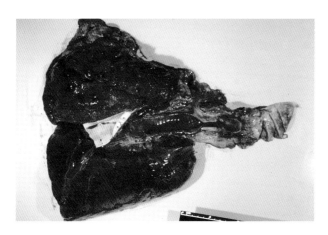

◀ **Figure 4.25** Adult respiratory distress syndrome
Adult respiratory distress syndrome, or diffuse alveolar damage, is a severe lung injury occurring most commonly in response to sepsis, aspiration, or trauma. The lungs are heavy, typically each weighing a kilogram or more, airless, and densely consolidated. Histopathological examination confirms the diagnosis.

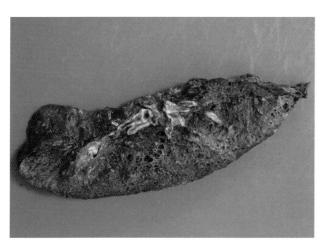

◀ **Figure 4.26** Emphysema
Emphysema is an irreversible enlargement of the alveolar airspaces of the lungs caused by damage to the alveolar walls, and it may involve the center of the acini (centriacinar emphysema) or entire acini (panacinar emphysema). It is a common autopsy finding, particularly among those with a history of tobacco smoking, although workers in certain occupations (including coal miners, metal workers (particularly cadmium), welders, stone masons, textile workers, quarry workers, flour and grain workers, petroleum workers, and rubber or plastics manufacturers) carry a risk of developing emphysema.[4] Consider examining the liver to exclude alpha-1-antitrypsin deficiency, particularly in the absence of a history of exposure to tobacco smoke or occupational causes. Emphysema is a part of the normal aging process of the lungs.

Emphysematous lungs appear hyperinflated, and the patient may be barrel-chested. On close examination, centriacinar emphysema results in the presence of multiple small cavities within the lung parenchyma, often associated with carbon pigment. Examination of the lung under running water may help to accentuate the appearance of emphysema.

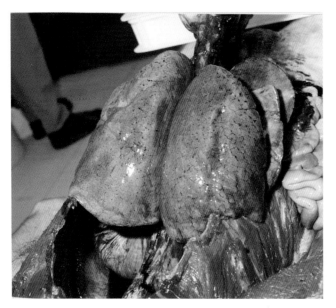

◀ **Figure 4.27** Hyperinflation secondary to drowning or asthma

Hyperinflation of the lungs is most commonly the result of emphysema, but it may also be caused by drowning or status asthmaticus. The hyperinflated lungs do not collapse when the chest is opened and may meet anteriorly in the midline, obscuring the pericardium. A review of the circumstances surrounding death generally allows the cause to be determined. When the cause of death is drowning (as shown here), the lungs are heavy and waterlogged, whereas asthma results in air trapping and mucus plugging within the lungs.

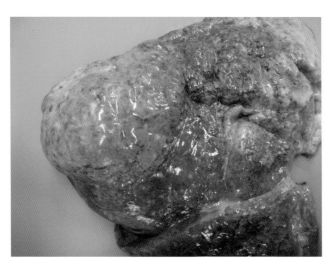

◀ **Figure 4.28a** Bullous emphysema

Bullous emphysema is a form of emphysema characterized by one or more cystic airspaces at least 10 mm in diameter and with a wall less than 1 mm thick. It may arise from either centriacinar or panacinar emphysema. Any part of the lung may be affected, although bullae commonly form beneath the pleura and at the apices of the lungs. Subpleural bullae may rupture spontaneously, giving rise to a pneumothorax.

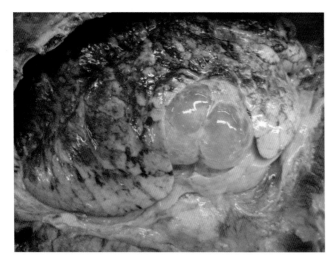

◀ **Figure 4.28b** Bullous emphysema

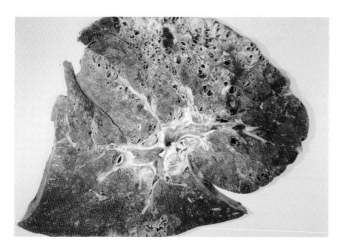

◀ Figure 4.29 Bronchiectasis

Bronchiectasis is the abnormal localized irreversible dilatation of the airways within the lungs. It results from the destruction of connective tissue in the wall of the airways and most frequently is a complication of pulmonary sepsis, although there are many acquired and congenital causes. The bronchi are found to be abnormally dilated and cystic, extending from the hilum to the pleura. Bronchiectasis predisposes to the development of pneumonia.

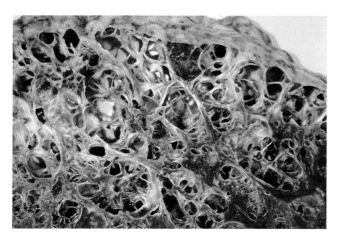

◀ Figure 4.30 Honeycomb lung

Honeycomb change in the lung describes the end-stage appearance of a variety of lung diseases, including bronchiectasis (as in this example), emphysema (where the change is often apical), and other interstitial lung disease such as usual interstitial pneumonia (where the change is typically basal). The affected lung is fibrotic and cystic, and it may undergo dystrophic calcification. Histopathological examination of the surrounding lung tissue may reveal the underlying cause.

93

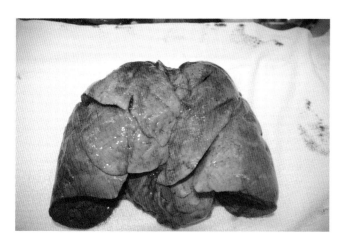

◀ Figure 4.31 Asthma

Asthma is a common cause of morbidity but an uncommon cause of mortality. Where asthma has not caused death, the lungs typically have a normal macroscopic appearance. In status asthmaticus, the lungs are hyperinflated, meet in the midline obscuring the pericardium, and do not collapse when the chest is opened. On slicing, the lungs are seen to be aerated, and mucus plugs may be seen within the bronchi. Consideration should always be given to the possibility that death was caused by an anaphylactic reaction.

◀ **Figure 4.32** Coal worker's pneumoconiosis
Coal worker's pneumoconiosis is caused by prolonged exposure to and inhalation of coal dust. Simple coal worker's pneumoconiosis manifests as the presence of numerous black macules throughout the lungs that are more prevalent in the upper lobes. As the disease progresses, the macules become fibrotic nodules. In patients with coexisting rheumatoid arthritis, the nodules are most commonly located at the periphery of the lungs. Nodules greater than 10 mm in diameter amount to progressive massive fibrosis and, unless associated with rheumatoid arthritis (Caplan syndrome), are most common in the upper lobes.

◀ **Figure 4.33** Asbestosis
Where there is also a history of previous asbestos exposure, the presence of diffuse interstitial fibrosis supports the diagnosis of asbestosis. Asbestosis has no pathognomonic features that allow it to be distinguished from other causes of interstitial fibrosis. The diagnosis is made by consideration of the occupational history, macroscopic and histopathological features of the lungs, radiographic appearance of the lungs, and mineral fiber counts.[5]

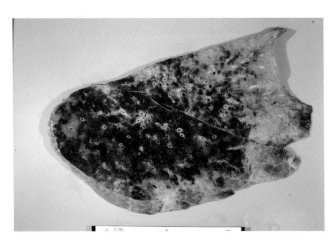

◀ **Figure 4.34a** Cryptogenic fibrosing alveolitis
Cryptogenic fibrosing alveolitis, better known to pathologists as usual interstitial pneumonia, is an idiopathic fibrotic lung disease seen in patients more than 50 years old. The lungs develop reticular fibrosis, most marked beneath the pleura and along the septa. The fibrosis is usually most prominent in the basal portions of the lower lobes, although any part of the lung may be affected. Honeycomb change in the bases of the lungs develops in advanced disease.

◀ **Figure 4.34b** Cryptogenic fibrosing alveolitis

◀ **Figure 4.35** Silicosis
Silicosis is a fibrotic interstitial lung disease caused by the inhalation of silica, the predominant component of sand. Typically, it develops at least 10 years after exposure. The silicotic lung contains multiple fibrotic nodules less than 10 mm in diameter that are most prevalent in the upper lobes. The cut surface of these nodules may have a glistening appearance. Nodules 10 mm or more in diameter indicate the development of progressive massive fibrosis. Patients with silicosis are at increased risk of pulmonary tuberculosis and lung cancer.

95

◀ **Figure 4.36** Sarcoidosis
Sarcoidosis is an idiopathic noncaseating granulomatous disease that may affect almost any tissue but that commonly affects the lungs. The pulmonary hilar lymph nodes are enlarged, and as the disease progresses, there are hilar reticulonodular infiltrates, pulmonary nodular infiltrates, and cystic and bullous changes. Histopathological examination of both the lung tissue and hilar lymph nodes confirms the diagnosis.

◀ **Figure 4.37a** Pulmonary thromboembolism
Pulmonary thromboemboli may be found coiled in the pulmonary trunk (so-called "saddle embolus"), in the main pulmonary arteries, or in the smaller branches of the pulmonary arteries.

Pulmonary thromboemboli must be distinguished from postmortem blood clots. In comparison with blood clots, thromboemboli are firm and have a matte surface and a laminated structure. They form casts of the vessels in which they originated, rather than the vessels in which they are found. Postmortem clot is soft, easily rubbed into a sponge, shiny, and has the appearance of red currant jelly and/or chicken fat.

Pulmonary thromboemboli in small pulmonary arteries can be readily found when the lung is sliced in the coronal plane. They stand proud of the cut surface of the lung, rather like toothpaste oozing from a tube.

◀ **Figure 4.37b** Pulmonary thromboembolism

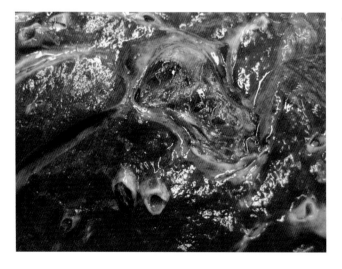

◀ **Figure 4.37c** Pulmonary thromboembolism

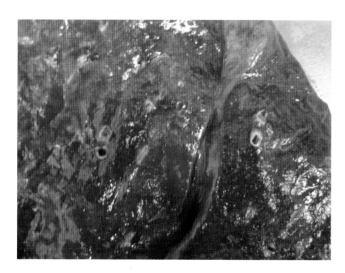

◀ **Figure 4.38a** Pulmonary infarction
Pulmonary infarction is most commonly the result of pulmonary thromboembolus. The infarcts are wedge shaped, with their base abutting the visceral pleura. There may be associated pleurisy. The infarcted tissue is firmer than the surrounding parenchyma and deep red. Healing may result in the formation of wedge-shaped scars.

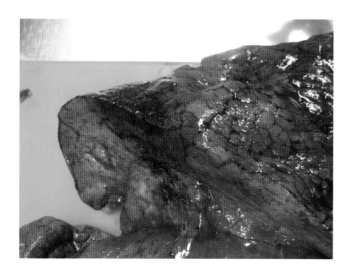

◀ **Figure 4.38b** Pulmonary infarction

◀ **Figure 4.38c** Pulmonary infarction

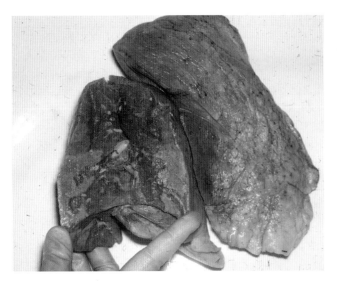

◀ **Figure 4.39** Multiple pulmonary thromboemboli with lung infarcts

This example demonstrates one of the typical wedge-shaped infarcts seen in individuals who have had multiple pulmonary thromboemboli.

Tumors of the Lungs

◀ **Figure 4.40** Chondroma

Chondromas are benign cartilaginous tumors, most typically observed as incidental findings in the peripheries of the lungs of young women. Clinically, they may be confused with pulmonary metastases.[6] They are readily enucleated from the surrounding parenchyma and have a bosselated gray cartilaginous surface. Slicing reveals that these tumors are solid and cartilaginous, and there may be calcification. Less commonly, chondromas may be hemorrhagic, cystic, or necrotic. Chondromas may occur as part of the Carney triad.[7]

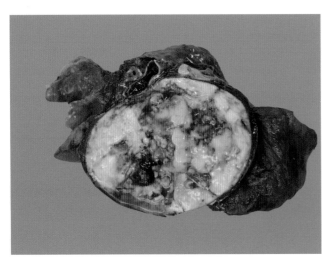

◀ **Figure 4.41** Metastatic malignancy

As in the brain, bones, and liver, malignant tumors found within the lungs are more likely to be metastatic than primary. Metastatic malignant disease in the lungs may range from multiple small white tumor deposits resembling miliary tuberculosis to a single gray-white tumor deposit within the parenchyma of the lungs. Malignant diseases from any site may metastasize to the lungs, although bowel, kidney, and breast are common primary sites. A careful review of the past medical history, coupled with a careful examination of the remaining organs, in addition to histopathological examination of the deposits, with immunohistochemistry if needed, usually reveals the primary site. (Image courtesy of Dr. S. K. Suvarna.)

◄ **Figure 4.42** Lymphangitis carcinomatosis
The surface of this lung shows an irregular, somewhat lumpy, quality. There is a widespread patchy discoloration of the pleura in this case of lymphangitis carcinomatosis. The primary tumor was a pulmonary adenocarcinoma situated centrally in the lung tissues. (Image courtesy of Dr. S. K. Suvarna.)

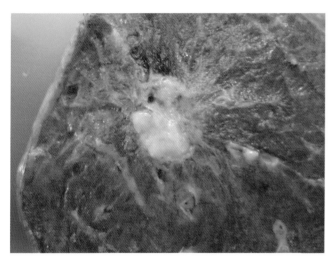

◄ **Figure 4.43a** Primary lung cancer
Primary lung carcinomas are common autopsy findings, and the diagnosis may be known or unsuspected before the examination. These tumors are typically solitary gray-white firm lesions, often with central necrosis, cavitation, and/or hemorrhage. Adenocarcinomas typically arise within the lung parenchyma near the periphery of the lung, whereas other types have a propensity to arise near to the hilum of the lung. Histopathological examination confirms the diagnosis. The finding of lung cancer should prompt a search for metastases in the brain, adrenals, liver, and bone marrow.

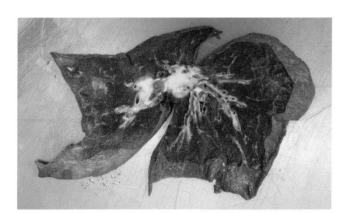

◄ **Figure 4.43b** Primary lung cancer

Pleura

◀ **Figure 4.44** Pleurisy

Pleurisy is inflammation of the pleura. Viral infection is the most common cause, but pleurisy can complicate underlying bacterial pneumonia, pulmonary infarction, cardiothoracic surgery, penetrating chest trauma, malignant disease, or inflammatory bowel disease. The pleura appears injected and inflamed, and it may be covered in a fibrinous or fibrinopurulent exudate.

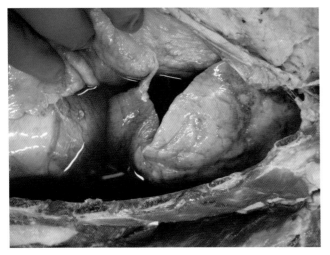

◀ **Figure 4.45** Effusion

The normal pleural cavity is a potential space containing approximately 3 to 5 mL of clear serous fluid. Pleural effusions are common autopsy findings and may be exudates (in patients with malignant diseases or sepsis) or transudates (in patients with cardiac failure, liver failure, or renal failure). At autopsy, examination of the lungs, heart, liver, and kidneys usually reveals the cause, although the fluid can be sampled for biochemical analysis and cytological examination if needed. Where sepsis is suspected, tissue samples are more likely to reveal the causative organism.

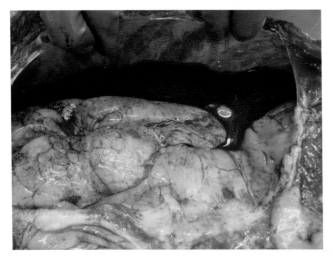

◀ **Figure 4.46** Hemothorax

Bleeding into the pleural cavity (hemothorax) typically results from chest trauma, but it may be caused by a ruptured thoracic aneurysm or insertion of chest drains or as a complication of anticoagulation, neoplasia, or rupture of pleural adhesions. In this example, hemothorax complicated a rib fracture. No other source of bleeding was identified.

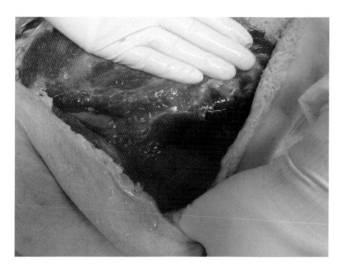

◀ Figure 4.47 Pneumothorax

Pneumothorax may result from the spontaneous rupture of emphysematous bullae caused by hyperinflation of the lung during mechanical ventilation or by penetrating chest trauma. At autopsy, pneumothorax may be demonstrated by chest radiography or by dissection. The intercostal muscles may be dissected away from the pleura to reveal that the lung is no longer in contact with the parietal pleura. Alternatively, as shown here, the skin and soft tissues of the chest wall may be dissected from the intercostal muscles. The resulting pouch is filled with water. When a blunt instrument is inserted under water through the intercostal muscles, bubbles are seen to escape.

◀ Figure 4.48 Pleural adhesions

Fibrous and/or fibrinous pleural adhesions are common autopsy findings and denote previous inflammation of the pleura. They are seen in patients who have had one or more episodes of pneumonia, and they are common in patients with chronic obstructive pulmonary disease. They are recognized by the presence of irregular fibrous (or fibrinous) connective tissue fusing the parietal and visceral layers of the pleura, and they may be extensive.

101

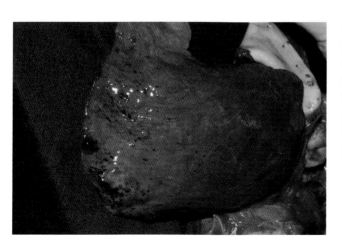

◀ Figure 4.49 Subpleural petechial hemorrhage

Subpleural petechial hemorrhages (Tardieu spots) are thought to develop post mortem following antemortem rupture of subpleural vessels. Although these hemorrhages were historically thought to be pathognomonic for strangulation or suffocation, it is now recognized that they may also arise as a result of sepsis, coagulopathies, and microembolic phenomena.[8]

◄ Figure 4.50 Benign fibrous plaques

Pleural plaques are common autopsy findings and denote previous exposure to asbestos. In England and Wales, pleural plaques diagnosed after 2007 in the absence of other asbestos-related disease are not considered a compensable disease, although patients diagnosed in other countries may be able to pursue a civil claim. These plaques are almost always asymptomatic. At autopsy, they are seen as irregular, white patches of fibrosis, and they are more common on the parietal than the visceral pleura. Over decades, they become calcified.[9]

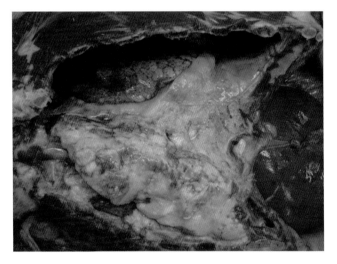

◄ Figure 4.51a Malignant mesothelioma

Malignant mesothelioma is almost always caused by occupational or paraoccupational exposure to asbestos or erionite. The tumor should be widely sampled for histopathological examination. The lungs should be widely sampled for histopathological examination, including a search for ferruginous bodies and asbestosis. Samples of lung tissue may be retained for mineral fiber count analysis.[10]

The tumor obliterates the pleural space, and evisceration of the lung may be difficult.

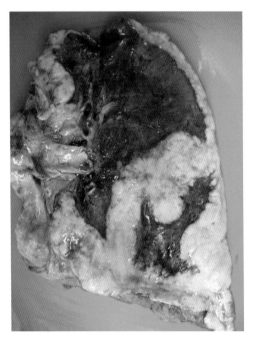

◄ Figure 4.51b Malignant mesothelioma

The lung is found to be encased by a firm-to-hard, gray-white tumor of variable thickness that may contain foci of hemorrhage and necrosis. The tumor may infiltrate the chest wall, diaphragm, underlying lung, pericardium, heart, or other mediastinal structures.

References

1. Hunt CR, Benbow EW, Knox WF, McMahon RF, McWilliam LJ. Can histopathologists diagnose bronchopneumonia? *Journal of Clinical Pathology* 1995;**48**:120–123.
2. Ridgway EJ, Harvey DJ. Microbiology of the autopsy. In: Burton JL, Rutty GN, editors. *The hospital autopsy: a manual of fundamental autopsy practice.* London: Hodder Arnold; 2010:227–245.
3. Butz RO, Zvetina JR, Leininger BJ. Ten-year experience with mycetomas in patients with pulmonary tuberculosis. *Chest* 1985;**87**:356–358.
4. UK Health and Safety Executive. COPD causes: occupations and substances. Available at: http://www.hse.gov.uk/copd/causes.htm. Accessed January 13, 2015.
5. Tossavainen A. Asbestos, asbestosis and cancer: the Helsinki criteria for diagnosis and attribution. *Scandinavian Journal of Work, Environment and Health* 1997;**23**:311–316.
6. Rodriguez FJ, Aubry MC, Tazelaar HD, Siezak J, Carney JA. Pulmonary chondromas: a tumor associated with Carney triad and different from pulmonary hamartoma. *American Journal of Surgical Pathology* 2007;**31**:1844–1853.
7. Carney JA. Gastric stromal sarcoma, pulmonary chondroma, and extra-adrenal paraganglionoma (Carney Triad): natural history, adrenocortical component, and possible familial occurrence. *Mayo Clinic Proceedings* 1999;**74**:543–552.
8. Geserick G, Krocker K, Wirth I. Tardieu's spots and asphyxia: a literature study. [in German] *Archiv für Kriminologie* 2010;**226**:145–160.
9. British Thoracic Society. Pleural plaques: information for health care professionals. Available at: https://www.brit-thoracic.org.uk/document-library/clinical-information/mesothelioma/pleural-plaques-information-for-patients. Accessed February 28, 2015.
10. British Thoracic Society Standards of Care Committee. BTS statement of malignant mesothelioma in the UK, 2007. *Thorax* 2007;**62**:ii1–ii19.

Chapter 5
The Gastrointestinal System

Introduction

The gastrointestinal tract is a common site for both fatal and non-fatal disease, and it should be examined carefully in every autopsy. This should begin with an inspection of the mouth and anus on external examination, followed by inspection of the gut once the body cavities have been opened, before evisceration. This is particularly important in postoperative deaths following gastrointestinal tract surgery. Surgical anastomoses must be handled gently but inspected closely before dissection. Recent anastomoses may be fragile, and careless traction on the bowel can cause artifactual anastomotic dehiscence that could be mistaken for a cause of death. In such cases, the task of eviscerating the bowel should be performed by the pathologist and never be delegated to an anatomical pathology technician.

The extent to which the gastrointestinal tract is then examined at autopsy and the way in which it is examined will depend in part on the clinical history and in part on the findings on inspection of the internal organs before evisceration.

The esophagus and stomach should be opened and examined in every autopsy examination. Care should be taken to collect the gastric contents (avoiding contamination with blood or other body fluids) for inspection. It is useful to note the state of digestion of any food within the stomach and the presence or absence of tablet residues. In cases where toxicology is needed, knowing the volume of the stomach contents allows the amount of drug actually present in the stomach to be determined. In cases of possible food-related anaphylaxis, photographs of the stomach contents provide useful information to the immunologist.

It is not at all uncommon to find a small quantity of blood within the stomach and some minor inflammation of the gastric mucosa. In the absence of a history of blood at the scene of death and the absence of blood elsewhere in the gastrointestinal tract, these findings can be accounted for by a physiological agonal stress response.

The intestines naturally harbor a range of potentially pathogenic microorganisms that pose a risk to the health of the pathologist. Consideration needs to be given to whether or not the intestines need to be opened.

In cases where there is no history to suggest bowel disease, no history of unexplained anemia, a cause of death in another organ, *and* the bowels appear normal externally, the small and large intestines need not be opened in full. Even then, it is wise to open the rectum because this is a common site for colorectal cancer and idiopathic inflammatory bowel disease. If abnormalities are found in the rectum, then the rest of the bowels should be examined.

The bowels should always be examined in cases where there is a history of bowel disease, a suspicion of gastrointestinal tract hemorrhage, unexplained anemia, bowel surgery, or where no cause of death is identified in the other organ systems. Obviously, the bowels should also be examined if they appear abnormal before evisceration. Eviscerating the intestines by dividing their mesenteries close to the bowel wall will make subsequent opening of the bowels much easier.

Before opening the bowels, some consideration must be given to whether or not there is interest in their contents. In cases of suspected gastrointestinal tract hemorrhage or bowel obstruction, it is useful to see the bowel contents *in situ*. Otherwise, the proximal intestine may be connected to a tap or hose and water instilled under low pressure to flush out the contents into a sink or sluice before opening the bowels.

Esophagus

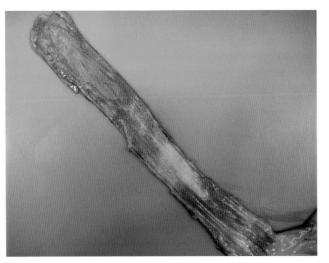

◀ **Figure 5.1** Normal esophagus
The esophagus is a muscular tube, approximately 25 cm long, lined by stratified squamous epithelium that connects the hypopharynx and stomach. The mucosa is a uniform tan-pink color, and it glistens. Gastric contents may be present within the esophagus at autopsy. This does not denote perimortem vomiting but more likely results from relaxation of the lower esophageal sphincter after death and passive redistribution of gastric contents.

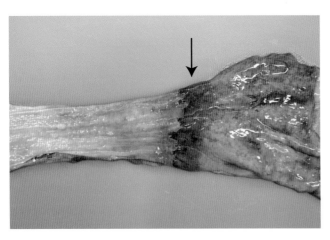

◀ **Figure 5.2** Barrett esophagus
Barrett esophagus is a glandular metaplasia affecting a variable length of the distal esophagus that is caused by repeated gastroesophageal acid reflux. It is a premalignant condition associated with an increased risk of esophageal cancer. At autopsy, the affected mucosa appears red. Histological examination can be used to confirm the diagnosis.

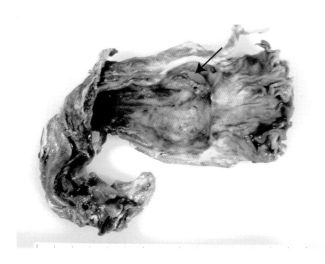

◀ **Figure 5.3** Esophageal ulcer

Esophageal ulcers are typically caused by the action of refluxed gastric acid, but viral infections (e.g., with *Herpes* simplex virus and *Cytomegalovirus*[1]) and many drugs (including oral potassium,[2] alendronic acid,[3] and some antibiotics[4]) are also known causes. The ulcers have the same typical morphology of peptic ulcers as described elsewhere in this chapter. Healing results in esophageal stricture formation. In the example shown, an esophageal ulcer has been complicated by perforation and posterior mediastinitis resulting from the action of refluxed gastric acid that caused death. There is an esophageal perforation (arrow), and the surrounding esophageal wall was necrotic and friable. Histological examination excluded malignancy.

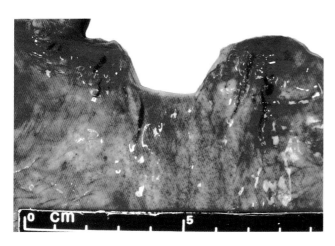

◀ **Figure 5.4** Mallory-Weiss tear

Mallory-Weiss tears are vertically orientated superficial lacerations in the mucosa at the gastroesophageal junction. They are caused by forceful or prolonged vomiting, but they are also seen in patients who have had an epileptic seizure. The history is typically one of vomiting followed by hematemesis. Bleeding may be torrential. In patients who have survived for several days, there may be nothing to see at autopsy because the lacerations typically heal quickly.

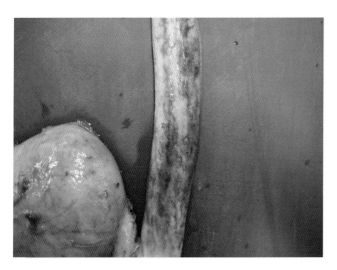

◀ **Figure 5.5** Varices

Esophageal varices are dilated veins in the submucosa of the esophagus. These veins are a site of portosystemic anastomosis between veins that drain into the azygos vein and veins that drain into the left gastric vein and thence the portal vein. Esophageal varices occur in patients who have portal hypertension, the most common cause of which is cirrhosis of the liver. The varices may rupture, resulting in torrential hemorrhage. At autopsy, they are most easily demonstrated by inverting the esophagus.

Stomach

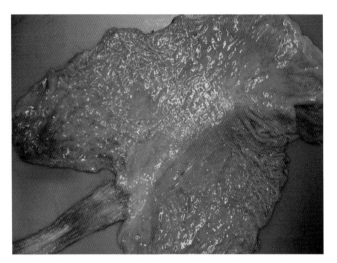

◀ **Figure 5.6** Normal stomach
The normal stomach is a highly distensible flask-like organ in the upper abdominal cavity. At autopsy, it is typically opened at the fundus, and this allows the collection of the gastric contents, which should be measured and described. In suspected deaths from anaphylaxis, the stomach contents should be photographed. The stomach can then be opened along the greater curve to permit inspection of the mucosa. Normal gastric mucosa is tan, glistening, and thrown into rugae.

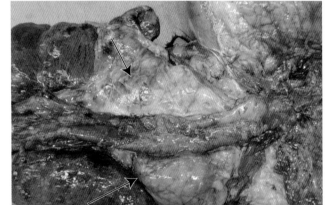

◀ **Figure 5.7a** Hiatus hernia
Hiatus hernia occurs when part of the stomach lies within the thorax. There are two types of hiatus hernias. In sliding hiatus hernias, the gastroesophageal junction and part of the stomach lie above the diaphragm. Rolling hiatus hernias are uncommon and occur when part of the stomach (typically the fundus) herniates through the esophageal hiatus to lie in the thorax alongside the esophagus. Hiatus hernias are easier to demonstrate at autopsy if the central portion of the diaphragm is left *in situ* until the upper gastrointestinal tract has been examined.

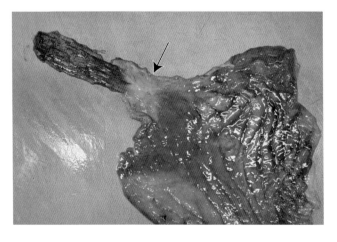

◀ **Figure 5.7b** Hiatus hernia

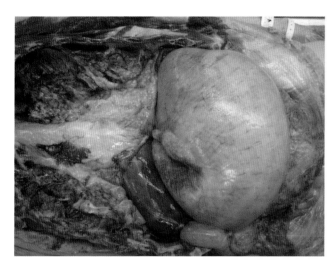

◀ **Figure 5.8** Gastric volvulus
Many parts of the gastrointestinal tract may twist on a fixed point of its mesentery and produce volvulus. Gastric volvulus is not common. It may cause symptoms of abdominal pain and retching and can result, as in this example, in gastric obstruction. As with volvulus at other sites, ischemia and infarction, and even perforation, of the tissue may occur.

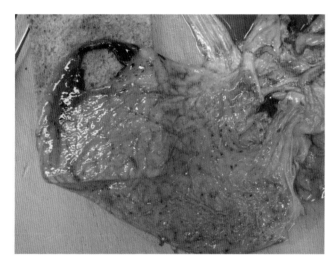

◀ **Figure 5.9** Gastric necrosis and perforation
The stomach has a rich vascular supply, and as a result gastric necrosis with subsequent perforation is rare. Fundal necrosis may complicate splenectomy, in which the short gastric branches of the splenic artery are divided. Gastric necrosis may also occur in patients with peripheral vascular disease who become hypotensive and/or develop multiple organ failure. The necrotic gastric wall is black and friable. Perforation results in chemical peritonitis.

109

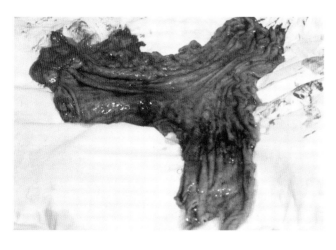

◀ **Figure 5.10** Soot in stomach (fire death)
In bodies that have been recovered following a fire, careful examination of the stomach and its contents is beneficial. The presence of soot in the stomach confirms that the deceased must have been alive when the fire started. This soot reaches the stomach after having been either swallowed from the mouth or expectorated from the lungs and swallowed.

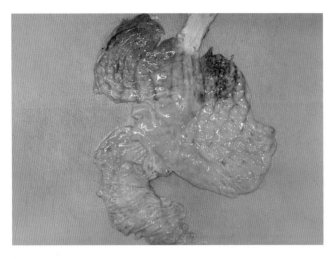

◀ Figure 5.11 Erosive gastritis
Erosive gastritis is typically a result of reduced mucosal defense in response to the ingestion of nonsteroidal anti-inflammatory drugs. Ingestion of alcohol and *Helicobacter pylori* infection can also cause erosive gastritis secondary to increased secretion of hydrochloric acid. Less common causes include viral infection, radiation, and direct trauma to the gastric mucosa. Erosions are breaches of the gastric mucosal surface that do not penetrate the muscularis mucosa.[5] At autopsy, erosive gastritis is recognized by the presence of multiple superficial ulcers that appear black because of the oxidizing action of gastric acid on hemoglobin. The surrounding mucosa may be edematous.

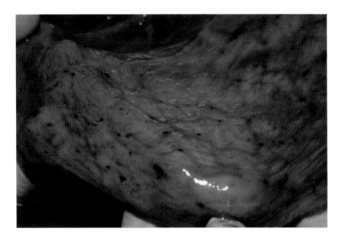

◀ Figure 5.12a Hypothermia: hemorrhagic gastritis
It is now well-recognized that acute hypothermia may result in a hemorrhagic gastritis (b). At autopsy there gastric mucosa contains multiple pin-prick hemorrhagic lesions, which turn black due to the oxidizing effect of gastric acid. Gastric ulcers may also be present. Concern that death may be due to hypothermia should prompt collection of urine for toxicological assessment of catecholamines.[6]

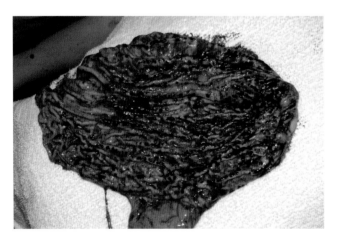

◀ Figure 5.12b Hypothermia: hemorrhagic gastritis

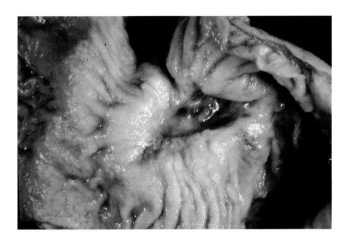

◀ **Figure 5.13a** Peptic ulcer

Most gastric ulcers are benign and are caused by mucosal attack by gastric acid (peptic ulcers). Peptic ulcers may occur anywhere in the stomach but are typically found in the gastric antrum. They are round or oval and have "punched out" or overhanging margins. Multiple ulcers may be present.[7] The ulcers are deep, with a smooth base lined by slough. The gastric rugae taper and converge on the ulcer. Complications include hemorrhage and perforation. Histological examination excludes malignancy and may reveal a causative *Helicobacter pylori* infection.

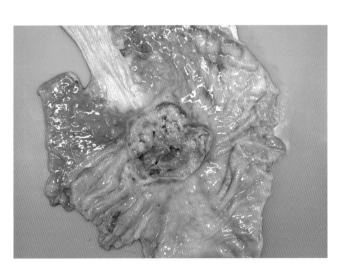

◀ **Figure 5.13b** Peptic ulcer

111

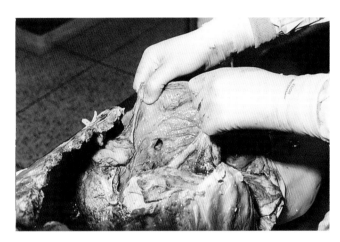

◀ **Figure 5.14** Malignant gastric ulcer

Approximately 4% of gastric ulcers will prove to be malignant on histological examination. Unlike their benign counterparts, malignant ulcers typically have raised rolled edges and asymmetrical irregular, angulated, or geographic margins. The ulcer base is uneven. The gastric rugae are disrupted and appear moth-eaten near the ulcer margin.[8]

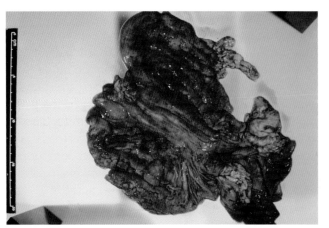

◄ Figure 5.15 Linitis plastica
Also known as leather bottle stomach, linitis plastica is a morphological description given to diffusely invasive, poorly differentiated signet-ring adenocarcinoma of the stomach. The stomach wall is thickened and fibrotic, with an appearance akin to a leather bottle. Linitis plastica is also seen in those who survive ingestion of caustic soda (sodium hydroxide) or acid.[9] Histological examination makes the distinction.

Duodenum

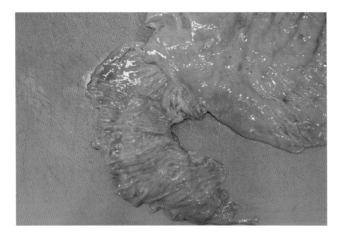

◄ Figure 5.16 Normal duodenum
The duodenum is the first part of the small intestine and is a C-shaped organ that arises at the pylorus and lies in the retroperitoneum. It is so named because it is 12 finger-widths long. The head of the pancreas lies within the concavity formed by the duodenum. The first and fourth parts of the duodenum lie almost horizontally within the abdomen. The second and third parts are vertical, with the ampulla of Vater marking the boundary between them. The first and second parts of the duodenum originate from the embryological foregut and so are supplied by branches of the celiac axis. The third and fourth parts of the duodenum originate from the embryological midgut and so are supplied by branches of the superior mesenteric artery.

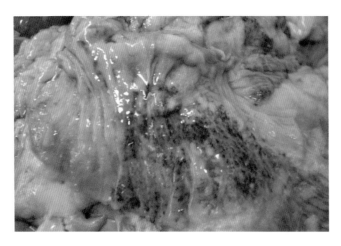

◄ Figure 5.17 Duodenitis
The duodenum may become inflamed as a consequence of infection (typically with *Helicobacter pylori*), peptic ulceration, and nonsteroidal anti-inflammatory drugs. Diffuse duodenitis has also been reported in patients with ulcerative colitis.[10] At autopsy, superficial erosions and inflammation are seen. Duodenitis may give rise to significant hemorrhage.

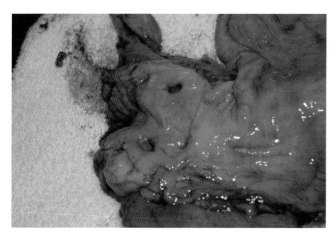

◀ **Figure 5.18a** Duodenal peptic ulcer
The duodenum, and particularly the first part of the duodenum, is a common site for peptic ulceration. These ulcers result from increased gastric acid secretion in the stomach, typically from *Helicobacter pylori* infection. Morphologically, peptic ulcers have sharp, "punched-out" margins and ulcer slough at the base. Malignant ulcers in the duodenum are rare. These images show duodenal peptic ulcers in the first (a) and second (b) parts of the duodenum.

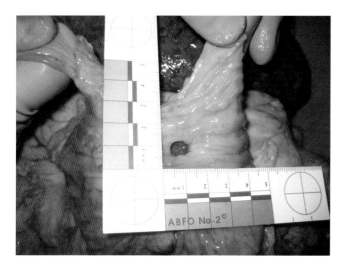

◀ **Figure 5.18a** Duodenal peptic ulcer

113

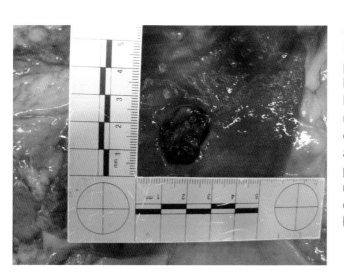

◀ **Figure 5.19** Duodenal peptic ulcer with vessel
Duodenal peptic ulcers may be complicated by perforation and subsequent peritonitis or by hemorrhage. Such hemorrhage may be profuse and life-threatening. Careful inspection of the ulcer may reveal a vessel in the base of the ulcer that is the source of the bleeding. This typically is the gastroduodenal artery, which runs on the posterior surface of the first part of the duodenum to supply the pylorus. There is no correspondingly named vein. The presence of blood clot adherent to the ulcer base also indicates that there has been bleeding from the ulcer.

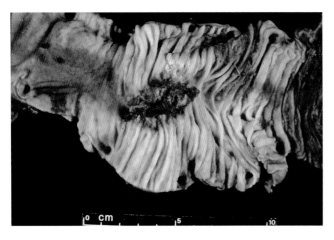

◀ **Figure 5.20** Ampullary carcinoma
Carcinoma of the ampulla of Vater typically arises on the background of an adenoma or polyp. It is often associated with bile duct dilatation resulting from distal obstruction. If advanced, it can be difficult to distinguish tumors originating from the ampulla, distal common bile duct, or pancreas.

Jejunum and Ileum

◀ **Figure 5.21** Normal jejunum and ileum
The jejunum and ileum form the majority of the small intestine and lie in the center of the peritoneal cavity. The loops of bowel are supported by a mesentery whose root runs from the upper left to lower right of the abdomen. Precise distinction between jejunum and ileum is difficult, but it is of little pathological relevance. The jejunum is typically of larger diameter, and has less fat in its mesentery, than the ileum. On opening the abdomen, the normal jejunum and ileum have a tan-pink serosa. Dependent loops of small intestine, particularly those lying in the pelvis, may appear dusky because of hypostasis, and this should not be mistaken for ischemia or infarction. On opening, the small intestinal mucosa is seen to be thrown into multiple circular folds (plicae circularis), and these are more prominent in the jejunum than in the ileum.

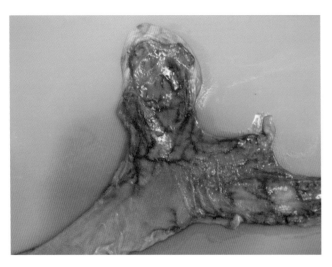

◀ **Figure 5.22** Meckel diverticulum
Meckel diverticulum, the most common congenital malformation of the midgut, is formed from a remnant of the vitellointestinal duct. These diverticula are found on the antimesenteric border of the ileum approximately 40 to 60 cm proximal to the ileocecal valve. Typically, they are a coincidental finding of no significance. In some cases, however, the diverticulum contains heterotopic gastric mucosa, and this can result in peptic ulceration of the surrounding ileal mucosa.

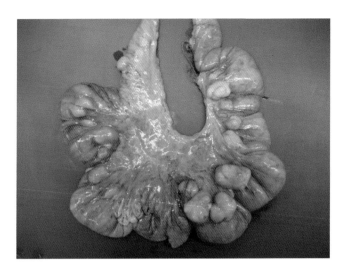

◀ **Figure 5.23** Small intestinal diverticulosis
Small intestinal diverticulosis is a rare condition in which there are multiple saccular pulsion diverticula along the mesenteric border of the small intestine, most notably in the jejunum. Small intestinal diverticulosis may be a coincidental finding, but it is increasingly recognized that such diverticula may be a cause of malabsorption or chronic abdominal pain,[11] and they may lead to perforation with abscess formation and/or generalized peritonitis.[12]

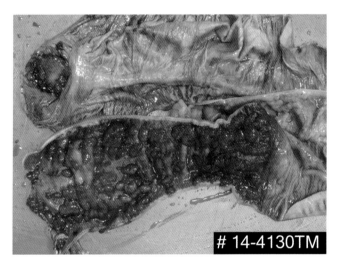

\# 14-4130TM

◀ **Figure 5.24** Crohn disease
Crohn disease can affect any part of the gastrointestinal tract from lips to anus, but the terminal ileum is most commonly involved. Several segments of the gut may be affected, with intervening normal tissue (skip lesions). The affected bowel is edematous. The mucosa has a "cobblestoned" appearance resulting from a combination of edema, inflammation, and deep fissuring ulcers. Crohn disease may be complicated by perforation with abscess formation, peritonitis, or fistula formation.

115

◀ **Figure 5.25a** Intussusception
Intussusception is the invagination of one part of the intestine into an adjacent segment. It is a rare cause of bowel obstruction in adults. It arises when peristalsis drags a mass in the lumen or wall of the bowel distally. Typically, intussusception complicates a benign tumor, inflammatory lesion, or diverticulum. (a) Small intestinal intussusception.

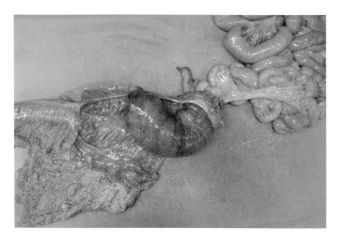

◀ **Figure 5.25b** Intussusception
Cecal intussusception caused by an annular stenosing carcinoma at the ileocecal valve.

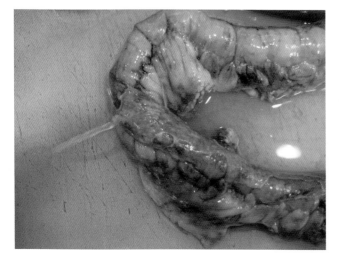

◀ **Figure 5.26** Demonstrating small intestinal perforation
The small intestine may perforate as a result of distal obstruction. Such perforations give rise to generalized peritonitis, but the site of perforation may be difficult to visualize. In such cases, the small intestine is first carefully inspected and then is divided from its mesentery, with care taken not to cut the bowel itself. The proximal end of the small intestine is then connected to a tap or hose, and cold water under low pressure is gently instilled into the bowel. Water can be seen leaking from the perforation site if this is still patent.

◀ **Figure 5.27** Small intestinal lymphangioma
Lymphangiomas of the small intestine are typically seen in children and are very rare in adults. Most intra-abdominal lymphangiomas are located in the mesentery. Other common sites in the body include the head, neck, and axillary regions. These lesions can be related to obstruction, abdominal pain, gastrointestinal bleeding, and intussusception.

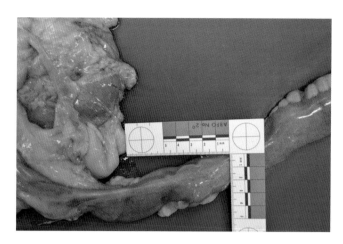

◄ Figure 5.28a Gallstone ileus
Gallstones are a rare cause of obstruction of the normal flow of material through the gut. In this patient, a gallstone 31 mm in diameter became lodged in the terminal ileum. A hard mass was palpable and visible before opening the bowel. The bowel proximal to the gallstone was dilated, and the terminal ileum distal to the stone was empty.

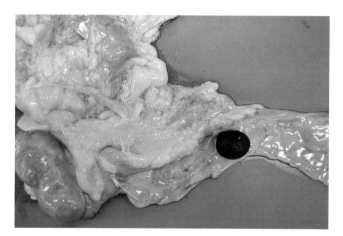

◄ Figure 5.28b Gallstone ileus
Opening the terminal ileum revealed a solitary gallstone. Examination of the duodenum revealed a choledochoduodenal fistula (see Figure 6.22).

117

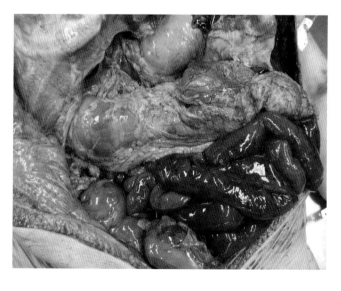

◄ Figure 5.29a Infarction
The jejunum and ileum originate from the embryological midgut and derive their blood supply from branches of the superior mesenteric artery. Infarction of the small intestine may be focal or generalized, and the diagnosis may have gone unrecognized in life. The affected bowel is black or necrotic and is typically distended by blood or blood-stained fluid. There is commonly an associated peritonitis. There may be an associated perforation. The affected bowel acts as an obstruction, and the proximal gut may contain feculent fluid. At autopsy, the affected bowel should be eviscerated *en bloc* with the retroperitoneal vasculature. This allows the superior mesenteric artery to be easily explored for the presence of thromboemboli. If no thromboemboli are found, histological sampling of the mesenteric vasculature is recommended to look for the presence of vasculitis.

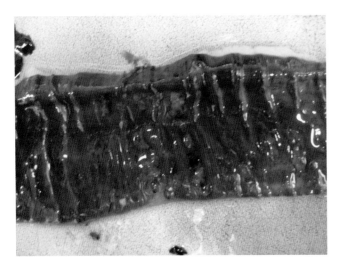

◄ Figure 5.29b Infarction

Focal infarction of one or more loops of small intestine may arise as a consequence of focal vasculitis, a small thromboembolus, strangulation within a hernia, or entrapment by a peritoneal band.

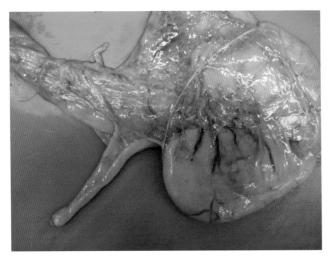

◄ Figure 5.29c Infarction

Infarction of the entire jejunum and ileum typically results from a thromboembolus in the proximal superior mesenteric artery or from vasculitis.

Appendix

◄ Figure 5.30 Normal appendix

The normal appendix is a vermiform (worm-like) organ that arises from the cecum at the point of confluence of the taenia coli. Typically approximately 8 to 10 cm in length, there is marked variation in the length and position of the appendix within the abdomen. The normal appendix has a smooth shiny tan peritonealized surface.

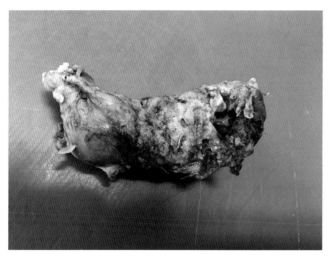

◀ Figure 5.31 Appendicitis

Although typically a disease of children and young adults, appendicitis can occur at any age and the mean age at diagnosis is rising. It is more common in males than in females.[13] The inflamed appendix is edematous, and the surface peritoneum becomes dull and then erythematous with a fibrinous or fibrinopurulent exudate. Acute appendicitis may be complicated by perforation, abscess formation, and generalized peritonitis. Acute appendicitis is a very rare adult autopsy finding. This example is of a surgical pathology specimen.

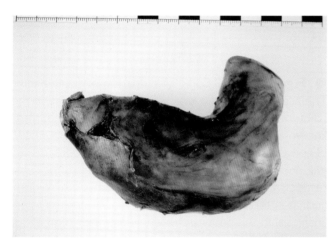

◀ Figure 5.32 Mucocele of the appendix

Mucoceles occur when the lumen of the appendix becomes dilated with a clear viscous mucoid material. The diagnosis is clinical rather than pathological. There are many causes such as mucinous cystadenoma or carcinoma, inspissated mucus (cystic fibrosis), hyperplastic or serrated polyp, or other obstruction to appendiceal drainage.

119

Colon and Rectum

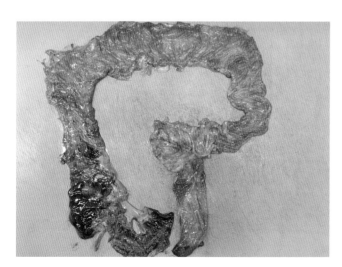

◀ Figure 5.33 Normal colorectum

The last part of the gastrointestinal tract comprises the cecum, ascending colon, transverse colon, descending colon, sigmoid colon, and rectum. The colon can be distinguished from the small intestine by its larger diameter, its location around the edges of the abdominal cavity, and the presence of taenia coli. The cecum, ascending colon, and transverse colon arise from the embryonic midgut and are supplied by branches of the superior mesenteric artery. The remainder of the large intestine arises from the embryonic hindgut, and it is supplied by the inferior mesenteric artery. The cecum, transverse colon, and sigmoid colon are supported by mesenteries and are intraperitoneal structures. The ascending colon and descending colon are retroperitoneal. On opening the large bowel, the mucosa is flat but thrown into haustra, thus giving it a segmented appearance.

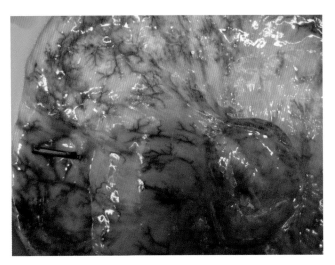

◄ Figure 5.34 Angiodysplasia

Angiodysplasia is the presence of fragile dilated vessels within the mucosa of the colon. It is more common with increasing age and typically affects the cecum and/or ascending colon. The etiology of angiodysplasia is uncertain. At autopsy, it can be recognized by the presence of prominent leashes of blood vessels in the mucosa. Angiodysplasia may give rise to torrential gastrointestinal tract hemorrhage. In this example of angiodysplasia of the cecum, a clip has been placed endoscopically in an attempt to control bleeding.

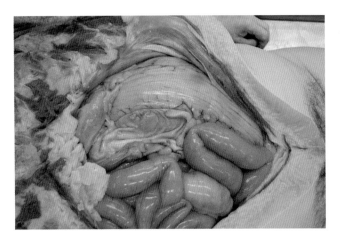

◄ Figure 5.35 Chronic constipation or fecal loading

The accumulation of a large quantity of feces within the colon of a chronically constipated patient is sometimes known as fecal loading. It may occur as a consequence of congenital or acquired neurological disorders (e.g., Hirschsprung disease and spinal cord injuries, respectively), autoimmune disease, and hypothyroidism and, as in this example, as a side effect of opiate analgesia. In this patient, the left side of the colon is markedly distended by firm feces. Compare this image with those of sigmoid volvulus (Figure 5.37).

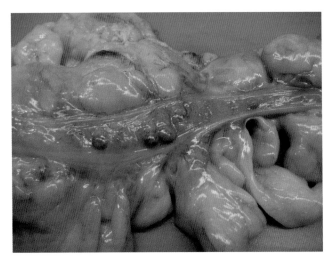

◄ Figure 5.36a Diverticulosis

Uncomplicated diverticulosis (diverticular disease) is a common incidental autopsy finding in middle-aged and older adults. Raised intraluminal pressure secondary to the consumption of a low-residue Western diet results in the formation of numerous colonic diverticula. These may be found in any part of the colon but are most prevalent in the sigmoid colon. The diverticula may be empty, or they may contain soft feces or fecaliths.

◀ **Figure 5.36b** Diverticulosis

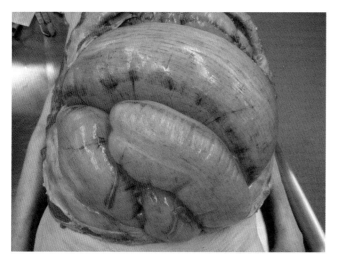

◀ **Figure 5.37a** Sigmoid volvulus
Volvulus occurs when part of the gut twists on its mesenteric axis.[14] The sigmoid colon is the most common site of volvulus. It becomes more frequent with increasing age, and there are associations between sigmoid volvulus and neuropsychiatric disease and constipation. At autopsy, the patient with a sigmoid volvulus typically has gaseous distention of the abdomen. Opening the abdomen reveals a markedly distended sigmoid colon that has twisted on its mesenteric axis, thus causing a closed-loop obstruction. The apex of the loop typically points toward or lies within the right upper quadrant of the abdomen.

121

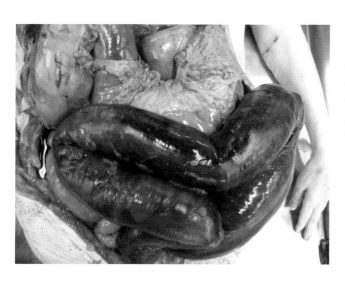

◀ **Figure 5.37b** Sigmoid volvulus
Sigmoid volvulus may be complicated by ischemia or infarction of the sigmoid. Such infarction may be extensive, but in all cases the affected bowel should be opened because infarction may be patchy. Hemorrhagic shock caused by sigmoid volvulus has also been reported.[15]

◀ Figure 5.38 Ulcerative colitis

Ulcerative colitis is a type of idiopathic inflammatory bowel disease characterized by continuous superficial inflammation and ulceration of the mucosa of the large intestine. It begins in the rectum and extends proximally in a continuous fashion toward the cecum. In patients with panproctocolitis, backwash ileitis may also be present. In patients who have been treated with topical therapy, the rectum may appear spared. Histological examination confirms the diagnosis.

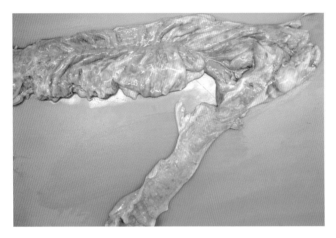

◀ Figure 5.39 Ischemic colitis

Ischemic colitis develops as a result of an insufficient blood supply to the colon. As may be expected, the watershed territory between the superior and inferior mesenteric arteries around the junction of the middle and distal thirds of the transverse colon is most commonly affected. Any disease process that results in reduced perfusion of the colon may cause ischemic colitis, and hence the list of potential causes is legion.[16] The macroscopic appearance depends on the duration and severity of the ischemia. The affected bowel is dusky, edematous, and hemorrhagic. Ulceration and gangrenous infarction may be present. Healing results in stricture formation and segmental mucosal atrophy. Histological examination is recommended to differentiate ischemic colitis from idiopathic inflammatory bowel disease, with which it may be readily confused.

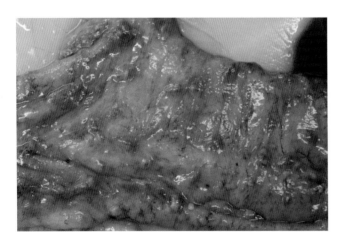

◀ Figure 5.40 Pseudomembranous colitis

Pseudomembranous colitis is typically the result of overgrowth of *Clostridium difficile* following antibiotic therapy. Clindamycin, cephalosporins, and penicillin-based antibiotics are common culprits. The antibiotic therapy may precede the development of pseudomembranous colitis by some months. A yellow-green pseudomembrane forms in plaques 2 to 10 mm in diameter on the surface of the colorectal mucosa. These plaques may become confluent. The disease causes diarrhea and may result in toxic megacolon. Death may ensue from electrolyte disturbance, systemic inflammatory response syndrome, or perforation. The macroscopic appearance is diagnostic, but histopathological examination and analysis of feces for the presence of *C. difficile* antigen and toxin are useful diagnostic adjuncts.

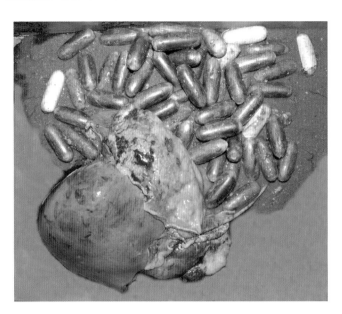

◄ Figure 5.41 Concealed narcotics
Individuals attempting to transport illicit drugs may do so by swallowing multiple small pellets or balloons that have been filled with narcotics such as heroin or cocaine. The balloons are often made from multilayered condoms and can appear throughout the gastrointestinal tract, as well as in body cavities such as the vagina. If a pellet or balloon ruptures, fatal drug toxicity may occur. A sample of the pellets or balloons can be submitted for toxicological examination. The remainder should be placed in custody of the police.

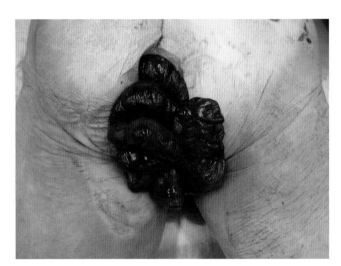

◄ Figure 5.42 Spontaneous rectal perforation and small bowel evisceration
Spontaneous rectal perforation is a rare complication of irritable bowel syndrome. It is thought to be caused by excessive straining. Chronic straining deepens the pouch of Douglas, thus weakening the wall of the rectum. Straining increases the pressure within the bowel, with resulting perforation. There may be a history of rectal prolapse. Rectal perforation may also occur as a result of preexisting disease such as diverticulosis, ulcers, colitis, or cancer, but there may be no evidence at autopsy that these diseases were present in the rectum. Rectal perforation may also occur as a complication of rectal instrumentation, for example, colonoscopy, or anorectal trauma. This patient had a history of irritable bowel syndrome. Spontaneous rectal perforation resulted in prolapse and evisceration of much of the small intestine, which subsequently infarcted (likely as a result of obstruction of the vascular supply secondary to compression of the anal sphincter). There was no evidence of trauma. On evisceration, there was no blood within the peritoneal cavity. Histological examination of the rectum revealed no evidence of solitary rectal ulcer, chronic idiopathic inflammatory bowel disease, or vasculitis.

123

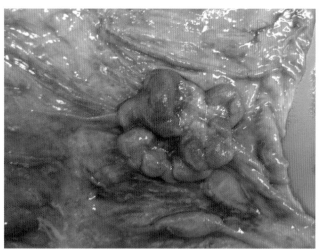

◀ **Figure 5.43a** Colorectal polyps
A polyp is a benign growth on a mucosal membrane. In the colorectum, most polyps are adenomas, but inflammatory and hyperplastic polyps also occur. Connective tissue neoplasms may manifest as colorectal polyps, but this is rare.[17] The risk of carcinoma within a polyp increases with the size of the lesion, and histological examination is recommended to exclude or confirm a malignant diagnosis. Colonic polyps may be sessile or pedunculated. Sessile polyps are flat lesions that lie on the surface of the colonic mucosa. They lack a stalk.

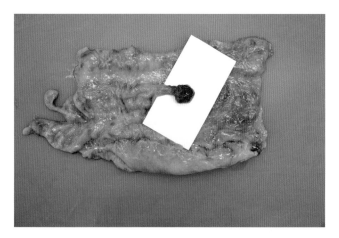

◀ **Figure 5.43b** Colorectal polyps
Pedunculated polyps are mushroom-shaped lesions that are attached to the colonic mucosa by a stalk.

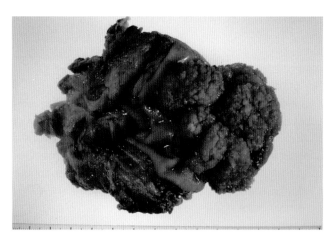

◀ **Figure 5.44** Villous adenoma of the rectum
Villous adenomas of the colon are typically several centimeters in diameter and may be as large as 10 cm. They have a cauliflower-like appearance with a fronded surface. They have a higher incidence of malignancy than other adenomas. Unlike tubular adenomas, they often do not have a stalk, and therefore the assessment of invasion can be difficult to assess. Because of their size, villous adenomas can cause obstructive symptoms.

◀ Figure 5.45 Familial polyposis coli

Familial adenomatous polyposis (FAP) is an autosomal dominant genetic condition in which patients have a defect in the *APC* gene at 5q21. This defect results in the development of hundreds of colonic polyps by adolescence that form a "carpet" of polyps. If patients with FAP are not treated by colectomy, adenocarcinoma will develop in nearly all these individuals. Polyps can occur in the stomach and small intestine. A thorough examination of the entire gastrointestinal tract for malignancy is essential at autopsy, although with elective colectomy in early life the incidence of this condition at autopsy is very small.

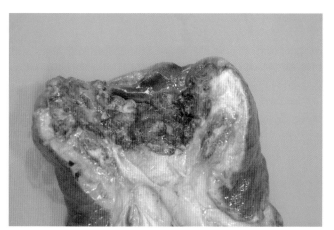

◀ Figure 5.46a Colorectal carcinoma

Malignant neoplasms of the colorectum are almost all adenocarcinomas. They may manifest as pedunculated polyps, ulcerated sessile polyps, or annular stenosing lesions. These adenocarcinomas invade locally and metastasize to the local lymph nodes, peritoneal cavity, liver, and lungs. Bone marrow metastases may also occur. Histopathological examination confirms the diagnosis and permits staging of the disease. Colorectal adenocarcinomas typically cause death by inducing a catabolic state, by causing bowel obstruction, and by causing hemorrhage.

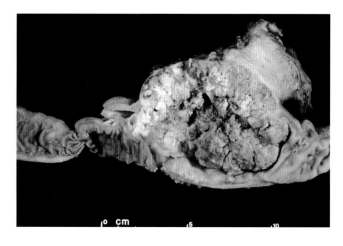

◀ Figure 5.46b Colorectal carcinoma

Anus

◀ **Figure 5.47** Normal anus

The anus is the sphincter that marks the distal end of the gastrointestinal tract. It consists of an internal sphincter and an external sphincter. The anus should be inspected at autopsy because failure to do so may result in missing the presence of foreign bodies or a focus of sepsis, bleeding, or trauma. The normal anus typically appears as a puckered sphincter lying within the natal cleft. The degree of relaxation of the sphincter at autopsy is highly variable. Funnel anus, in which there is a deep, skin-lined anal funnel, is a normal congenital anatomical variant,[18] and it should *not* be taken to indicate that there has been anal sexual intercourse.

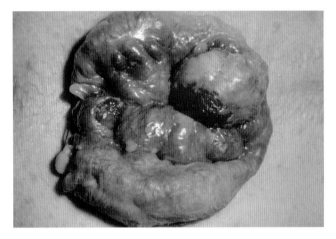

◀ **Figure 5.48** Hemorrhoids

Hemorrhoids are engorged anal vascular cushions and, with the patient in the lithotomy position, are present at the 7-o'clock, 11-o'clock, and 3-o'clock positions. They should not be confused with rectal varices. Hemorrhoids are easily recognizable as fleshy masses present at the anal margin. When uncomplicated, they are known colloquially as piles. Hemorrhoids may thrombose or give rise to hemorrhage. Bleeding from hemorrhoids may be fatal, although this is rare.

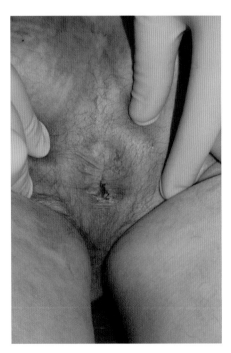

◀ **Figure 5.49** Fissure

Anal fissures are lacerations in the anus and are a common cause of anorectal pain, pain on defecation, and bleeding. They commonly arise as a complication of constipation (passing hard stool), childbirth, chronic diarrhea, and idiopathic inflammatory bowel disease. They may also be a feature of sexual assault or trauma.

◀ **Figure 5.50** Fistula in ano

Anal fistula, or fistula in ano, is an abnormal tract or cavity with an external opening in the perianal area that is communicating with the rectum or anal canal. Most fistulas are thought to arise as a result of an infection of the anal glands with resultant perirectal abscess. This image shows a fissure with a pink base to the left of the anal canal. There is a small skin tag to the left of the fistula.

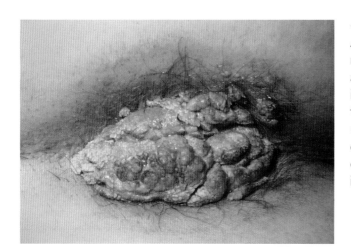

◀ **Figure 5.51** Condylomata acuminata

Anogenital warts (condylomata acuminata) are the most common viral sexually transmitted disease, and they are caused by human papillomavirus (HPV) infection. These warts affect the mucosa and skin of the anorectum and genitalia. They present as warty (verrucous) excrescences and may develop into cauliflower-like masses (as in this picture) in moist, occluded areas such as the perianal skin, vulva, and inguinal folds.

127

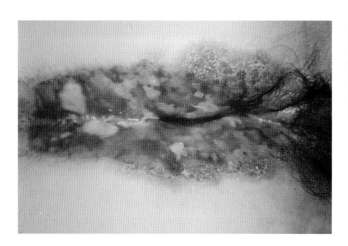

◀ **Figure 5.52** Paget disease of the anus

Perianal Paget disease is a rare malignant disease. It is often associated with an underlying adenocarcinoma (estimated at 33%). It usually manifests with anal itchiness and discomfort and intermittent rectal bleeding, and it can be misdiagnosed as hemorrhoids.

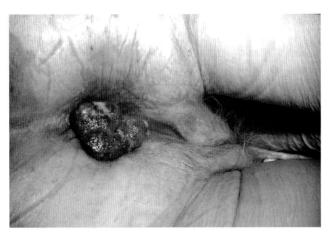

◀ **Figure 5.53** Anal malignancy
Anal cancer is an uncommon malignant disease, accounting for only about 1% of all cancers of the lower alimentary tract. This image shows a polypoid tumor protruding from the anal canal. In this instance, the tumor was a malignant melanoma; however, 80% of anal cancers are squamous cell carcinomas. Other tumor types include lymphoma and adenocarcinoma.

Peritoneum

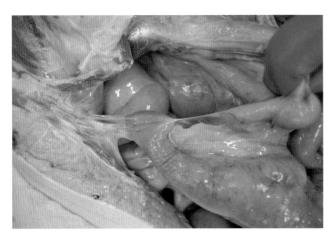

◀ **Figure 5.54** Peritoneal adhesions
Any process that results in peritoneal inflammation may give rise to peritoneal adhesions. Thus, these adhesions are seen in patients who have undergone abdominal surgery or who have a history of a localized or generalized inflammatory process affecting the abdominal contents. Adhesions begin as strands of fibrin and organize into fibrous connective tissue over time. Adhesions may mat loops of bowel together and are a cause of bowel obstruction.[19] In severe examples, all the loops of small intestine, the large intestine, and the abdominal wall are matted together, and in such cases it may be impossible to eviscerate the intestines separate from the other organs.

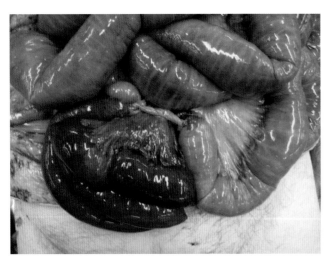

◀ **Figure 5.55** Peritoneal band
Peritoneal bands are congenital malformations resulting from nonabsorption of portions of omentum and mesentery during embryological development. They comprise a sheet or band of fibrous connective tissue. They may be present anywhere within the peritoneal cavity but are most common around the duodenum, duodenojejunal flexure, ileocecal valve, and ascending colon.[20] They may be asymptomatic. Their significance at autopsy lies in their role as potential causes of bowel obstruction[21] and infarction.[22] Peritoneal bands extending from the cecum to the subhepatic region, posterior peritoneum, or abdominal wall are known as Ladd bands and may cause duodenal obstruction.[23]

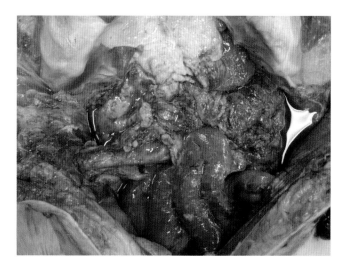

◀ Figure 5.56a Peritonitis

Inflammation of the peritoneum can result from a wide variety of causes. It is recognized at autopsy as an inflamed erythematous peritoneum that may be associated with a fibrinous exudate and/or pus. Peritonitis may be sterile or infected. Sterile peritonitis results from spillage of gastric contents, bile, pancreatic fluid, blood, or urine into the peritoneal cavity. Secondary infection is common.

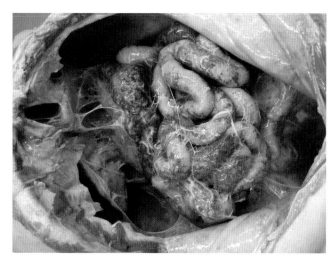

◀ Figure 5.56b Infected peritonitis

Infected peritonitis most commonly occurs as a consequence of perforation of the intestines. A diagnosis of fecal peritonitis is manifestly obvious on opening the abdomen as the pathologist is met by a severely inflamed peritoneum and a strong fecal odor. Infected peritonitis may also complicate penetrating abdominal trauma, systemic infection, or ambulatory peritoneal dialysis. Patients with ascites secondary to cirrhosis may have infected spontaneous bacterial peritonitis[24] resulting from bacterial translocation from the bowel into the blood, prolonged bacteremia, and intrahepatic shunting of blood away from Kupffer cells.[25]

129

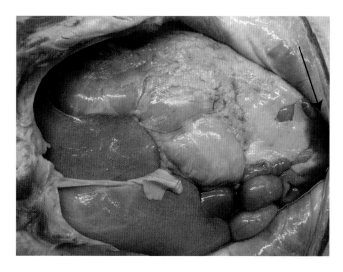

◀ Figure 5.57 Ascites

Ascites is the accumulation of fluid within the peritoneal cavity. Transudative ascites occurs in patients with right ventricular failure or renal failure and in those with cirrhosis and portal hypertension. Raised venous pressure causes transudation of fluid into the peritoneal cavity. Hypoalbuminemia and activation of the renin-angiotensin-aldosterone pathway potentiate the condition. Transudative ascites is a clear yellow fluid. Exudative ascites develops in patients with abdominal or pelvic malignant and/or inflammatory diseases. Exudative ascites may be turbid and blood-stained. The presence of ascites should prompt a search for the underlying cause. Microbiological examination assists in the diagnosis or exclusion of spontaneous bacterial peritonitis. Many liters of fluid may accumulate, resulting in diaphragmatic splinting and respiratory embarrassment.

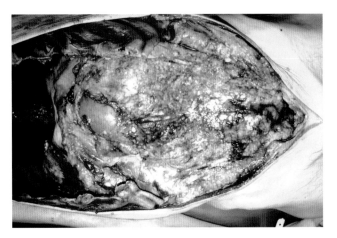

◀ **Figure 5.58** Peritoneal mesothelioma

Malignant peritoneal mesothelioma is a rare aggressive tumor of the peritoneum, regarded as a universally fatal disease. It accounts for approximately 30% of all mesotheliomas. Patients usually present with abdominal pain, abdominal distention, and widespread tumor. It is linked, as with pleural mesothelioma, to asbestos exposure. It can be very difficult to differentiate from disseminated primary ovarian malignant mesothelioma, which is also exceedingly rare; therefore, histological sampling is prudent.

References

1. Wilcox CM, Schwartz DA, Clark WS. Esophageal ulceration in human immunodeficiency virus infection: causes, response to therapy, and long term outcome. *Annals of Internal Medicine* 1995;**123**:143–149.

2. Rosenthal T, Adar R, Deutsch V. Esophageal ulceration and oral potassium chloride ingestion. *Chest* 1974;**65**:463–465.

3. Abraham SC, Cruz-Correa M, Lee LA, Yardley JH, Wu TT. Alendronate-associated esophageal injury: pathological and endoscopic features. *Modern Pathology* 1999;**12**:1152–1157.

4. Carlborg B, Lindqvist C, Densert O. Tetracycline induced esophageal ulcers: a clinical and experimental study. *Laryngoscope* 1983;**93**:184–187.

5. Yardley JH, Hendrix TR. Gastritis, duodenitis, and associated ulcerative lesions. In: Yamada T, Alpers DH, Owyang C, Powell DW, Silverstein FE, editors. *Textbook of gastroenterology*. Philadelphia: Lippincott; 1995:1456–1493.

6. Hirvonen J, Huttunen P. Increased urinary concentration of catecholamines in hypothermia deaths. *Journal of Forensic Sciences* 1982;**27**:264–271.

7. Karsner HT. The pathology of peptic ulcer of the stomach. *Journal of the American Medical Association* 1925;**85**:1376–1380.

8. Chen CY, Kuo YT, Lee CH, Hsieh TJ, Jan CM, Jaw TS, Huang WT, Yu FJ. Differentiation between malignant and benign gastric ulcers: CT virtual gastroscopy versus optical gastroendoscopy. *Radiology* 2009;**252**:410–417.

9. Skapinker S, Crawshaw GR. Acid burns of the stomach. *South African Medical Journal* 1954;**28**:356–359.

10. Endo K, Kuroha M, Shiga H, Kakuta Y, Takahashi S, Kinouchi Y, Shimosegawa T. Two cases of diffuse duodenitis associated with ulcerative colitis. *Case Reports in Gastrointestinal Medicine* 2012;**2012**:396521.

11. Meagher AP, Porter AJ, Rowland R, Ma G, Hoffmann DG. Jejunal diverticulosis. *Australian and New Zealand Journal of Surgery* 1993;**63**:360–366.

12. Lempinen M, Salmela K, Kemppainen E. Jejunal diverticulosis: a potentially dangerous entity. *Scandinavian Journal of Gastroenterology* 2004;**39**:905–909.

13. Buckius MT, McGrath B, Monk J, Grim R, Bell T, Ahuja V. Changing epidemiology of acute appendicitis in the United States: study period 1993-2008. *Journal of Surgical Research* 2012;**175**:185–190.

14. Levsky JM, Den EI, DuBrow RA, Wolf EL, Rozenblit AM. CT findings of sigmoid volvulus. *AJR American Journal of Roentgenology* 2010;**194**:136–143.

15. Sato H, Tanaka T, Tanaka N. Hemorrhagic shock caused by sigmoid colon volvulus: an autopsy case. *Medical Science Monitor* 2011;**17**:CS145–CS148.
16. Theodoropoulou A, Koutroubakis IE. Ischemic colitis: clinical practice in diagnosis and treatment. *World Journal of Gastroenterology* 2008;**14**:7302–7308.
17. Kemp CD, Arnold CA, Torbenson MS, Stein EM. An unusual polyp: a pedunculated leiomyoma of the sigmoid colon. *Endoscopy* 2011;**43**:E306–E307.
18. Suomalainen A, Wester A, Koivusalo A, Rintala RJ, Pakarinen MP. Congenital funnel anus in children: associated anomalies, surgical management and outcome. *Pediatric Surgery International* 2007;**23**:1167–1170.
19. van Goor H. Consequences and complications of peritoneal adhesions. *Colorectal Disease* 2007;**9**(Suppl 2):25–34.
20. Oelhafen K, Shayota BJ, Muhleman M, Klaassen Z, Shoja MM, Loukas M. Peritoneal bands: a review of anatomical distribution and clinical implications. *American Surgeon* 2012; **78**:377–384.
21. Sozen S, Emir S, Yazar FM, Altinsoy HK, Topuz O, Vurdem UE, Cetinkunar S, Ozkan Z, Guzel K. Small bowel obstruction due to anomalous congenital peritoneal bands: a case series in adults. *Bratislavske lekarske listy* 2012;**113**:186–189.
22. Kotán R, Bittner R, Sápy P. A duplicate peritoneal sheet of the lateral abdominal wall may create internal hernias: a rare case of intestinal obstruction. *Chirurgische Gastroenterologie* 2005;**21**:188–190.
23. Macías Robles MD, Martínez Mengual BM, Amador Tejón MJ, García Arias F, Fernández San Martín A. Ladd's band duodenal obstruction. *Emergency* 2007;**19**:162–163.
24. Lata J, Stiburek O, Kopacova M. Spontaneous bacterial peritonitis: a severe complication of liver cirrhosis. *World Journal of Gastroenterology* 2009;**15**:5505–5510.
25. Căruntu FA, Benea L. Spontaneous bacterial peritonitis: pathogenesis, diagnosis, treatment. *Journal of Gastrointestinal and Liver Diseases* 2006;**15**:51–56.

Chapter 6
The Hepatobiliary System and Pancreas

Introduction

Diseases of the liver, gallbladder, bile ducts, and pancreas are common autopsy findings. They may be coincidental to the cause of death or highly pertinent to it.

In the Western world, the most common causes of significant liver injury are alcohol, viral hepatitis, and paracetamol (acetaminophen) poisoning. The clinical history may give important clues to the causation of the liver disease, but histopathological examination, coupled with histochemistry, is typically needed to determine the cause. In chronic viral hepatitis, the liver typically looks macroscopically normal until fibrosis or cirrhosis intervenes.

The external manifestations of liver disease, including palmar erythema, Dupuytren contractures, spider nevi, jaundice, and peripheral edema, may be evident on external examination. Internal findings may include the presence of pleural effusions and ascites. Where ascites is present it should be sampled for microbiological examination to exclude spontaneous bacterial peritonitis. However, an individual may have significant liver disease without external manifestations. The author has undertaken a number of autopsies in which liver disease caused significant metabolic derangement, resulting in toxic levels of prescribed medications taken at therapeutic doses but metabolized by the liver while those medications that are excreted by the kidney were present at therapeutic concentrations.

As in the lungs, brain, and bones, malignant tumors within the liver are far more likely to be metastases than primary tumors. Careful inspection and palpation of the capsular surface of the liver when the abdomen is first opened will usually alert the pathologist to the presence of tumor deposits within the liver, and this should prompt a careful search for the primary site.

In the biliary system, by far the most common abnormal finding is that of gallstones, followed by cholesterolosis of the gallbladder. Gallstones are frequently asymptomatic, and their presence is rarely related to the cause of death.

The most common abnormality seen within the pancreas is chronic pancreatitis. There may or may not be a history of diabetes mellitus, gallstones, or alcoholism, although in the West these are the most frequent causes.

This chapter considers the common and some of the not-so-common disorders to affect these organs.

Liver

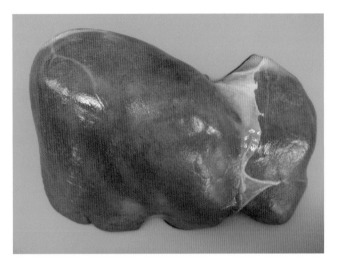

◀ **Figure 6.1** Normal liver

The normal liver has a uniformly smooth and shiny capsule. Smooth slices made no more than 1 cm apart with a long-bladed knife reveal a dark red-brown homogenous cut surface in which larger branches of the hepatic veins and bile ducts can be readily discerned. The weight of the normal liver depends upon the body mass index of the deceased. Livers that weigh more than 1800 g are generally abnormal, even if the cut surface is unremarkable, and histological sampling may be warranted.

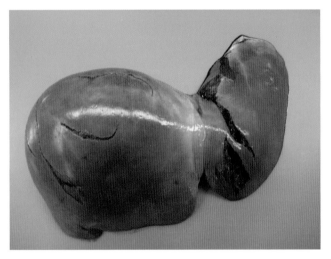

◀ **Figure 6.2** Lacerated liver

Lacerations of the liver result from the application of blunt force trauma to the abdomen and may be associated with injuries to other intra-abdominal organs. They are frequently multiple and of varying length, and they may result in complete or almost complete transection of the liver and severe disruption of the hepatic parenchyma. When death has occurred rapidly, there may be very little associated bleeding, but with prolonged survival there is usually significant hemoperitoneum.

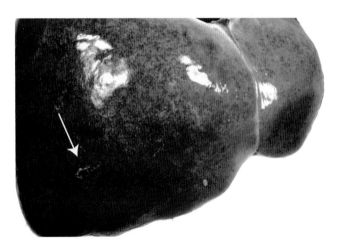

◀ **Figure 6.3** Liver hemorrhage following liver biopsy

Most biopsies are currently performed for parenchymal disease not to make specific diagnosis but to assess the liver damage (the degree of inflammation, fibrosis) or the response to therapy. One of the main complications of the procedure, after pain, is bleeding, which can be major or minor. The risk of major bleeding is reported to be around 0.16%. In this case, the needle entry site and the surrounding parenchyma hemorrhage are clearly visible.

◀ **Figure 6.4a** Chronic hepatic venous congestion
Chronic hepatic venous congestion is one of the most common abnormalities seen within the liver, but it is also one of the most overdiagnosed by those learning autopsy pathology. In the mildest form of this disorder, the cut surface appears mottled, with dark zones approximately 1 mm in diameter interspersed with liver of normal color. This is hepatic congestion.

◀ **Figure 6.4b** Chronic hepatic venous congestion
In chronic hepatic venous congestion, the liver contains a mixture of dark red-brown zones that correspond to venous congestion centered on central veins interspersed with pale yellow zones corresponding to the accumulation of fat within the hepatocytes of acinar zones 1 and 2. True chronic hepatic venous congestion is therefore also known as "nutmeg" liver because of the alleged resemblance to the cut surface of a nutmeg.

135

◀ **Figure 6.4c** Chronic hepatic venous congestion
The cut surface of a nutmeg (*Myristica fragrans*) for comparison with (b). Note the interspersed dark and light areas.

◄ Figure 6.5 Fatty liver

Fatty change is one of the most common abnormalities seen within the liver at autopsy. Severe fatty change can be seen with the liver *in situ*. The liver is enlarged and bright yellow.

The fatty liver has a smooth, greasy cut surface that typically smears along the blade of the knife. Histopathological examination is required to distinguish pure steatosis from steatohepatitis. The finding of a bright yellow fatty liver should prompt toxicological investigation for the presence of alcoholic and diabetic ketoacidosis, even in the absence of a history of these disorders.

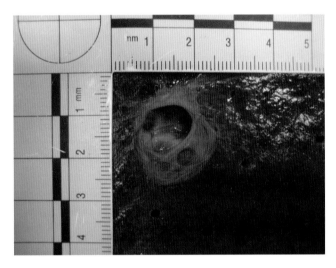

◄ Figure 6.6 Cysts

Hepatic cysts, also known as simple cysts, are common and typically solitary lesions within the liver. They have thin, fibrous walls and are filled with clear fluid. They are typically asymptomatic in life, although they may exert clinically significant effects as a result of mass effect, rupture, hemorrhage, and infection.[1,2]

◄ Figure 6.7a Cirrhosis

The presence of cirrhosis should prompt further investigation in an attempt to determine the underlying cause, as well as a search for complications of cirrhosis including portal hypertension and malignant disease. Although the most common causes of cirrhosis in the West are alcoholism and viral hepatitis (particularly hepatitis B and hepatitis C), other causes exist and may be identified with histopathological examination, virology, and immunology using materials retained at autopsy. Such investigations are important because diagnoses such as hemochromatosis, alpha-1-antitripsin deficiency, and Wilson disease (hepatolenticular degeneration) may have implications for surviving first-degree relatives. Other causes such as autoimmune hepatitis and primary biliary cirrhosis should also be considered. Individuals with cirrhosis need not be jaundiced.

◀ **Figure 6.7b** Cirrhosis

The cirrhotic liver may be of normal weight, enlarged, or shrunken compared with the body habitus of the deceased. The capsule has a firm, nodular texture. On slicing the cirrhotic liver at intervals no more than 1 cm apart, the liver is felt to be firm, and it may have a "gritty" texture under the knife. The cut surface is typically pale and waxy, with a nodular architecture. The size of the nodules may be used to classify the cirrhosis as either micronodular (<3 mm in diameter) or macronodular. Although alcoholic cirrhosis typically has a micronodular architecture, such a classification has little practical value in clinical practice and should not replace histopathological investigation.

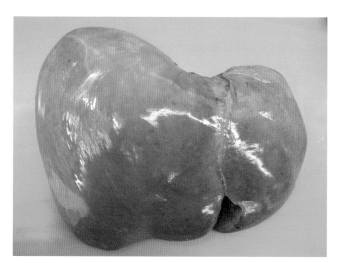

◀ **Figure 6.8a** Infarction

Global infarction of the liver is rare, but it may result from periods of profound hypotension secondary to hemorrhage, sepsis, or other causes. It may also result from toxic insult to the liver, for example, from paracetamol (acetaminophen) poisoning. The infarcted liver has an abnormally firm texture and a gray-green cut surface.

137

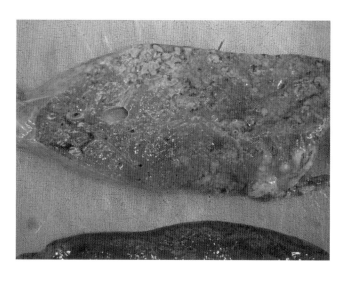

◀ **Figure 6.8b** Infarction

Localized infarcts within the liver may result from embolic events and appear as sharply demarcated wedge-shaped lesions with a firm, white-gray cut surface.

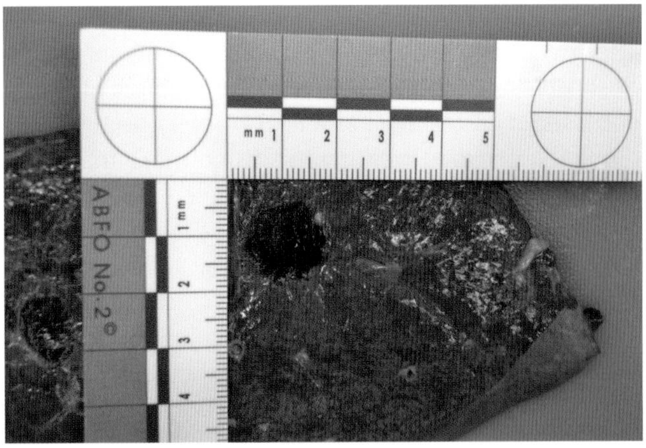

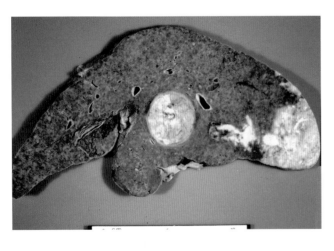

◀ Figure 6.9 Hemangiomas

Hemangiomas are the most common benign tumors of the liver and are a frequent autopsy finding. They are more common in women than in men and more common in the right lobe than the left. Although these tumors are typically asymptomatic, pregnancy, steroid use, and estrogen therapy may cause hemangiomas to enlarge. Hemangiomas are typically solitary, but they may be multiple. They may appear as reddish-brown solid and cystic masses or as solid white masses, the latter mimicking metastatic malignant disease. Histopathological examination confirms the diagnosis. Large hemangiomas may rupture spontaneously or with blunt force trauma, giving rise to hemoperitoneum.

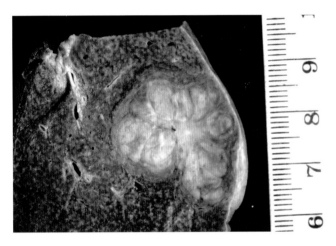

◀ Figure 6.10 Focal nodular hyperplasia

Focal nodular hyperplasia is a benign tumor of the liver. It is usually asymptomatic and has no malignant potential. The tumor can be very difficult to distinguish from hepatic adenoma. There is a strong female preponderance, and there is thought be an association with oral contraceptives (66% to 95% of cases). The tumors can show hemorrhage, necrosis, and even infarction.

◀ Figure 6.11 Hepatocellular carcinoma

Hepatocellular carcinoma (HCC) is the most common primary malignant disease of the liver,[3] although most malignant tumors within the liver are metastases from elsewhere, most notably the gastrointestinal tract, lungs, and breast. Alcoholism, hepatitis B, hepatitis C, and cirrhosis resulting from any cause are risk factors for the development of HCC. Macroscopically, HCC is a nodular-infiltrative solid tumor that may vary in color from gray through green to tan. Diffuse HCC spreads through the portal veins and may give rise to multiple masses. Foci of hemorrhage and necrosis may be present.

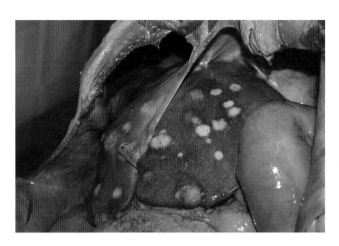

◀ **Figure 6.12** Metastatic malignancy capsular surface

The presence of metastatic malignancy within the liver may be evident from its capsular surface. Subcapsular metastases appear as firm gray/white masses that give rise to puckering of the capsular surface. Such an appearance should prompt a careful search for the primary malignancy, including complete examination of the gastrointestinal tract and breasts.

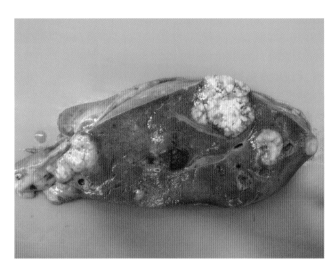

◀ **Figure 6.13a** Metastatic malignancy cut surface

Metastases within the liver most commonly originate from primaries within the gastrointestinal tract. They are firm white/gray tumor deposits with irregular infiltrative margins and often contain central necrosis. The tumor deposits may be extensive, and may almost entirely replace the substance of the liver. Histopathological examination helps to determine the primary site, but does not negate the need for a careful macroscopic search for the primary. Malignant melanoma may metastasise to the liver, giving rise to heavily pigmented/black tumor deposits. A careful search should be made for the primary tumor (which may have been excised), remembering that ocular melanoma can also spread to the liver.

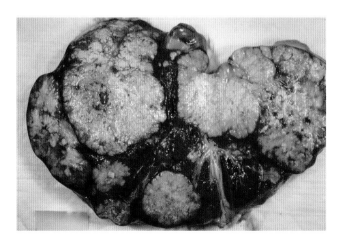

◀ **Figure 6.13b** Metastatic malignancy cut surface

Gallbladder

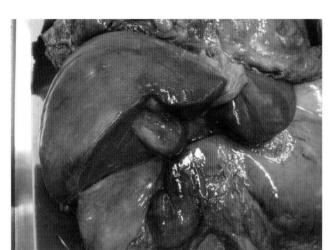

◀ **Figure 6.14** Normal gallbladder
The normal gallbladder has a uniformly smooth, shiny, brown or green serosal surface. Opening the gallbladder reveals that the wall is typically 1 to 2 mm thick. The mucosa is a uniform dark brown and has a roughened texture, corresponding to its villous architecture. The bile within the gallbladder may variably be green, light brown, or dark brown, but it is clear, and there are no gallstones. The gallbladder may be folded near the fundus, giving it an appearance of a Phrygian cap. This is a normal anatomical variant of no significance.

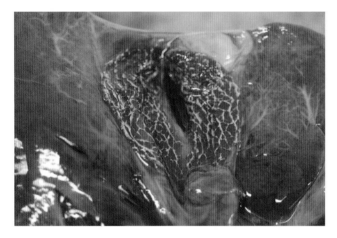

◀ **Figure 6.15a** Cholesterolosis
Also known as "strawberry gallbladder," cholesterolosis is a common autopsy finding, but one of little clinicopathological significance. The wall of the gallbladder is of normal thickness, but the mucosa contains innumerable small yellow or white patches that resemble the seeds of a strawberry and correspond to the presence of foamy histiocytes histologically.

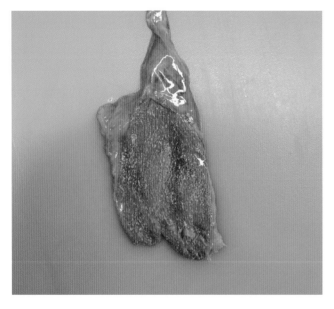

◀ **Figure 6.15b** Cholesterolosis

◀ **Figure 6.16a** Gallstones

Gallstones are a common, and frequently incidental, autopsy finding. They range in size from little bigger than a grain of sand to the size of a duck egg that fills the gallbladder. They may be yellow (pure cholesterol stones), green, or black (pigment stones). Mixed cholesterol and pigment stones may be encountered. Gallstones may be spherical or ovoid, faceted, or spiculated.

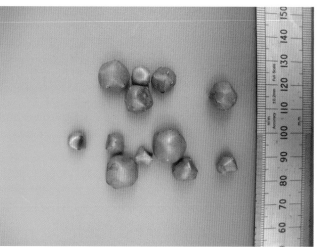

◀ **Figure 6.16b** Gallstones

141

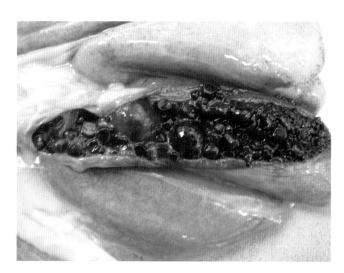

◀ **Figure 6.16c** Gallstones

◀ **Figure 6.17** Mucocele

Mucocele of the gallbladder occurs when the cystic duct becomes obstructed, typically by a gallstone. Externally, the gallbladder appears distended and white. On opening, the wall of the gallbladder appears thinned and fibrotic, and the gallbladder is filled with clear, colorless mucin secreted by the epithelium.

142

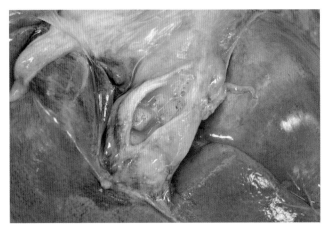

◀ **Figure 6.18** Empyema

Empyema of the gallbladder is uncommon. It occurs when the neck of the gallbladder or cystic duct becomes obstructed, typically by a gallstone, and there is secondary bacterial infection. Externally, the gallbladder appears inflamed. On opening, the wall of the gallbladder is thickened, and the gallbladder contains purulent fluid or frank pus. Empyema of the gallbladder may be associated with liver abscesses. Microbiological examination of the pus may reveal the causative microorganism.

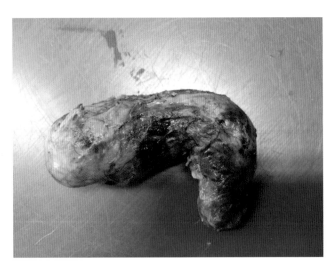

◀ **Figure 6.19** Acute cholecystitis

The acutely inflamed gallbladder has a thickened edematous wall, and there is inflammation of the peritoneum overlying the gallbladder and surrounding structures. Opening the gallbladder and biliary tree frequently reveals the presence of gallstones.

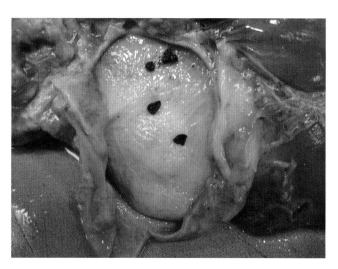

◀ **Figure 6.20** Chronic cholecystitis
Chronic cholecystitis most commonly results from repeated episodes of inflammation and scarring caused by gallstones. The gallbladder is shrunken, thick walled, and fibrotic. The mucosa may appear ulcerated. In some cases, the gallbladder may fibrose completely, leaving only a mass of fibroadipose tissue in the gallbladder bed. This can be distinguished from operative removal by the absence of clips on the bile ducts.

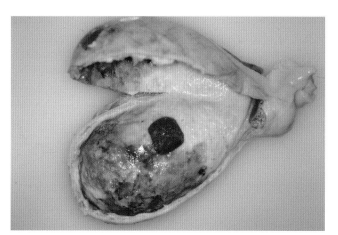

◀ **Figure 6.21** Porcelain gallbladder
This is a rare complication of chronic cholecystitis. The gallbladder becomes heavily calcified, and the condition is aptly named as the organ takes on the appearance of porcelain. A saw may be needed to open the gallbladder. The condition is typically seen in women with gallstones, and it may also be associated with carcinoma of the gallbladder.

143

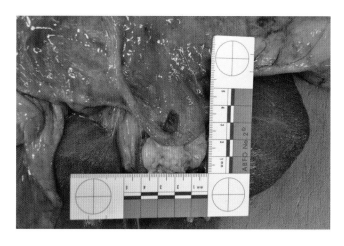

◀ **Figure 6.22** Choledochoduodenal fistula
A choledochoduodenal fistula is an abnormal connection between the gallbladder and the first part of the small intestine. Such a fistula can arise as a result of a peptic ulcer eroding through the wall of the duodenum into the gallbladder. Less commonly, it can result from a gallstone eroding out of the gallbladder into the duodenum. It is not possible to distinguish between the two mechanisms accurately or definitively at autopsy. Choledochoduodenal fistula can be complicated by gallstone ileus (see Figure 5.28b).

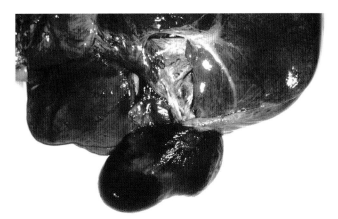

◀ **Figure 6.23** Torsion of the gallbladder
Torsion of the gallbladder is rare. In patients whose gallbladder hangs freely, it may twist along its long axis, resulting in ischemic infarction, as shown here. If left untreated, biliary sepsis, rupture, and biliary peritonitis may ensue.

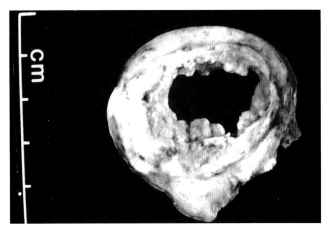

◀ **Figure 6.24** Carcinoma of the gallbladder
Carcinoma of the gallbladder may manifest with biliary peritonitis caused by rupture of the gallbladder. Macroscopically, there is localized thickening of the wall of the gallbladder, often at the fundus, and invasion of surrounding structures may be evident. Gallstones are virtually always also present within a gallbladder in which there is a primary carcinoma. The tumors, which are almost all adenocarcinomas, spread to local lymph nodes, the liver, stomach, and duodenum.

144

Bile Ducts

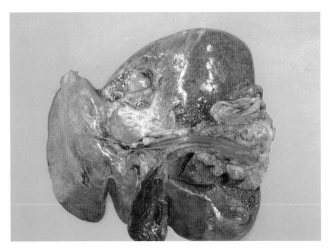

◀ **Figure 6.25** Normal bile ducts
The normal common bile duct is a tube 4 to 5 mm in diameter that contains bile. Having opened the duodenum, the patency of the duct can be confirmed by squeezing the gallbladder and seeing bile flow through the ampulla of Vater. The common bile duct can be opened, and this allows the common bile duct, cystic duct, and hepatic ducts to be examined. The ducts are thin walled and do not contain stones, as shown here.

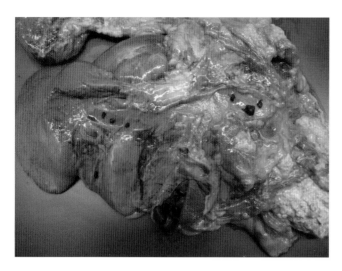

◄ Figure 6.26 Dilated: stone
Gallstones are the commonest cause of dilatation of the gallbladder, and the causative stone(s) may be found at any point from the ampulla of Vater to the hepatic ducts. Any malignancy that surrounds the bile ducts may give rise to dilatation of the bile ducts. Carcinomas within the head of the pancreas are the commonest cause.

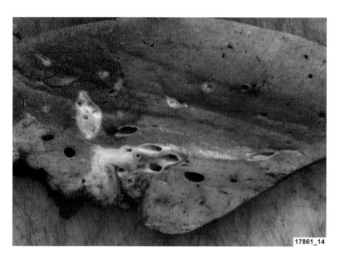

◄ Figure 6.27 Cholangiocarcinoma
Cholangiocarcinoma is rare. Most patients have no known risk factor for the disease, but cholangiocarcinoma is associated with ulcerative colitis, primary sclerosing cholangitis, and infestation with liver flukes such as *Clonorchis sinensis*. Cholangiocarcinoma may affect any portion of the intrahepatic or extrahepatic bile ducts, and it appears as a solid, firm, yellow-white tumor mass. Histopathological examination confirms the diagnosis. (Image courtesy of Dr. J. Denson.)

145

Pancreas

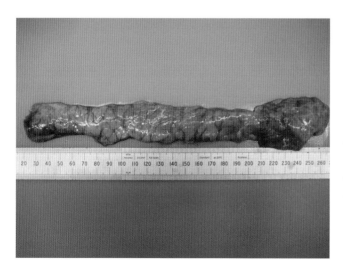

◄ Figure 6.28 Normal pancreas
The normal pancreas is a light tan organ with a lobulated architecture that surrounds a central duct. The gland should contain no hemorrhage. It typically lies encased in fat, which should be a uniform bright yellow. Anteriorly, the pancreas is separated from the posterior wall of the stomach by the lesser sac. Release of enzymes after death may cause significant autolysis of the pancreas that leads to atypical appearances. Any concerns regarding whether the pathologist is examining an inflamed or autolytic pancreas should prompt histopathological examination, and this is essential if acute pancreatitis is a potential cause of death.

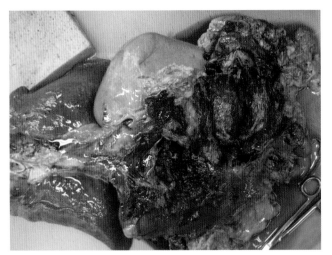

◀ **Figure 6.29** Acute hemorrhagic pancreatitis
In the Western world, the most common causes of acute hemorrhagic pancreatitis are gallstones and alcohol. Other causes, such as trauma, steroids, scorpion stings, mumps, autoimmune disease, hypothermia, hypocalcaemia, and other drugs, should always be considered. The pancreas appears inflamed, necrotic, and hemorrhagic, and there are usually white flecks in the surrounding adipose tissue as a result of saponification.

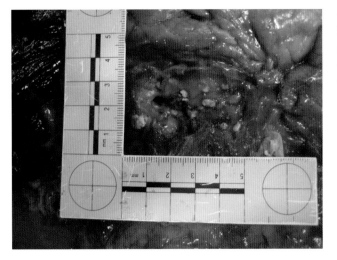

◀ **Figure 6.30a** Saponification
Saponification is the hydrolysis of triglycerides into soap, and it is the result of acute pancreatitis. The saponified fats appear as pale yellow-white flecks in the adipose tissue surrounding the pancreas.

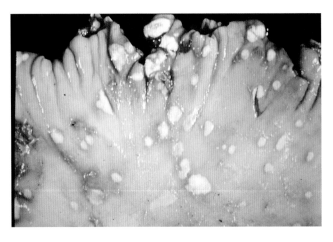

◀ **Figure 6.30b** Saponification
Where there has been severe pancreatitis, such flecks may also be seen in the adipose tissue of the intestinal mesenteries.

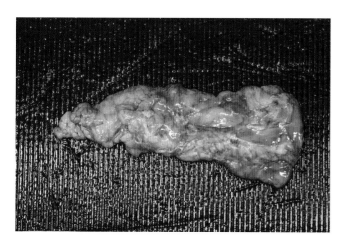

◄ Figure 6.31 Chronic pancreatitis
Chronic pancreatitis is a common autopsy finding. The pancreas becomes shrunken, and on slicing it has a firm, variably white and tan fibrotic cut surface. There is no hemorrhage. The lesser sac may be obliterated by fibrous adhesions.

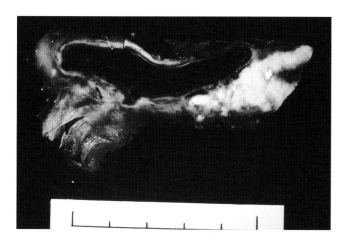

◄ Figure 6.32 Pancreatic pseudocyst
Pancreatic pseudocyst is a complication of acute pancreatitis, although it may also complicate chronic pancreatitis. It is the most common cause of a unilocular pancreatic lesion with a cystic appearance, although because it lacks an epithelial lining, technically it is not a true cyst.[4] It is recognized by the presence of a circumscribed, fluid-filled space, typically in the lesser peritoneal sac. The fluid is rich in pancreatic enzymes and may contain necrotic pancreatic tissue and blood. A pancreatic abscess ensues if the pseudocyst becomes infected.

147

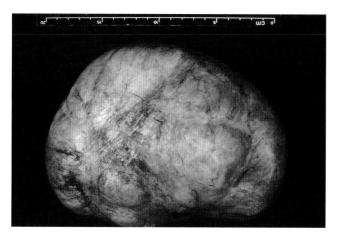

◄ Figure 6.33 Mucinous cystadenoma
Mucinous cystadenomas are the most common cystic tumors of the pancreas and have the potential to evolve into malignant neoplasms. Almost all mucinous cystadenomas occur in women.[5] These lesions are seen as a unilocular or multilocular cystic pancreatic mass, typically within the body or tail of the gland. The mucinous cysts are typically large and thin walled.

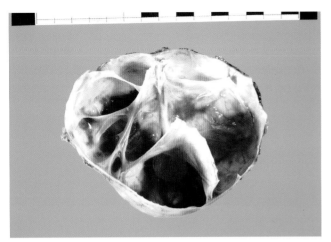

◀ **Figure 6.34** Serous cystadenoma

In contrast to mucinous cystadenomas, serous cystadenomas most commonly affect the head and neck of the pancreas. These tumors appear as a solid mass containing numerous small, serous cysts arranged around a central scar, giving rise to a honeycomb appearance on slicing.[4]

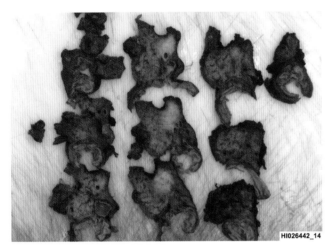

◀ **Figure 6.35** Pancreatic adenocarcinoma

Adenocarcinoma of the pancreas may affect any part of the gland, but it is most commonly seen within the head and neck of the gland. The entire gland should be carefully palpated. Adenocarcinoma results in thickening of the affected portion and appears as a firm or hard, white, solid mass within the pancreas that has an irregular margin. The common bile duct should be opened, to look for evidence of obstruction, and the local and regional lymph nodes should be examined and sampled to look for evidence of metastasis. Histological examination confirms the diagnosis. (Image courtesy of Dr. J. Denson.)

References

1. Yanai H, Tada N. A simple hepatic cyst with elevated serum and cyst fluid CA19-9 levels: a case report. *Journal of Medical Case Reports* 2008;**2**:329.
2. Yoshida H, Onda M, Tajiri T, Mamada Y, Taniai N, Mineta S, Hirakata A, Futami R, Arima Y, Inoue M, Hatta S, Kishimoto A. Infected hepatic cyst. *Hepatogastroenterology* 2003;**50**:507–509.
3. El-Serag HB. Hepatocellular carcinoma. *New England Journal of Medicine* 2011;**365**: 1118–1127.
4. Sahani DV, Kadavigere R, Saokar A, Fernandez-del Castillo C, Brugge WR, Hahn PF. Cystic pancreatic lesions: a simple imaging-based classification system for guiding management. *Radiographics* 2005;**25**:1471–1484.
5. Lee WA. Mucinous cystadenoma of the pancreas with predominant stroma creating a solid tumour. *World Journal of Surgical Oncology* 2005;**3**:59.

Chapter 7
The Genitourinary System

Introduction

The genitourinary tract comprises the kidneys, ureters, bladder, and the sexual organs. Diseases of these organs are common, are often encountered at autopsy, and frequently have relevance to the cause of death. Consequently, the genitourinary tract should be examined in every autopsy.

Urinary Tract

The urinary tract comprises the kidneys, ureters, and bladder. Diseases of these organs are common, and they may be congenital or acquired.

Congenital abnormalities of the kidneys and ureters are not infrequently encountered at autopsy and arise as a result of errors in organogenesis. Horseshoe kidney, congenital absence of a kidney, pelvic kidney, and duplex ureters are frequently encountered abnormalities. They typically have little or no pathological significance.

Many different localized and systemic diseases affect the kidneys. The kidney has a limited range of responses to pathological insult, and consequently histopathological, immunological, and electron microscopic examination may be required to elucidate the underlying cause. Benign neoplasia is fairly uncommon, but malignancy is often encountered, and it may be an unexpected finding at autopsy. Renal cell carcinomas metastasize to bones, and the finding of a renal cell carcinoma should prompt examination of the vertebral bone marrow for the presence of metastatic disease. This is done by performing a simple vertebral strip.

Disease of the ureters most typically arises as a consequence of disease elsewhere in the urinary tract. Calculi that formed in the kidney may lodge in the ureter, and the ureter may become dilated because of more distal urinary tract obstruction. Ureteric malignant diseases are rare.

The appearance of the normal bladder varies considerably, depending on the volume of urine within it. The bladder is a common site of infection, and this can result in fatal sepsis. Trabeculation and the formation of diverticula are commonly encountered, particularly in men, as a result of bladder outflow obstruction, typically secondary to benign prostatic hyperplasia. Bladder calculi, once common, are now rarely encountered at autopsy. The decline in bladder calculi is multifactorial and is partly the result of better nutrition and partly the result of improved treatment of lower urinary tract infections and bladder outflow obstruction. Bladder cancers remain common. In the West, these are typically transitional cell carcinomas, but in those parts of the world where schistosomiasis is endemic, squamous cell carcinomas predominate.

Male Genital Tract

The male genital tract includes the prostate, seminal vesicles, penis, testes, and scrotum. It should be examined in every autopsy examination.

Given that most autopsies are performed on older adults, the normal prostate is not commonly encountered. Prostatic enlargement resulting from hyperplasia is common, and the incidence increases with increasing age. The prostate is the most common site for malignant disease in the male genital tract and the second most common site of malignancy in men. It is not possible to reliably detect prostate cancer macroscopically, and if there is clinical suspicion histopathological examination is required. The incidence of prostate cancer increases with age, but many men with prostate cancer will die *with* their disease rather than *of* it. Prostate cancers have a predilection for metastasizing to bones (where they typically produce osteosclerotic metastases). The vertebral bone marrow should be examined for the presence of metastases in any individual with a history of prostate cancer.

The testes should be examined in every autopsy for evidence of trauma, infection, and malignancy. The testes are the most common site of malignant tumors in young men, and they may harbor an occult primary malignant tumor in a case of metastatic disease of unknown origin. Blunt trauma to the scrotum rarely causes bruising of the skin (being pliable) but often causes bruising to the firm testis. Postmortem drying artifact of the scrotum should not be confused with injury.

Disease of the male urethra is uncommon. The urethra can suffer traumatic rupture either from a fall astride a hard object or as a consequence of traumatic decatheterization. The autopsy pathologist should be familiar with techniques needed to dissect out the penile urethra in continuity with the remainder of the urinary tract, but this is not necessary in all cases.

Female Genital Tract

The female genital tract comprises the ovaries, fallopian tubes, uterus, cervix, vagina, and external genitalia. The external genital structures are discussed in Chapter 1, but the breasts are included here. All these structures may have different appearances at different stages of life (prepubertal stage, puberty, pregnancy, maturity, and after menopause). During the reproductive years, the cyclical nature of the menstrual cycle gives rise to different appearances, particularly of the uterus and ovaries. Pregnancy also causes identifiable changes.

The diseases that arise in the reproductive years are often very different from those of the postmenopausal years, and pregnancy itself is associated with many disorders that are outside the scope of this chapter.

The genital tract should be examined in all autopsies. The cervix and uterus may harbor tumors that may not be immediately apparent or an occult primary tumor in a case of metastatic carcinoma of unknown origin. Similarly, the breasts should be examined for evidence of previous surgery, radiation therapy, or active tumors.

Examination of the breasts and genital tract should also look for injuries. Although injuries to the vagina or breasts are in no way diagnostic of sexual assault (and, indeed, the absence of genital injury does not exclude nonconsensual intercourse), any injuries should always be considered in the overall context of the case, and if any concerns exist, a senior colleague or forensic pathologist should be consulted. Most of the diseases that may be a cause of death are most commonly (although by no means exclusively) seen in the postmenopausal years. Deaths that appear to be associated with pregnancy or the postpartum period (so-called maternal deaths) present their own unique challenges, and the autopsy should be undertaken by a pathologist experienced in such deaths or with the assistance of such an individual.

Anatomical variants may be encountered, particularly of the uterus, such as bicornuate, septate, unicornuate, and didelphic uterus. Bicornuate uteri are described as "heart shaped," where the upper uterine body is formed by two horns. Septate uterus describes a uterus in which the uterine cavity is partitioned by a longitudinal septum. A unicornuate uterus has a single horn and a banana-like shape. A didelphic uterus is a double uterus with two separate cervices, and often a double vagina as well. These variants rarely have direct relevance to death, but documentation of such anomalies is best practice for the thorough autopsy pathologist.

The pathologist should record the presence or absence of the pelvic organs (hysterectomy with or without salpingo-oophorectomy is a relatively common procedure), along with whether the organs appear atrophic (as is often the case in older patients), and the presence of any lesions such as fibroids, cysts, or polyps should be recorded. The author tends to refer to benign, well-circumscribed lesions in the uterine wall as "fibroids" when they are examined only macroscopically and reserves the term "leiomyoma" for histologically diagnosed lesions.

Kidney

◀ **Figure 7.1** Normal kidney
The normal kidney lies encased within fat, the thickness of which depends on the deceased's body habitus. A shallow incision into the lateral border allows the capsule to be easily lifted, revealing a smooth, shiny, dark red-brown cortical surface. The author places no significance on the presence of an adherent capsule in an otherwise normal kidney. Fetal lobations may be evident but are normal. Slicing the kidney with a long-bladed knife from the lateral border toward the hilum in the coronal plane reveals the cortex, medulla, and renal pelvis. The renal cortex is 7 mm or more thick, and the corticomedullary junction is well defined. The medullary pyramids are brown, typically darker than the cortex, and becoming paler toward the renal pelvis as a result of the formation by the collecting ducts of visible pale medullary rays.

151

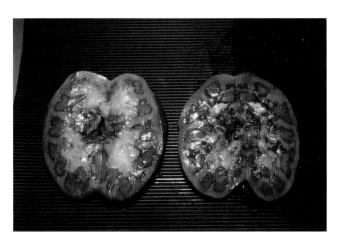

◀ **Figure 7.2** Pale kidneys
In patients who have exsanguinated, the kidneys are pale, a change that first affects the cortex and then the medullary pyramids. Such renal pallor should prompt a search for the cause of the blood loss.

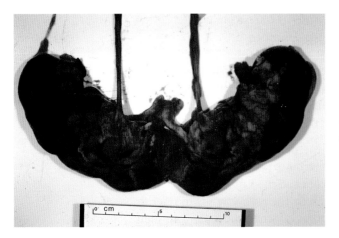

◀ **Figure 7.3** Horseshoe kidney
Horseshoe kidney, the most common congenital abnormality of the kidneys, occurs in approximately 1 in 500 individuals. It is more common in men than in women. The lower poles of the kidneys are fused by an isthmus of fibrous tissue or functioning renal tissue. By itself, horseshoe kidney is asymptomatic, but the abnormality predisposes to hydronephrosis, renal calculi, infections, and certain neoplasms.

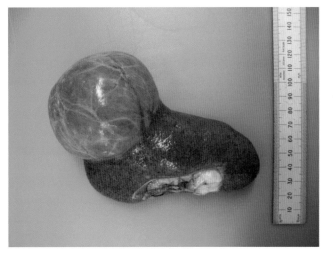

◀ **Figure 7.4** Simple cortical cysts
Simple renal cortical cysts are extremely common autopsy findings, and they are seen most frequently in individuals 50 years old or older. Their cause is unknown. They may be single or multiple but are typically unilocular, with a thin wall that is easily punctured when stripping the renal capsule. They contain a watery yellow serous fluid. More complex cystic masses within the kidney should raise the possibility of a cystic renal cell carcinoma. The presence of one or several cysts should not be confused with polycystic kidney disease.

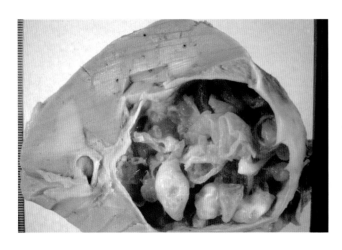

◀ **Figure 7.5** Renal hydatid cyst
Hydatid cysts are caused by the ingestion of the ova of the canine tapeworm *Echinococcus granulosus,* found in the feces of infected dogs. These complex cysts can develop in the kidney (as shown here), brain, lung, liver, and spleen. Rupture, which may be spontaneous, traumatic, or iatrogenic, may be complicated by fatal anaphylaxis.

◀ **Figure 7.6** Autosomal dominant polycystic kidney disease

Autosomal dominant polycystic kidney disease is the most common hereditary cystic renal disease. It is characterized by the progressive development of numerous fluid-filled cysts throughout the substance of both kidneys. As the disease progresses through adult life, the kidneys become enlarged, and renal failure may ensue. Cysts may also be present in the liver, spleen, and pancreas. Autosomal recessive polycystic kidney disease is much less common and typically manifests in the first days of life.

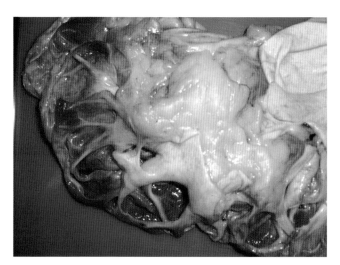

◀ **Figure 7.7** Hydronephrosis

Hydronephrosis may be unilateral or bilateral and arises as a result of urinary tract obstruction. Whether the condition affects one or both kidneys depends on the site or sites of the obstruction or obstructions. As the condition progresses, there is increasing dilatation of the renal pelvis and calyces, with thinning of the renal medulla. The condition may be associated with renal calculi and with hydroureter.

153

◀ **Figure 7.8a** Renal calculi

Renal calculi (nephrolithiasis) are more commonly seen in men than in women and arise as a consequence of supersaturation of urine. Approximately 80% of these stones consist of calcium oxalate. There are many possible causes, although high dietary intake of oxalates and low fluid intake likely predominate. Renal calculi lie within the pelvicalyceal system and range in size from grains of sand to staghorn calculi that fill the collecting system of the kidney.

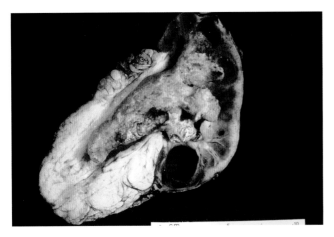

◄ Figure 7.8b Renal calculi
Staghorn calculi (also known as coral calculi) form a cast of the renal pelvis and calyces and are named for their characteristic shape that resembles antlers or coral. Calculi within a kidney act as a nidus for infection (pyelitis). There may be associated hydronephrosis and pyelonephritis.

◄ Figure 7.9 Hypertensive renal disease
Hypertensive damage results from disease in small arteries and arterioles. In patients with malignant hypertension, petechial hemorrhages may also be evident. On slicing, the hypertensive kidney is seen to have a thinned cortex. Small infarcts may also be evident.

◄ Figure 7.10a Acute tubular necrosis
Acute tubular necrosis may result from renal ischemia or exposure to nephrotoxins. The cortex is abnormally pale, and there may be linear hemorrhages in the cortex, medulla, and papillae. Cortical thickness is unaffected.

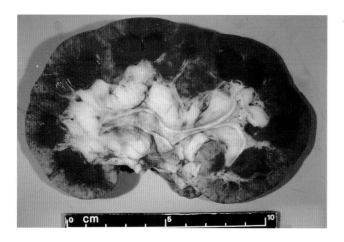

◀ **Figure 7.10b** Acute tubular necrosis

◀ **Figure 7.11a** Pyelonephritis
Acute pyelonephritis is purulent inflammation of the kidney and renal pelvis. It is characterized by the presence of abscesses throughout the kidney. In the cortex, these abscesses are 1 to 2 mm in diameter and white-yellow. In the medulla, they form yellow-white linear streaks that converge on the papillae. The author has seen tuberculosis and lymphoma mimic pyelonephritis, and sampling of the kidney for histological and microbiological examination is recommended. Chronic pyelonephritis is associated with renal scarring.

155

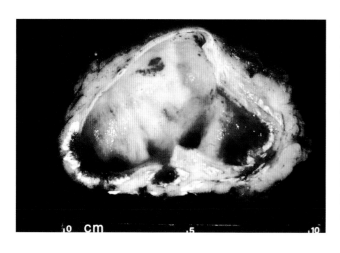

◀ **Figure 7.11b** Pyelonephritis
Xanthogranulomatous pyelonephritis is a rare granulomatous condition of the kidney, typically caused by recurrent infection with *Escherichia coli* and/or *Proteus mirabilis*.[1] The kidney is scarred, with yellow granulomas destroying the renal parenchyma. The disease is typically diffusely distributed through the kidney, although it can be focal. The inflammatory process may extend into the perinephric fat and adjacent retroperitoneal structures. Histological and microbiological examination is recommended to distinguish the disease from tuberculosis.

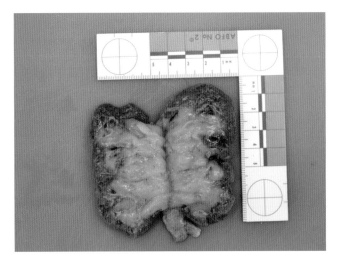

◀ **Figure 7.12** End-stage kidney

The end-stage kidney is the end result of a wide variety of diseases that affect the kidneys. Once this point is reached, it is often impossible to determine the underlying cause. The end-stage kidney is shrunken and fibrotic, and it has a capsule that is difficult to strip from the underlying cortex. The cortical surface is granular, pitted, and scarred, and there is marked cortical atrophy.

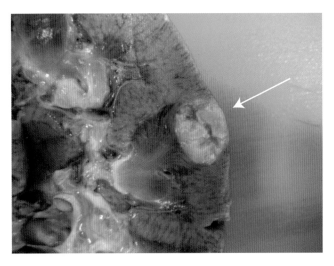

◀ **Figure 7.13** Angiomyolipoma

Angiomyolipomas are the most common benign tumors of the kidney. They comprise variable amounts of fat, smooth muscle, and blood vessels. They range in size from a few millimeters to several centimeters in diameter and have a solid yellow variegated cut surface and a well-demarcated margin. They are typically a coincidental autopsy finding, and their importance lies in not confusing them with tumor metastases or primary renal malignant diseases. The presence of multiple angiomyolipomas raises the possibility of tuberous sclerosis. Histological examination confirms the diagnosis if needed.

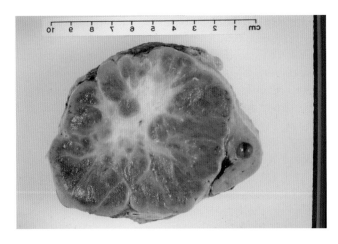

◀ **Figure 7.14** Renal oncocytoma

These benign renal neoplasms are typically an incidental finding at autopsy. Macroscopically, they can be distinguished from renal cell carcinomas by their solid tan or brown cut surface that typically contains a central scar. Where there is doubt or concern, histopathological examination confirms the diagnosis.

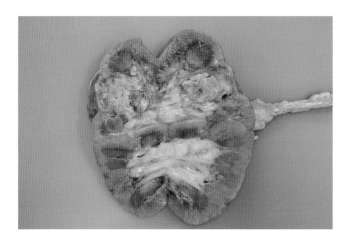

◀ Figure 7.15 Renal cell carcinoma
Renal cell carcinomas arise from the renal tubules and are by far the most common malignant neoplasms of the kidneys. On slicing, they are fleshy and typically solid, with a characteristic yellow cut surface with focal hemorrhage and necrosis. Histological examination confirms the diagnosis. These tumors have a predilection for growth into and along the renal vein and inferior vena cava, and these vessels should be examined thoroughly. The tumor metastasizes to para-aortic lymph nodes and the lungs. Renal cell carcinoma also commonly spreads to bone, and a vertebral strip should be performed to examine for the presence of bony metastases.

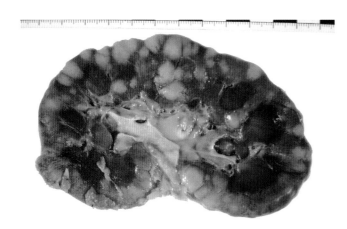

◀ Figure 7.16 Metastases to the kidney
Because the kidneys are highly vascular organs, they are prone to hematogenous spread of malignancy from other sites. The finding of multiple tumor deposits in the kidney, as in this example, should prompt the autopsy pathologist to search for the primary site (including opening the bowels and examining the testes). Histopathological examination confirms the diagnosis and may assist in determining the nature of an unidentified primary tumor.

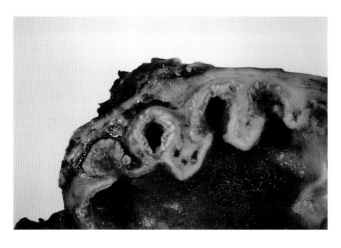

◀ Figure 7.17 Transitional cell carcinoma of the pelvis
Transitional cell carcinomas arise from the renal pelvis and account for 5% to 10% of renal malignant diseases. They are more common in men than in women.[2] They may form polypoid projections in the renal pelvis, infiltrative tumors, or only mild thickening of the renal pelvis. Histological examination confirms the diagnosis.

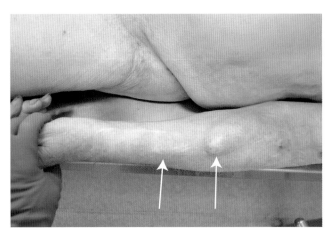

◀ **Figure 7.18** Arteriovenous fistula for dialysis
Patients undergoing hemodialysis may have an arteriovenous fistula to facilitate vascular access for dialysis. The fistula is a surgically fashioned anastomosis between an artery and vein, typically in the forearm or arm. The increased blood flow in the vein causes it to dilate and become "arterialized," thus allowing repeated cannulation. These fistulas are readily identified by the presence of surgical scars and a varix.

Ureter

◀ **Figure 7.19** Normal ureter
The normal ureter is a muscular tube 20 to 25 cm in length connecting the renal pelvis to the bladder. The ureters are pale tan-pink and are uniformly 3 to 5 mm in diameter. The ureter can be opened easily with artery scissors via the renal pelvis, although there is little point if the ureter appears normal externally and in the absence of hydronephrosis.

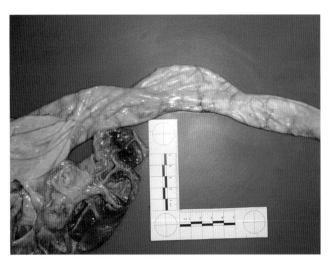

◀ **Figure 7.20** Hydroureter
Hydroureter is distention of the ureter as a result of urinary tract obstruction. It may be unilateral or bilateral (depending on the site or sites of obstruction), and there is commonly associated hydronephrosis, as in this example. The dilated ureter should be opened to seek a cause for obstruction.

Bladder

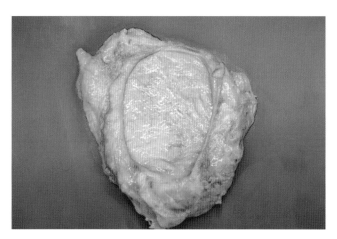

◄ Figure 7.21 Normal bladder

The urinary bladder is a hollow, distensible muscular organ varying in shape from tetrahedral to oval, depending on the degree of filling. The appearance and thickness of the mucosa vary from rugous and thick to smooth and thin, depending on the volume of urine present, but it should be shiny and a pale cream color. The mucosa of the trigone, delimited by the ureters and urethra, is always smooth.

◄ Figure 7.22 Trabeculation of the bladder

Bladder outflow obstruction from any cause (most commonly benign prostatic hyperplasia) increases the force needed to expel urine from the bladder. This causes hypertrophy of the detrusor muscle and gives the bladder wall a trabeculated appearance.

159

◄ Figure 7.23 Bladder diverticula

Where there is marked bladder outflow obstruction, increased intraluminal pressure may result in the formation of bladder diverticula (arrowheads). These structures may be solitary but are more commonly multiple. Large diverticula predispose to incomplete voiding and stagnation of urine, which in turn predisposes to urinary tract infection and bladder calculi.

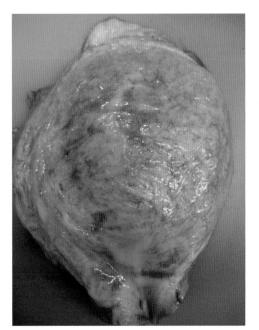

◀ **Figure 7.24a** Catheter artifact
Urinary catheterization is a commonly encountered medical intervention at autopsy. The presence of a urinary catheter can induce a localized reaction in the bladder wall, seen as erythema of the posterior wall of the bladder. This is common, normal, and should not be mistaken for cystitis.

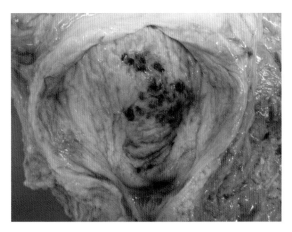

◀ **Figure 7.24b** Catheter artifact

◀ **Figure 7.25a** Bladder stones
Bladder calculi are now uncommon in the developed world. They arise against a background of bladder outflow obstruction and urinary stasis. Calculi vary widely in shape and size, and they may be smooth, faceted, or spiculated. They may be single or multiple, soft or hard. Most bladder calculi are composed of uric acid, but calcium oxalate, calcium phosphate, ammonium urate, cysteine, or magnesium ammonium phosphate bladder calculi also occur. Magnesium ammonium phosphate stones are typically associated with *Proteus mirabilis* infection.

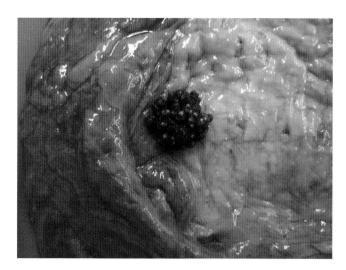

◀ **Figure 7.25b** Bladder stones

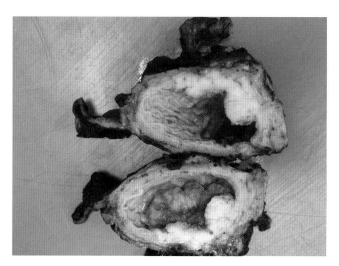

◀ **Figure 7.26** Bladder cancer
Most bladder cancers are transitional cell carcinomas. The appearance of the tumor varies with the stage. Low-stage lesions have a polypoid architecture. With advancing stage, the tumors develop an increasingly endophytic growth pattern, and the surface of the tumor appears hemorrhagic, ulcerated, and necrotic. Histopathological examination confirms the diagnosis.

161

Prostate

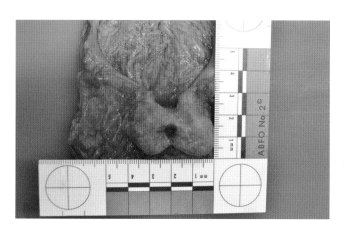

◀ **Figure 7.27** Normal prostate
The normal prostate lies at the base of the male bladder. It is a rounded, inverted pyramidal structure approximately 4×3×2 cm in size (approximately the size of a walnut in young adults). Slicing reveals that the prostate has a uniform dense, firm, pale pink-gray cut surface. The posterior surface is flattened, and the anterior surface is convex. The seminal vesicles lie on the posterior surface.

◀ **Figure 7.28** Benign prostatic hyperplasia
Enlargement of the prostate is extremely common with advancing age. On slicing, the hyperplastic prostate has a pale nodular architecture and a firm rubbery texture. The hyperplastic middle and lateral lobes may project into the lumen of the prostatic urethra, with resulting bladder outflow obstruction.

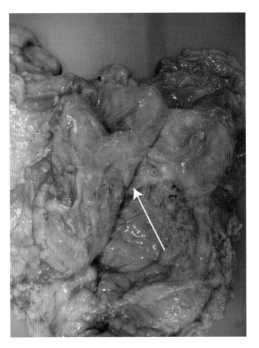

◀ **Figure 7.29** Carcinoma of the prostate
Prostate cancer is the most common malignant disease of the male genitourinary tract, and the incidence rises with increasing age. Prostate cancers most commonly arise in the posterior zone of the gland, and almost all are adenocarcinomas. Prostate cancers may be evident as hard, craggy, yellow-white masses. Ultimately, however, as in surgical pathology, the macroscopic identification of cancer within the prostate is notoriously unreliable.[3] Where there is a suspicion that death may have been contributed to by prostate cancer, the entire prostate should be submitted for histological examination. Adenocarcinoma of the prostate also commonly spreads to bone, and a vertebral strip should be performed to examine for the presence of bony metastases.

Testis

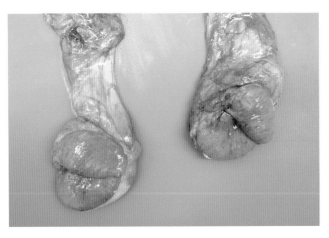

◀ **Figure 7.30** Normal testis
The normal testes are ovoid organs present as a pair within the scrotum. Although there is considerable variation in size, the average testis has a volume of 18 cm³. It is normal for one testis to be larger than the other, and typically one lies lower in the scrotum than the other. The eviscerated testis has a dense white fibrous capsule, the tunica albuginea, which is covered by an extension of the peritoneal mesothelium, the tunica vaginalis. Sectioning in the sagittal plane reveals a tan pulp comprising the seminiferous tubules, and these can be teased out with a pair of forceps. The epididymis lies on the posterior surface of the testis.

◀ Figure 7.31 Hydrocele
A hydrocele is a collection of clear, pale yellow serous fluid beneath the tunica vaginalis. Hydroceles vary in size, may be unilateral or bilateral, and lie predominantly anterior to the testis. Causes include trauma, epididymo-orchitis, testicular tumors, and torsion.

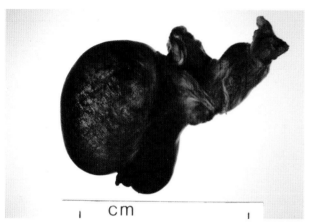

◀ Figure 7.32 Testicular torsion and infarction
The testis is prone to complete infarction from torsion, incarcerated hernia, trauma, vasculitis,[4] or as a complication of epididymo-orchitis.[5] Segmental infarction of the testis is very rare but may complicate cystoprostatectomy.[4] The infarcted testis is edematous, black, and hemorrhagic.

163

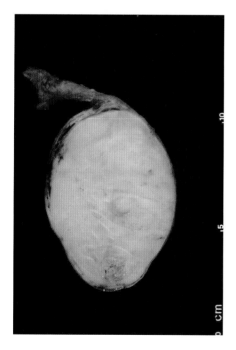

◀ Figure 7.33 Testicular tumors
Seminoma, the most common germ cell tumor of the testis, accounts for approximately 40% of all cases.[6] On sectioning, seminoma is a fleshy, nodular, solid, cream-colored tumor that may replace all or part of the testis. Histopathological sampling is recommended to confirm the diagnosis, and a search should be made for distant metastases. Teratomas are tumors containing derivatives of all three embryological germ layers. Testicular teratomas are associated with distant metastases in at least 60% of cases.[7] Macroscopically, they are nodular and have a solid and cystic gray and white cut surface. Foci of hemorrhage may be present. Histopathological sampling is recommended to confirm the diagnosis because these tumors may occur in combination with other germ cell testicular tumors, particularly when in adults. Pure embryonal carcinoma of the testis, shown in this example, is uncommon, accounting for approximately 16% of nonteratomatous testicular tumors. The tumor is typically solid with a pale white-gray cut surface. However, macroscopic diagnosis of tumor type is likely to be inaccurate, and histopathological examination of all testicular tumors is recommended.

Ovary

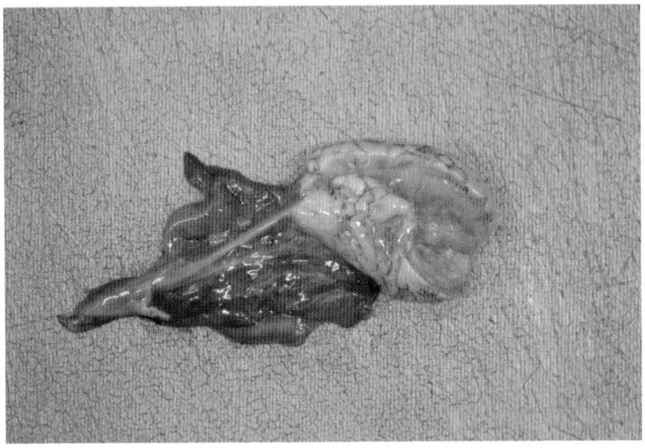

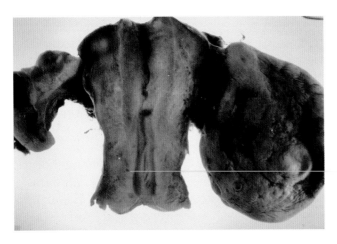

◀ Figure 7.34 Normal ovary

The ovaries are the female gonads and produce ova. They lie deep within the pelvis and are usually small, whitish, walnut-like structures. There may be follicles present as part of the normal cyclical changes. Histologically, the ovary is composed of follicles of various degrees of maturation with associated stroma.

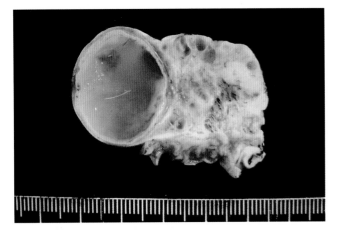

◀ Figure 7.35 Follicular simple cysts

Simple cysts in the ovaries are not unusual autopsy findings. Simple cysts have a thin, smooth wall (on external and internal surfaces) and are filled with serous or mucinous fluid. They may be unilateral or bilateral. The presence of features such as papillary excrescences on the wall should alert the pathologist to the possibility of a more sinister pathological finding. Simple cysts tend to have limited pathological significance unless they become large and cause mass effect or undergo torsion.

◀ Figure 7.36 Endometriosis

Endometriosis is the presence of endometrial tissue in locations other than the uterus. Endometriosis has been recognized for many years, but the pathogenesis remains obscure. A detailed discussion of the theories is beyond the scope of this volume, but retrograde menstruation and peritoneal metaplasia have been proposed. The misplaced endometrial tissue may appear as a nodule, often within the pelvis or abdomen, and it responds to hormonal stimulation and therefore can shed during the menses. In the ovary, endometriosis may give rise to a cystic mass filled with altered blood (the so-called "chocolate" cyst). The appearance, both macroscopically and microscopically, varies depending on the phase of the menstrual cycle.

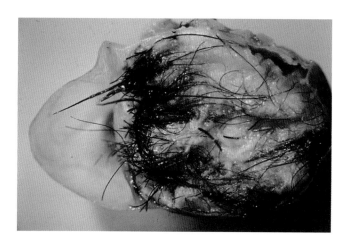

◀ Figure 7.37a Ovarian teratomas

Mature teratoma. Teratomas (also known as dermoid cysts) are neoplasms containing tissues from all three germ cell layers. In mature ovarian teratomas, all of the tissues identified resemble normal adult tissue. Hair, teeth and sebaceous secretions are commonly found, and point to the diagnosis. Mature ovarian teratomas are benign, and likely to represent an incidental finding at autopsy. Large mature teratomas may compress the pelvic veins, predisposing to deep vein thrombosis and pulmonary thromboembolus.

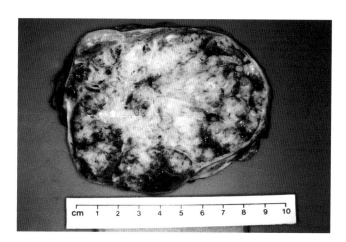

◀ Figure 7.37b Ovarian teratomas

Immature teratoma. Immature ovarian teratomas are considered to be malignant neoplasms. They have a variegated solid and cystic cut surface, and foci of hemorrhage or necrosis may be evident. Histopathological examination confirms the diagnosis and reveals the presence of embryonic tissues from multiple germ cell layers.

165

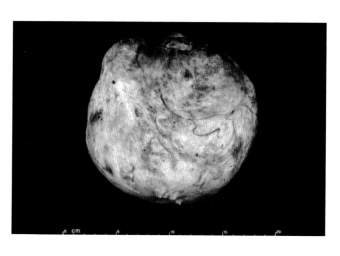

◀ Figure 7.38 Ovarian fibroma

These benign sex cord stromal tumors are most commonly encountered in perimenopausal and postmenopausal women. They have a smooth-bosselated capsule and a solid, firm, white-tan cut surface. Histopathological examination confirms the diagnosis. Although they are typically coincidental asymptomatic tumors, they can cause abdominal pain. Large fibromas may compress the pelvic veins, predisposing to deep venous thrombosis and fatal pulmonary thromboembolism.

◄ Figure 7.39 Ovarian cancer
The ovary can be the source of various malignant diseases. The most common form of ovarian malignant disease is adenocarcinoma (arising from the epithelium or stroma), but many of the other cell types may give rise to malignant lesions such as dysgerminoma. Even adenocarcinomas can have highly divergent macroscopic appearances, such as serous cystadenocarcinoma or mucinous cystadenocarcinoma. Thus, detailed histological analysis of a suspected ovarian malignant tumor is necessary for accurate diagnosis of the precise nature of the lesion.

Fallopian Tube

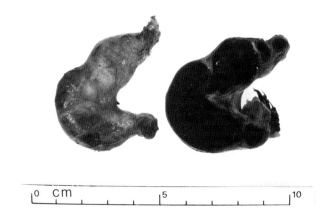

◄ Figure 7.40 Ectopic pregnancy
Ectopic pregnancy occurs when the fertilized ovum implants outside the uterine cavity. This occurs most commonly within a fallopian tube, and it can be associated with damage to the cilia from infection with organisms such as *Chlamydia trachomatis*. Ectopic pregnancy may also occur in other locations, such as the cervix or even the abdominal cavity. Ectopic pregnancies are usually not viable, and as the fetus grows it places pressure on the structures around it, thus causing pain that can be mistaken for appendicitis. Untreated ectopic pregnancy can cause rupture of the structure within which the gestational sac is located, with potentially lethal consequences such as catastrophic hemorrhage.

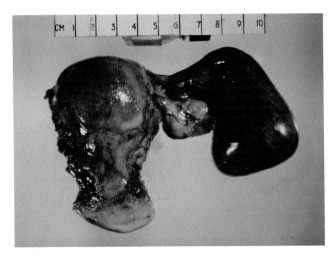

◄ Figure 7.41 Hydrosalpinx
Pelvic inflammatory disease is a blanket term for infection within the upper female genital tract, often involving the fallopian tubes. Inflammation and infection can cause occlusion of the tubes, with consequent infertility and/or risk of ectopic pregnancy. Tubal occlusion may result in a hydrosalpinx, in which the fallopian tube becomes filled with serous fluid and markedly distended.

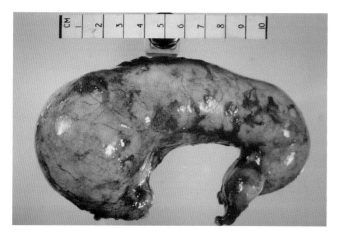

◀ Figure 7.42 Pyosalpinx
Patients with pelvic inflammatory disease may develop a pyosalpinx, in which the fallopian tube becomes filled with pus. This condition may act as the source for disseminated sepsis, a possibility that becomes more likely should the pyosalpinx rupture.

Uterus

◀ Figure 7.43 Normal uterus and cervix
The uterus comprises a fundus, body, and cervix and lies within the pelvis, posterior to the urinary bladder. The normal nongravid uterus in reproductive life is a small, gourd-shaped organ with a smooth, cream-colored external surface. The uterine wall is composed of smooth muscle and has a striated but regular appearance on incision. The endometrium varies in appearance, depending on the phase of the menstrual cycle. Particularly during the menses, the endometrium has a dark, hemorrhagic appearance, but at other times in the cycle it is pale. Autolysis can cause breakdown of the endometrium at the time of autopsy, thereby limiting the information available on histological examination.

167

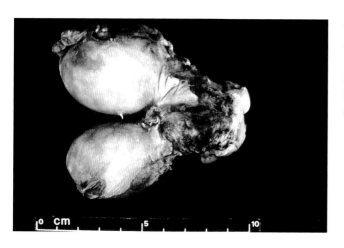

◀ Figure 7.44 Bicornuate uterus
A bicornuate uterus results from partial failure of the Müllerian ducts to fuse during embryonic life. The bicornuate uterus has two discrete endometrial cavities. Its incidence is estimated at around 0.4%. It is typically an incidental finding at autopsy.

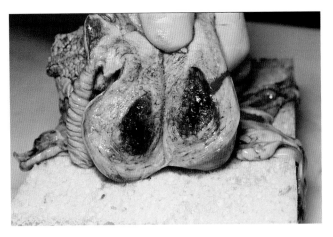

◀ **Figure 7.45** Uterus in early pregnancy

The macroscopic appearance of the gravid uterus at autopsy depends on the gestation of the pregnancy. The history of pregnancy in the second trimester onward is most often known, and such autopsies should be conducted by a pathologist with expertise in maternal deaths. However, it is not unfeasible for an unexpected finding of early pregnancy to occur, as in this case. The uterus appears larger and feels boggy. Products of conception are visible inside the endometrial cavity. If necessary, the whole uterus should be removed for fixation and examination by a pediatric pathologist.

◀ **Figure 7.46** Ruptured uterus

Uterine rupture can occur during childbirth, and can result in sudden and catastrophic collapse, with the health of the mother and child at risk. However, it can also be seen in pregnant women involved in road traffic crashes and other major trauma.

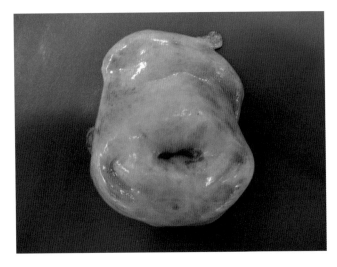

◀ **Figure 7.47** Parous cervix

The parous cervix has a very similar overall appearance to that seen in a nullipara. Once a vaginal delivery has occurred, the os becomes slit-like rather than circular.

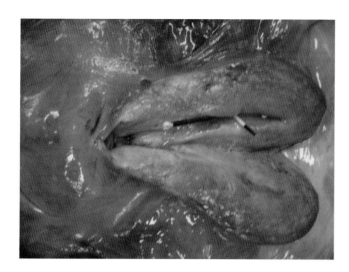

◀ Figure 7.48 Intrauterine contraceptive device
Intrauterine contraceptive devices are inserted via the cervix into the uterine cavity and act to prevent implantation of the fertilized egg. Many are made of copper, although some devices elute hormones (See also Figure 14.44).

◀ Figure 7.49 Endometrial polyps
Endometrial polyps can be accurately identified at autopsy only by opening the uterus. These polyps may be sessile or pedunculated, the latter being more common. Large pedunculated polyps may protrude through the cervical os and be mistaken for endocervical polyps. They are generally benign, although histological examination may reveal adenocarcinomatous elements in around 0.5% of lesions. When seen, these polyps are almost always incidental findings at autopsy.

169

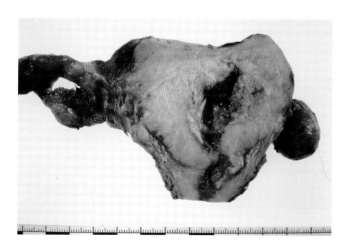

◀ Figure 7.50 Endometrial carcinoma
The endometrium is prone to the development of adenocarcinoma. Early menarche, late menopause, obesity, nulliparity, increasing age, positive family history, and use of the drug tamoxifen all increase the risk of endometrial adenocarcinoma. Endometrial adenocarcinoma is usually seen as a fungating tumor mass that extends into the uterine cavity and often invades the myometrium. Local spread and metastasis occur. Histological features are usually typical of an adenocarcinoma, although as with other glandular linings such as the stomach or intestine, histology may be compromised by autolysis. Therefore obtaining the results of histological examinations undertaken in life may be valuable in evaluating the significance of autopsy findings.

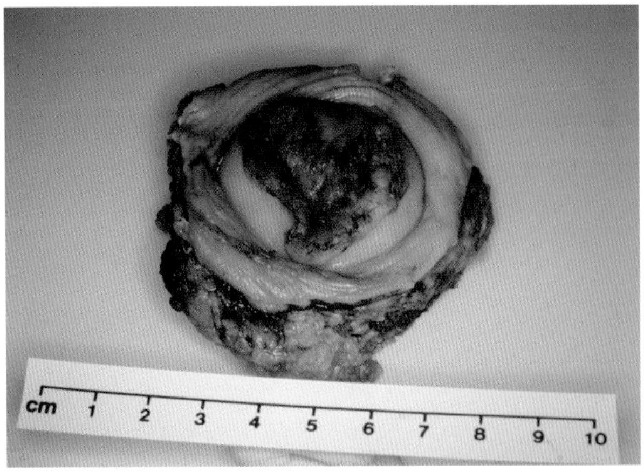

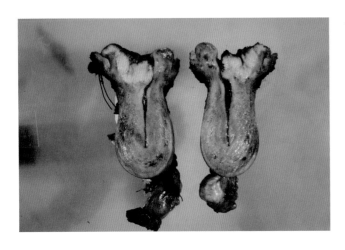

◀ **Figure 7.51a** Cervical carcinoma

The cervix bears both stratified squamous (on the vaginal aspect) and glandular (within the canal) epithelium, and both squamous carcinoma and adenocarcinoma may develop. Squamous carcinomas may occur in young women and are associated with human papillomavirus (HPV). Most cases are associated with HPV types 16 and 18. Such tumors usually appear as fungating lesions. Many countries have screening programs aimed at identifying cellular atypia to allow treatment before an invasive carcinoma develops. Adenocarcinoma may also develop, and although this is less common than squamous carcinoma, it is also thought to be associated with HPV infection.[8]

◀ **Figure 7.51b** Cervical carcinoma

◀ **Figure 7.52** Leiomyomas

Leiomyomas are benign tumors of the smooth muscle of the uterus and are the most common uterine neoplasms. They vary greatly in size and may be single or multiple. They may be associated with infertility, menstrual symptoms, and postmenopausal bleeding. They are well circumscribed and do not invade adjacent tissues. The texture is usually firm, and the cut surface is pale with a whorled architecture. These tumors are increasingly common with increasing age and usually do not cause life-threatening problems, although large lesions may compress the pelvic veins and cause deep venous thrombosis. Leiomyomas may undergo dystrophic calcification, particularly in postmenopausal women.

◄ Figure 7.53 Leiomyosarcoma
Malignant myometrial neoplasms (leiomyosarcomas) are rare. As with most malignant tumors, they are not well circumscribed and invade adjacent structures. The cut surface is variably hemorrhagic and necrotic, and it may be solid and cystic. Histologically, in comparison with the bland, repetitive cellular structure of a leiomyoma, the sarcoma shows the typical features of malignancy, including pleomorphism. If there is any concern about a lesion seen with the naked eye, histological samples should be taken to clarify the nature of the lesion.

Breast

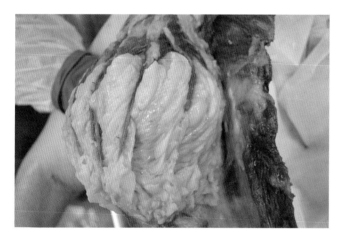

◄ Figure 7.54 Normal breast
The breasts develop with the onset of puberty and become atrophic after menopause, although this may be altered by the use of hormone replacement therapy. The size and shape of the normal human breast are highly variable. The nipples are also variable in size and shape and tend to become darker with pregnancy. Decorative tattoos and piercings are not uncommon findings, particularly in younger women. Small, pinpoint tattoos on or close to the breast may have been made in a woman undergoing radiation therapy to assist in accurately positioning the beams. This finding is usually associated with scars from breast surgery.

171

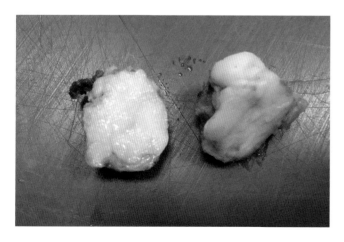

◄ Figure 7.55 Fibroadenoma
Fibroadenomas are small, well-circumscribed, firm lesions that may develop in the breast. As the name suggests, they are fibrous and benign. They are not tethered and therefore can move within the breast when palpated (hence their colloquial description as a "breast mouse").

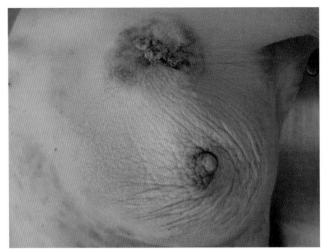

◀ **Figure 7.56a** Breast carcinoma

Carcinoma of the breast remains a common cause of morbidity and mortality, and great efforts have been put into screening programs in the United Kingdom and elsewhere. However, it is still the second most common cause of cancer-related deaths in the United Kingdom (after lung). There are many features that the pathologist may see, including a frank, fungating mass, *peau d'orange* change in the skin (literally "skin of the orange" where the skin of the breast takes on the appearance of the skin of the fruit), and Paget disease of the nipple. As with cancerous lesions elsewhere, histological diagnosis is essential for precise identification of the nature of the lesion. Breast cancer commonly metastasizes to bone. The vertebral bone marrow should be examined for the presence of metastatic disease in patients with breast cancer or a history of it.

◀ **Figure 7.56b** Breast carcinoma

The example shown is a lobular carcinoma. This is not the same patient shown in Figure 7.56a.

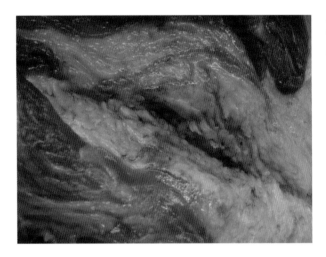

References

1. Kuo CC, Wu CF, Huang CC, Lee YJ, Lin WC, Tsai CW, Wu VC, Chen YM, Wu MS, Chu TS, Wu KD. Xanthogranulomatous pyelonephritis: critical analysis of 30 patients. *International Urology and Nephrology* 2011;**43**:15–22.
2. Leder RA, Dunnick NR. Transitional cell carcinoma of the pelvicalices and ureter. *AJR American Journal of Roentgenology* 1990;**155**:713–722.
3. Renshaw AA. Correlation of gross morphologic features with histologic features in radical prostatectomy specimens. *American Journal of Clinical Pathology* 1998;**110**:38–42.
4. Alleemudder AI, Amer T, Roa A. Segmental testicular infarction following cystoprostatectomy. *Urology Annals* 2011;**3**:42–43.
5. Bird K, Rosenfield AT. Testicular infarction secondary to acute inflammatory disease: demonstration by B-scan ultrasound. *Radiology* 1984;**152**:785–788.
6. Looijenga LH, Oosterhuis JW. Pathogenesis of testicular germ cell tumours. *Reviews of Reproduction* 1999;**4**:90–100.
7. Carver BS, Al-Ahmadie H, Sheinfeld J. Adult and pediatric testicular teratoma. *Urology Clinics of North America* 2007;**34**:245–251.
8. Burton JL, Lopez JM, Wells M. Adenocarcinoma of the cervix. *Current Obstetrics and Gynaecology* 1999;**9**:124–129.

Chapter 8
The Endocrine System

Introduction

The endocrine organs are the pituitary, thyroid, parathyroid, and adrenal glands, along with the endocrine pancreas and gonads.

Endocrine disease is commonly encountered at autopsy, particularly among the aging autopsy population, but it is rarely the cause of death. By and large, the diseases that affect the endocrine organs lack reliable macroscopic pathognomonic features, and histopathological examination is required to confirm the diagnosis. With the exception of the thyroid, primary malignant diseases of these organs are rare.

Pituitary

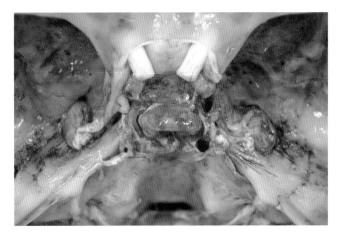

◀ **Figure 8.1** Normal pituitary gland
The normal pituitary gland resides entirely within the sella turcica directly beneath the optic chiasm. It is a tan, bean-shaped organ with a stalk that passes through the diaphragm sellae to the hypothalamus. The gland normally weighs less than 1 g and is approximately 10 mm in diameter.

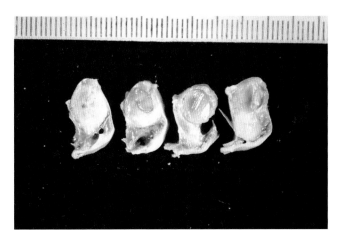

◀ **Figure 8.2** Pituitary cyst
Small, simple cysts within the anterior pituitary gland are common incidental autopsy findings. Most often, they arise from embryological remnants of Rathke pouch and lie between the anterior and posterior components of the pituitary. Larger cysts may cause visual disturbance and diabetes insipidus. Histopathological examination allows distinction of these simple cysts from neoplasms with a cystic element, such as craniopharyngioma.

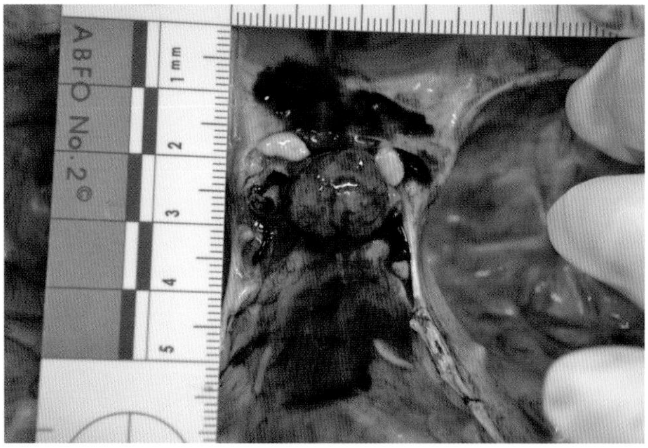

◀ **Figure 8.3** Pituitary adenoma

Adenomas are the most common neoplasms arising within the pituitary gland.[1] Clinically relevant pituitary adenomas are relatively common, occurring in approximately 1 in 1000 individuals. Of these more than two-thirds are prolactinomas, and one-fifth of patients have hypopituitarism.[2] Pituitary adenomas less than 10 mm in diameter are termed microadenomas, whereas those greater than 40 mm in diameter are macroadenomas. Microadenomas may be clinically silent and go unnoticed at autopsy unless a specific search for them is made. With increasing size, these tumors expand, erode the sella turcica, and eventually grow to compress the optic chiasm. They are solid, fleshy brown tumors, lacking a true capsule. Pituitary adenomas have a propensity to invade their surrounding tissues, and this risk increases with increasing size of the tumor. The tumor may invade the surrounding dura mater and bone. Careful sampling for histopathological examination is required to distinguish invasive pituitary adenoma from the exceptionally rare pituitary carcinoma.[1]

Thyroid

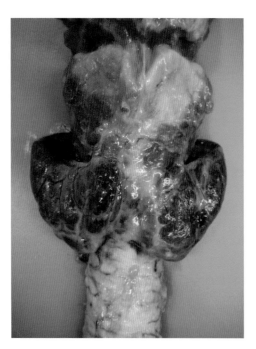

◀ **Figure 8.4a** Normal thyroid

The normal thyroid is a brown, fleshy H- or U-shaped bilobed organ located beneath the strap muscles of the anterior neck. The gland lies anterolateral to the trachea and inferior to the thyroid cartilage.

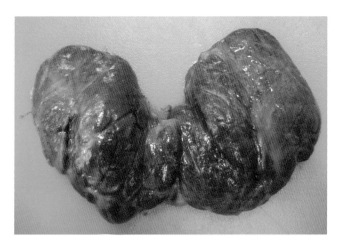

◀ **Figure 8.4b** Normal thyroid
The two lateral lobes are connected by an anterior isthmus.

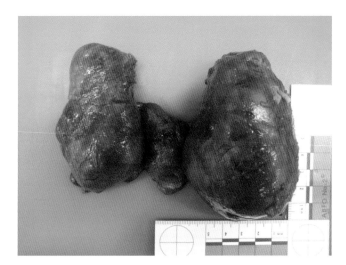

◀ **Figure 8.5a** Colloid nodular goiter
Colloid nodular goiter is the most common abnormality of the thyroid encountered at autopsy. The gland is enlarged, often with a bosselated capsule.

175

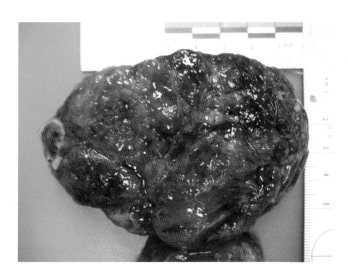

◀ **Figure 8.5b** Colloid nodular goiter
Slicing reveals numerous variously sized colloid nodules that have a glistening tan cut surface. Untreated, and with increasing age, these nodules may undergo dystrophic calcification. Calcified colloid nodular goiter should not be confused with thyroid cancer.

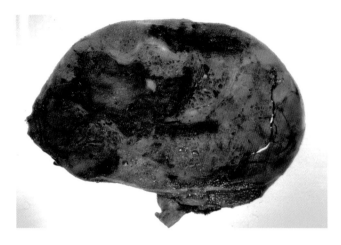

◄ Figure 8.6 Follicular adenoma
As in surgical pathology, the only way to differentiate between follicular adenoma and follicular carcinoma reliably is to submit the entire lesion for histological examination.

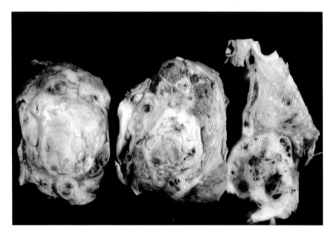

◄ Figure 8.7 Carcinoma of the thyroid
Thyroid carcinoma may be follicular, papillary, anaplastic, or medullary. The tumor may be solid or cystic, and there may be associated hemorrhage. Although follicular thyroid cancers typically result in a solitary mass within the thyroid, the other variants may be solitary or multiple, and there may be diffuse involvement of the gland. Histopathological examination is required to type the neoplasm accurately. The presence of medullary carcinoma should prompt consideration that the patient may have a multiple endocrine neoplasia syndrome (MEN). Thyroid cancers commonly metastasize to bone, and a search for bony as well as local metastases should be made.

176

Parathyroid

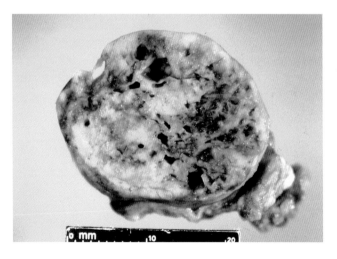

◄ Figure 8.8 Parathyroid neoplasms
Parathyroid adenomas are the most common cause of primary hyperparathyroidism. Typically, there is tumorous enlargement of one of the parathyroid glands, whereas the remaining glands become atrophic. Parathyroid carcinoma is very rare and beyond the scope of this atlas.

Adrenal

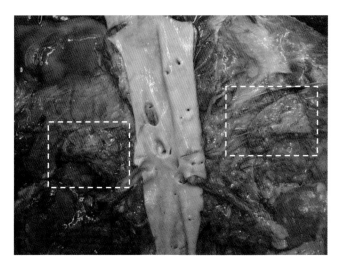

◀ **Figure 8.9** Normal adrenal glands
The adrenal glands are richly vascular retroperitoneal endocrine organs that lie in fat above the kidneys. The right adrenal gland is triangular, and the left adrenal gland is semilunar. The outer cortex is bright yellow because of its high cholesterol content. The inner medulla is brown. The medulla rapidly degrades and undergoes cavitation after death, and this change should not be mistaken for disease.

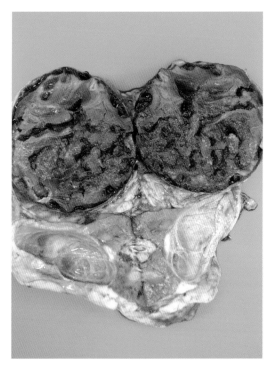

◀ **Figure 8.10** Adrenal hemorrhage
Hemorrhage into the adrenal glands is uncommon. Causes include trauma, thrombocytopenia, adrenal vein thrombosis, sepsis (including meningococcal septicemia [Waterhouse-Friderichsen syndrome[3]]), and disseminated intravascular coagulation. However, adrenal hemorrhage may complicate a wide range of medical and surgical conditions and treatments. Symptoms are nonspecific, but life-threatening adrenal insufficiency may result.

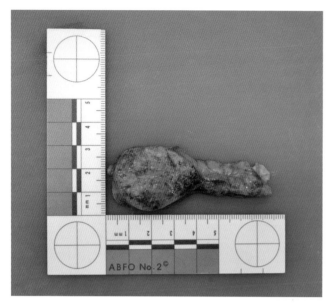

◀ **Figure 8.11a** Adrenal cortical adenoma
Adrenocortical adenomas, the most common tumors encountered in the adrenal glands at autopsy, are seen in up to 8.7% of autopsy examinations.[4,5] Macroscopically, these adenomas are recognized as discrete, solid yellow cortical tumors. They are typically unilateral and nonfunctional, and so the background adrenal cortex is normal. As in surgical pathology, the weight of the tumor gives an indication of the likelihood that the tumor is benign. The risk of malignancy increases with the size of the lesion. Hemorrhage (which may be life-threatening) can occur into adrenal tumors.

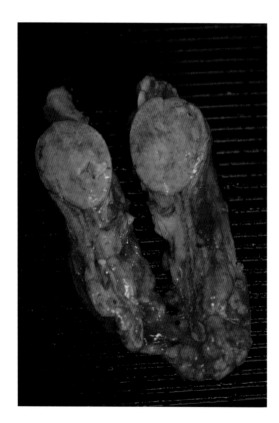

◀ **Figure 8.11b** Adrenal cortical adenoma

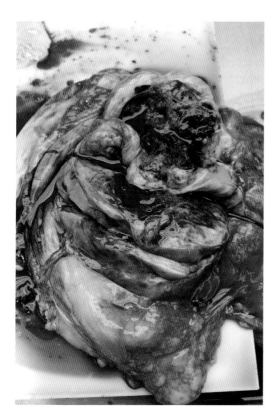

◀ Figure 8.12 Metastasis to the adrenal
The adrenal glands are richly vascular, and it is therefore unsurprising that they are a common site of metastasis from primary tumors elsewhere. Cancers of the breast, gut, lungs, and kidneys, as well as melanomas and lymphomas, commonly metastasize to the adrenal glands. The presence of a tumor deposit in an adrenal gland should therefore prompt a diligent search for the primary malignant disease. The example shown is of metastatic melanoma in the adrenal gland.

179

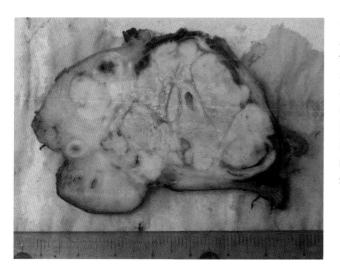

◀ Figure 8.13 Adrenocortical carcinoma
Adrenocortical carcinomas are rare. They are typically larger than adrenal cortical adenomas, with a more complex cut surface that may contain areas of hemorrhage and/or necrosis. The presence of metastatic deposits confirms the malignant diagnosis, but in most cases, histopathological examination is required. These tumors may secrete hormones, resulting in Cushing syndrome, virilization, Conn syndrome, or feminization.

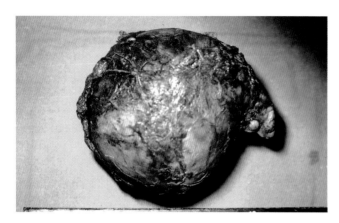

◀ **Figure 8.14a** Pheochromocytoma
These neuroendocrine malignancies secrete catecholamines. The adrenal medulla is the most common site for the development of pheochromocytoma, and the tumor may be unilateral or bilateral.

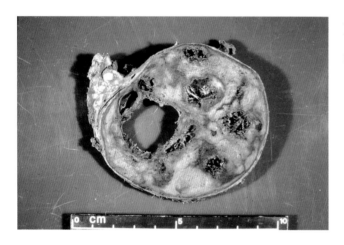

◀ **Figure 8.14b** Pheochromocytoma
The tumors have a dark brown cut surface and may contain foci of hemorrhage and necrosis. Histopathological examination confirms the diagnosis.

References

1. Ironside JW. Best practice no. 172: pituitary gland pathology. *Journal of Clinical Pathology* 2003;**56**:561–568.
2. Daly AF, Rixhon M, Adam C, Dempegioti A, Tichomirowa MA, Beckers A. High prevalence of pituitary adenomas: a cross-sectional study in the province of Liege, Belgium. *Journal of Clinical Endocrinology and Metabolism* 2006;**91**:4769–4775.
3. Tormos LM, Schandl CA. The significance of adrenal hemorrhage: undiagnosed Waterhouse-Friderichsen syndrome: a case series. *Journal of Forensic Science* 2013;**58**(4):1071–1074.
4. Saeger W, Reinhard K, Reinhard C. Hyperplastic and tumourous lesions of the adrenals in an unselected autopsy series. *Endocrine Pathology* 1998;**9**:235–239.
5. Hedeland H, Östberg G, Hökfelt B. On the prevalence of adrenocortical adenomas in an autopsy material in relation to hypertension and diabetes. *Acta Medica Scandinavica* 1968;**184**:211–214.

Chapter 9
The Lymphoreticular System

Introduction

The lymphoreticular system comprises the lymph nodes, thymus, spleen, and mucosa-associated lymphoid tissue. This system plays a crucial role in the defense against infection, antigen processing, and the removal of effete cells from the blood. Given the propensity of humans to acquire infectious, autoimmune, and neoplastic diseases, it is not surprising that abnormalities of the lymphoreticular system are commonly found at autopsy. Such abnormalities do, however, present a particular challenge because the range of responses of these structures to disease is limited. Enlargement resulting from congestion, hyperplasia, or neoplastic infiltration is common.

Isolated macroscopic examination of the tissues of the lymphoreticular system is unlikely to reveal an accurate diagnosis. Consideration of the clinical history is crucial, and it is often necessary to use further laboratory investigations including microbiology, virology, histopathology, and genetic analysis to reach a final diagnosis.

This chapter contains some of the more common disorders to affect this organ system that present difficulties to the autopsy pathologist.

Spleen

◀ **Figure 9.1** Normal spleen
The normal adult spleen is a bean-shaped organ with an anterior notch that is located in the left upper quadrant of the abdominal cavity. Bounded by a thin fibrous capsule, it has a smooth reddish blue-gray appearance. The normal anatomy of the spleen can be remembered by using the 1×3×5×7×9×11 rule: it is 1×3×5 inches across, weighs approximately 7 oz (150 to 200 g), and lies between the ninth and eleventh ribs adjacent to the greater curvature of the stomach. Slicing reveals that the spleen is largely composed of a red pulp, within which the malpighian corpuscles of the white pulp are interspersed.

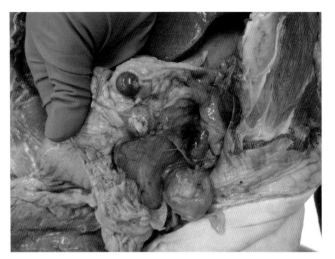

◀ **Figure 9.2a** Splenunculus

Splenunculi, or accessory spleens, are common autopsy findings, present in approximately 10% of the population.[1] Typically approximately 1 cm in diameter, they are usually found at the splenic hilum, on or in the tail of the pancreas, or along the path of the splenic vessels.

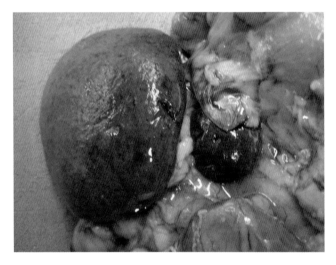

◀ **Figure 9.2b** Splenunculus

Splenunculi most commonly represent a congenital abnormality, although they can also result from splenic trauma and implantation of splenic fragments into the well-vascularized surfaces within the abdominal cavity or thorax, sometimes referred to as "traumatic splenosis." They may be affected by the same disease processes found in the normal spleen and may hypertrophy following splenectomy.[2]

◀ **Figure 9.3** Polysplenism

Unlike splenunculi, polysplenism is rare and is associated with a variety of other congenital abnormalities and syndromes. Also unlike splenunculi (which are typically single accessory spleens), polysplenism is characterized by the presence of multiple splenic masses that replace the normal spleen.

◀ Figure 9.4 Perisplenitis

Perisplenitis, also known colloquially as "icing sugar spleen," is a common autopsy finding. The capsule of the spleen becomes nodular, thickened, and fibrotic, and it appears as though the spleen has been dipped in white icing. Over time, calcification may supervene. Perisplenitis can complicate any inflammatory process in the abdomen or pelvis and splenic sepsis, and it is also seen in patients with chronic obstructive pulmonary disease. It has been reported as part of Curtis-Fitz-Hugh syndrome.[3] Capsular fibrosis of the spleen is typically asymptomatic and of little clinical significance. Its importance is in recognizing that it is a benign indolent process and in not confusing it with primary or metastatic malignant disease.[4]

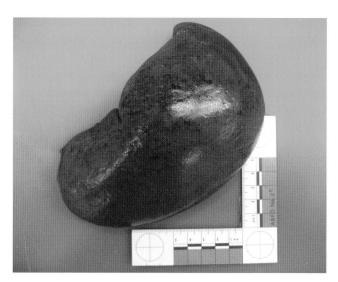

◀ Figure 9.5 Splenomegaly

Splenomegaly is a common autopsy finding. There are many causes, ranging from simple congestion through hemoglobinopathies, infections, autoimmune diseases, extramedullary hematopoiesis, inborn errors of metabolism, and neoplastic infiltration. By and large, these causes cannot be readily distinguished by macroscopic examination of the spleen, and correlation of the clinical history, histopathological features, and microbiological findings is required to reach a diagnosis. The example shown demonstrates the splenomegaly seen in Felty syndrome.

183

◀ Figure 9.6a Congested spleen

Congestion of the spleen is a common cause of splenomegaly and results from any condition that elevates the pressure in the splenic vein. Thus, it is seen in patients with cirrhosis and portal hypertension, right ventricular cardiac failure, and thrombosis of the portal and/or splenic veins. Sepsis may also result in acute congestion of the spleen. The congested spleen is enlarged, with a smooth capsule.

◀ **Figure 9.6b** Congested spleen

On slicing, the cut surface is a dusky red in which the red pulp is expanded and the white pulp is discernible. Prolonged congestion results in fibrosis, thus increasing the firmness of the organ.[5]

◀ **Figure 9.7** Diffluent spleen

In patients with septicemia, the spleen may become diffluent. On slicing, the spleen is noted to be enlarged, congested, and markedly softened, such that the red pulp may ooze out over the bench, as shown here. The appearance is not specific, and microbiological investigations are required to identify the causative organism.[6] Softening of the spleen occurs as part of putrefactive decomposition, and caution must be taken not to overinterpret a decomposing spleen as evidence of systemic sepsis.

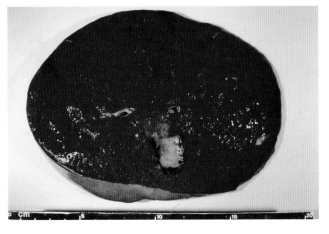

◀ **Figure 9.8** Splenic abscess

Abscesses within the spleen are rare, but they are associated with a high mortality rate. They are most commonly encountered in patients with alcoholism, diabetes, and immunosuppression. Splenic abscesses typically result from the hematogenous spread of infection from another site, and they may be caused by a wide variety of microorganisms. Microbiological culture and a search for infection at other sites are recommended.

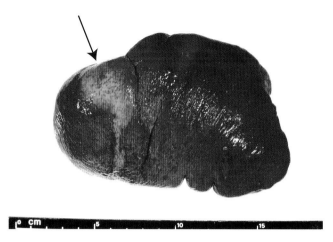

◀ Figure 9.9a Splenic infarct

Splenic infarction may complicate any disease in which the vascular supply to the spleen is impaired, there is an increased tendency to thrombus formation, or that causes splenomegaly. Splenic infarction may range from localized, wedge-shaped infarcts to complete infarction of the organ, which is uncommon but may be complicated by pneumococcal sepsis. Splenic infarcts initially appear as firm, dark red hemorrhagic areas beneath the splenic capsule, and they evolve into white masses as fibrosis develops. Splenic infarction may be complicated by splenic rupture or abscess formation.[7]

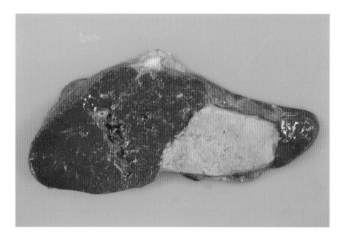

◀ Figure 9.9b Splenic infarct

185

◀ Figure 9.10 Splenic cyst

Splenic cysts are rare, found in only 0.07% of autopsies.[8] Most commonly, splenic cysts are the result of parasitic infection with *Echinococcus granulosus* (hydatid cysts). Nonparasitic causes include pseudocysts resulting from trauma, congenital cysts, epidermoid cysts, splenic abscess, and cystic neoplasms.[9] Splenic cysts grow slowly and may reach a large size before becoming symptomatic. Histopathological examination assists in determining the cause of the cyst.

◀ **Figure 9.11** Sarcoidosis

Splenic involvement by sarcoidosis is a cause of splenomegaly. The enlargement of the spleen may range from minor, as in this example, to massive. The splenic capsule remains smooth. On slicing, the cut surface of the spleen has a prominent white pulp, and this may be mistaken for lymphomatous involvement (compare with Figure 9.12a) or miliary tuberculosis. Histopathological examination is required to confirm the diagnosis.

◀ **Figure 9.12a** Lymphoma

Lymphomas confined to the spleen are rare. More commonly, lymphomatous involvement of the spleen results from infiltration by Hodgkin or non-Hodgkin lymphoma arising at another site. Lymphomatous deposits appear as firm, white or yellow masses within the spleen. The deposits may range in size from a miliary appearance that can be confused with tuberculosis (a) to large deposits several centimeters across that virtually replace the normal splenic pulp (b). Histopathological examination, coupled with immunohistochemistry and in some cases molecular genetic analysis, is required to establish the diagnosis.

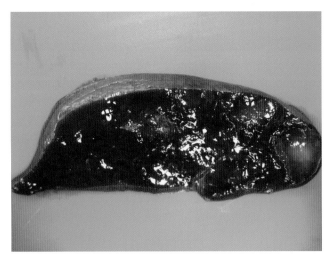

◀ **Figure 9.12b** Lymphoma

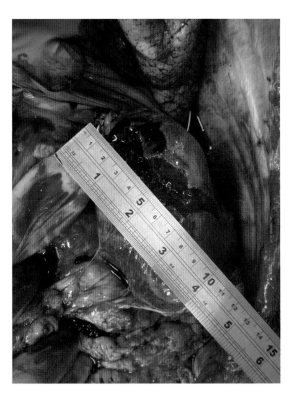

◀ **Figure 9.13** Splenic rupture

Splenic rupture most commonly results from blunt force trauma to the abdomen, although it is also a recognized complication of colonoscopy.[10] Splenomegaly increases the risk of splenic rupture following minor trauma. Spontaneous splenic rupture secondary to infectious mononucleosis[11] or to neoplastic or hematological disease[12] is rare. The capsule and parenchyma of the spleen are typically seen to be lacerated, and subcapsular hematoma formation is common. There may be extensive hemoperitoneum.

Thymus

187

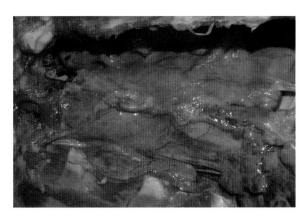

◀ **Figure 9.14** Normal thymus

The normal thymus is a soft, pinkish-gray asymmetrical bilobed lobulated organ located within the anterior mediastinum overlying the pericardium, aortic arch, left innominate vein, and trachea.[13] It is largest during puberty and then undergoes marked involution in early adult life, when it is largely replaced with fat and becomes difficult to identify at autopsy. Consequently, although the normal thymus may be readily identified in adults up to 25 to 30 years old, it is usually not readily apparent in adults who are more than 60 to 70 years old.

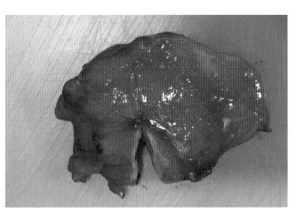

◀ **Figure 9.15a** Thymoma

Thymomas are usually located in the anterior mediastinum and are the most common anterior mediastinal tumors in adults.[14] They are recognized as variably encapsulated masses within the anterior mediastinum.

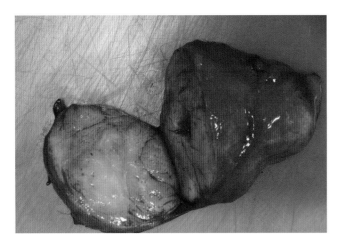

◀ **Figure 9.15b** Thymoma

On section, thymomas are usually solid, soft yellow tumors, although cyst formation and necrosis may be evident and extensive. Histopathological examination is required for both typing and staging of the disease. Invasive thymomas may metastasize to the pleura, bones, liver, and brain.[15]

Lymph Nodes

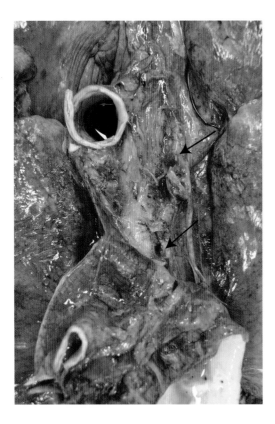

◀ **Figure 9.16a** Benign lymph nodes

Normal lymph nodes are bean-shaped, light-brown structures ranging in size from a few millimeters to 20 mm, typically up to 10 mm in maximum dimension. They have a smooth capsule and a soft texture.[16]

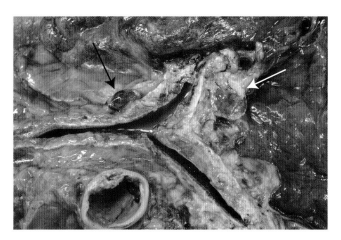

◀ **Figure 9.16b** Benign lymph nodes

Benign reactive enlargement of the lymph nodes at the pulmonary hila and around the carina is a common autopsy finding, particularly in those individuals with respiratory tract infections. The lymph nodes retain their soft consistency but are frequently laden with carbon pigment, particularly in city dwellers and in tobacco smokers. Disseminated lymphadenopathy raises the possibility of human immunodeficiency virus infection.

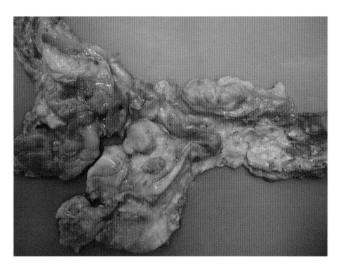

◀ **Figure 9.17a** Malignant lymph nodes

Carcinoma. Carcinomas commonly metastasize to local and then regional lymph nodes. Involved lymph nodes are enlarged and may be partially or completely replaced by tumor, which is typically solid, firm and white/yellow in appearance. A careful search should be made for the primary malignancy. It should be remembered that lymph nodes draining a tumor may enlarge due to sepsis as well as due to neoplastic involvement.

189

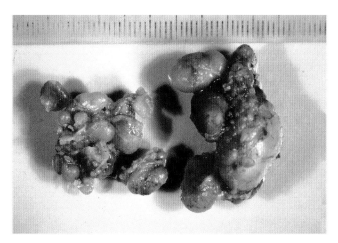

◀ **Figure 9.17b** Malignant lymph nodes

Lymphoma. Involved lymph nodes in patients with lymphoma are enlarged, frequently exceeding 20 mm in diameter. They have a rubbery or fleshy texture and a solid pink/gray cut surface. Sampling the largest lymph nodes for histopathological examination is most likely to yield the diagnosis. Having found lymphomatous nodes at one site a careful examination of other lymph node groups should be made to assist with staging of the disease.

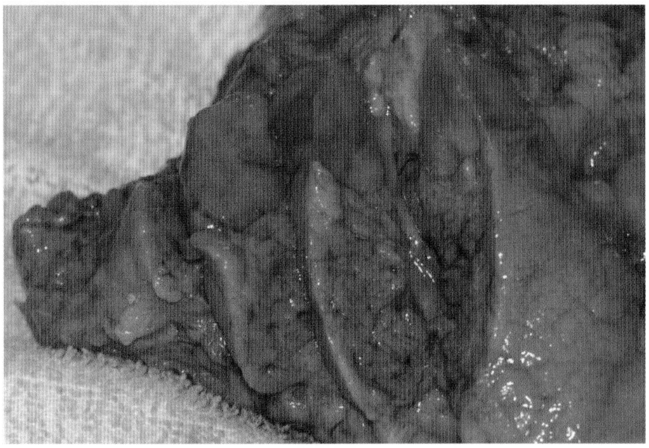

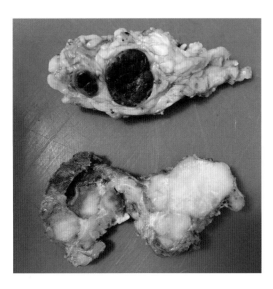

◀ **Figure 9.17c** Malignant lymph nodes

Lymphoma. Involved lymph nodes in patients with lymphoma are enlarged, frequently exceeding 20 mm in diameter. They have a rubbery or fleshy texture and a solid pink/gray cut surface. Sampling the largest lymph nodes for histopathological examination is most likely to yield the diagnosis. Having found lymphomatous nodes at one site a careful examination of other lymph node groups should be made to assist with staging of the disease.

◀ **Figure 9.17d** Malignant lymph nodes

Melanoma. Malignant melanoma metastases in lymph nodes can show considerable macroscopic variation. The top axillary dissection shows a very classical darkly pigmented, almost black deposit within a lymph node. Compare this to the bottom dissection that, on histopathological examination, was confirmed as amelanotic malignant melanoma.

Mucosa-Associated Lymphoid Tissue

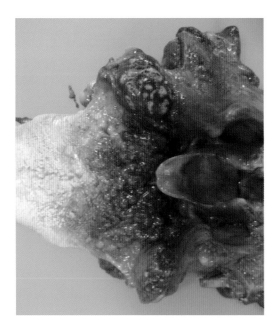

◀ **Figure 9.18** Tonsillitis

Inflammation of the tonsils is rarely seen at autopsy and is even less commonly the cause of death. It is most often the result of a viral infection, but can also be caused by bacterial infection, typically group A *Streptococcus*. The inflamed tonsils are enlarged, erythematous, and edematous. A purulent exudate may be seen arising from the tonsillar crypts. There may be associated enlargement of the tonsillar lymph nodes and those in the upper anterior cervical chain. Unilateral enlargement of a tonsil may be a marker of underlying malignant disease, but the prevalence of malignancy in such tonsils is low.[17]

Bone Marrow

◀ Figure 9.19 Metastatic disease

Normal hematopoietic bone marrow is red, lying within the trabecular bone of the vertebral bodies, ribs, sternum, cranium, and pelvis, as well as in the proximal ends of long bones. Any of these sites may contain metastatic malignant disease, but it is most easily demonstrated in the marrow of the vertebral bodies. Almost any cancer can metastasize to bone marrow, but carcinomas of the breast, bronchus, thyroid, kidney, and prostate have a particular predilection for doing so. A history or the presence of primary carcinomas at these sites should prompt a search for metastatic disease, which is recognized by the presence of white solid tumor deposits. Metastatic adenocarcinoma of the prostate frequently gives rise to osteosclerotic deposits, whereas metastases from other sites are more usually osteolytic.

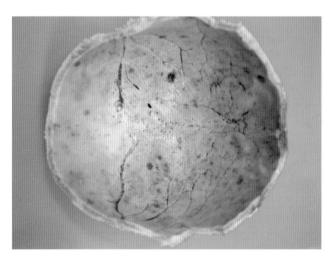

◀ Figure 9.20 Multiple myeloma

Multiple myeloma is characterized by osteolytic aggregates of malignant plasma cells within the bone marrow of the vertebrae, ribs, skull, pelvis, and long bones. In this skull cap from a patient with multiple myeloma, multiple tumor deposits are evident as dark red-purple ovoid-spherical lesions, which correspond to the classic "pepper pot" appearance of the skull on radiographs.

191

References

1. Merran S, Karila-Cohen P, Servois V. CT anatomy of the normal spleen: variants and pitfalls. *Journal of Radiology* 2007;**88**:549–558 [in French].
2. Slater LA, Naidoo PS. Traumatic rupture of hypertrophic splenunculus; MDCT findings, literature review and clinical recommendations. *European Journal of Radiology Extra* 2006;**59**:123–126.
3. Gatt D, Jantet G. Perisplenitis and perinephritis in the Curtis-Fitz-Hugh syndrome. *British Journal of Surgery* 1987;**74**:110–112.
4. Janaki M, Hayath MS, Rao GM, Chennappa Y. Marked perisplenitis in gastric carcinoma. *Indian Journal of Gastroenterology* 1998;**17**:66–67.

5. University of Connecticut Department of Diagnostic Imaging and Therapeutics. Available at: http://radiology.uchc.edu/eAtlas/HEM/269.htm.
6. Wilkins BS, Wright DH. The spleen in immunodeficiency and systemic infections. In: *Illustrated Pathology of the Spleen*. Cambridge: Cambridge University Press; 2000:63–74.
7. Nores M, Phillips EH, Morgenstern L, Hiatt JR. The clinical spectrum of splenic infarction. *American Surgeon* 1998;**64:**182–188.
8. Morgenstern L. Nonparasitic splenic cysts: pathogenesis, classification and treatment. *Journal of the American College of Surgeons* 2002;**194:**306–314.
9. Adas G, Karatepe O, Altiok M, Battal M, Bender O, Ozcan D, Karahan S. Diagnostic problems with parasitic and non-parasitic splenic cysts. *BMC Surgery* 2009;**9:**9.
10. Fishback SJ, Pickhardt PJ, Bhalla S, Menias CO, Congdon RG, Macari M. Delayed presentation of splenic rupture following colonoscopy: clinical and CT findings. *Emergency Radiology* 2011;**18:**539–544.
11. Farley DR, Zeitlow SP, Bannon MP, Farnell MB. Spontaneous rupture of the spleen due to infectious mononucleosis. *Mayo Clinic Proceedings* 1992;**67:**846–853.
12. Laseter T, McReynolds T. Spontaneous splenic rupture. *Military Medicine* 2004;**169:**673–674.
13. Nasseri F, Eftekhari F. Clinical and radiologic review of the normal and abnormal thymus: pearls and pitfalls. *Radiographics* 2010 **30:**413–428.
14. Singh G, Rumende CM, Amin Z. Thymoma: diagnosis and treatment. *Acta Medica Indonesiana* 2011;**43:**74–78.
15. Thomas CR, Wright CD, Loehrer PJ. Thymoma: state of the art. *Journal of Clinical Oncology* 1999;**17:**2280–2289.
16. Willard-Mack CL. Normal structure, function, and histology of lymph nodes. *Toxicologic Pathology* 2006;**34:**409–424.
17. Sunkaraneni VS, Jones SE, Prasai A, Fish BM. Is unilateral tonsillar enlargement alone an indication for tonsillectomy? *Journal of Laryngology and Otology* 2006;**120:**E21.

Chapter 10
The Locomotor System

Introduction

The locomotor, or musculoskeletal, system comprises the axial skeleton, the appendicular skeleton, and the musculature. By far the most common abnormalities encountered in this regard by the autopsy pathologist are traumatic, although primary or secondary diseases may occasionally be identified. In cases where skeletal trauma is likely to be pertinent to the cause of death, consideration should be given to radiological examination (plain films or computed tomography if available), although if the deceased was admitted to hospital before death, then such investigations may have been undertaken in life, and results should be made available to the pathologist.

The location, nature, and extent of muscular injury or fractures should be recorded. Accurate recording of the location of fractures is extremely important for reconstruction of any incident leading to trauma.

Soft Tissue Injuries

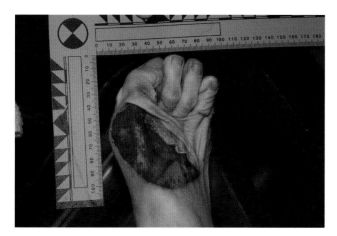

◀ Figure 10.1 Degloving

Degloving injuries occur when tangential force is applied to the body. They are most often seen when the wheels of a vehicle overrun the lower limbs. The natural tissue plane between the subcutaneous tissue and musculature becomes disrupted, and the overlying skin lacerates. Such trauma is often associated with patterned surface injures from the object traversing the limb, for example tire tread patterns.

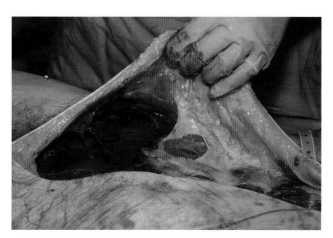

◀ Figure 10.2 Closed degloving injury

Although most injuries that disrupt subcutaneous tissue planes are associated with surface lacerations, some may simply involve the deep tissues. Patterned injuries or surface bruising may give the astute pathologist a clue to their presence. Dissection reveals the extent of injury. Closed degloving injuries may produce a tissue "pocket" into which there may be significant blood loss.

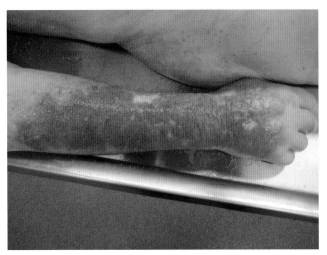

◄ **Figure 10.3a** Necrotizing fasciitis

Necrotizing fasciitis is a severe, rapidly progressive limb- and life-threatening infection of the skin and subcutaneous tissues. It is caused by a variety of microorganisms. Group A *Streptococcus* may cause this disease either alone or in combination with other microorganisms. The disease is characterized by extensive necrosis of the soft tissues, systemic toxicity, and a high mortality rate. It is commonly referred to in the press as "flesh-eating disease." The disease often follows trauma, and this can be minor. In this patient the skin of the right forearm and hand was erythematous and edematous, with blister formation.

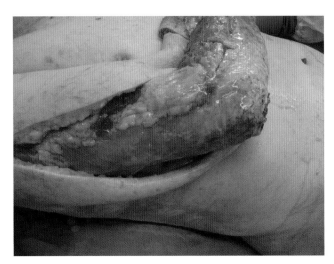

◄ **Figure 10.3b** Necrotizing fasciitis

Dissection revealed purulent necrosis of the subcutaneous tissues, fascia, and muscles that extended beyond the area of erythema. Histological examination confirmed the presence of severe acute inflammation with abscess formation and necrosis of fibrofatty connective tissue and skeletal myocytes. Colonies of gram-positive cocci, some arranged in chains, were present, and cultures yielded Group A *Streptococcus*.

◄ **Figure 10.4** Calcinosis

The formation of calcium deposits within the soft tissues is known as calcinosis. It may occur in any soft tissues, but it is common around the knee joint in patients who have undergone total knee replacement. In such patients, as in this example, calcinosis may result from dystrophic calcification as a result of a synovial leak or in response to talc from surgical gloves. The finding is typically coincidental to the cause of death.

Bones and Joints: Degenerative, Infective, and Metabolic Diseases

◀ **Figure 10.5a** Osteoporosis

Osteoporosis is common in the older population, particularly women, and is characterized by reduced bone mineral density. It predisposes to fractures, most commonly in the femoral neck and ribs. Compression fractures of the spine may be seen. Fractures in people with osteoporosis may require minimal trauma (pathological fractures), and a history of trauma may be absent. Osteoporosis is most easily identified by the pathologist when removing the ribs because, with experience, the ease with which osteoporotic ribs can be cut can be appreciated. Artifactual postmortem fractures of the osteoporotic spine may be seen with rough handling of the body, and lower cervical postmortem fractures are sometimes colloquially referred to as "undertaker's fractures." These postmortem fractures can be distinguished from fractures that occurred in life by the presence of only minimal associated bruising.

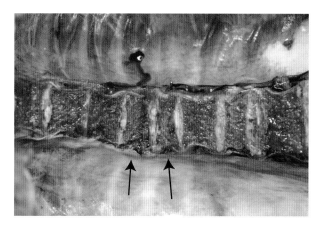

◀ **Figure 10.5b** Osteoporosis compression fractures

195

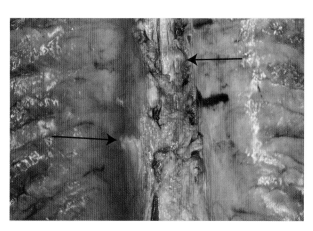

◀ **Figure 10.6** Osteoarthritis: spine

Osteoarthritis of the spine is characterized by osteophytes which are visible both radiologically and to the naked eye. These may cause spinal nerve root compression that cause signs and symptoms in life, although rarely cause potentially lethal complications.

◀ **Figure 10.7** Ochronosis of the vertebral discs
Ochronosis results from the accumulation of homogentisic acid in connective tissues. Affected tissues have a blue-gray discoloration. The disorder may result from an autosomal recessive mutation or from the topical use of hydroquinone or phenolic compounds on the skin. Ochronosis is typically an incidental finding at autopsy, but it may cause stenosis of the cardiac valves.

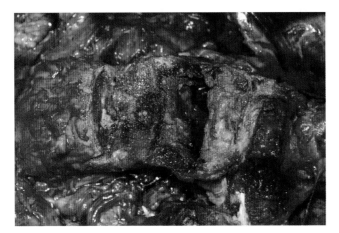

◀ **Figure 10.8** Infective lumbar discitis
A history of pyrexia of unknown origin, back pain, and/or abdominal pain, particularly in an individual who is immunosuppressed or who was an intravenous drug user, should point the pathologist toward a diagnosis of lumbar discitis. In this patient, deroofing of the lumbar spine reveals infective lumbar discitis. The intervertebral disc is swollen and focally necrotic. Microbiological culture and histopathological examination confirm the diagnosis.

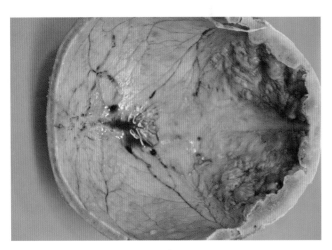

◀ **Figure 10.9** Hyperostosis frontalis interna
Hyperostosis frontalis interna is a relatively common incidental autopsy finding. The inner table of the frontal bone of the skull becomes irregular, with nodular growths of bone. It is not a condition that in itself is pathologically significant, but if associated with obesity, virilism, and hirsutism, it is part of Morgagni syndrome.

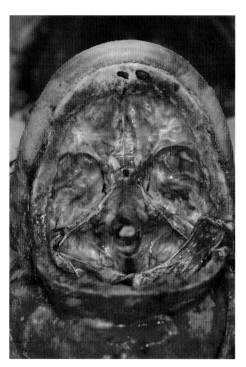

◄ Figure 10.10 Paget disease of the skull
Paget disease of bone (not to be confused with the unrelated Paget disease of the nipple) is a condition of older people and is associated with several genetic mutations. It is characterized by disordered osteoblastic and osteoclastic activity leading to disorganized and weakened bone structure. This condition increases the risk of fractures. Rarely, in severe cases, there may be hypervascularization of the abnormal bone with associated arteriovenous shunting that can cause high-output cardiac failure. Malignant disease (osteosarcoma) is a rare complication.

Fractures

197

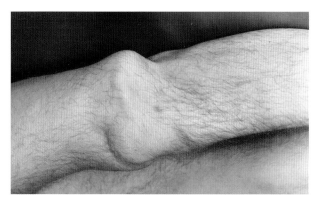

◄ Figure 10.11 Simple fractures
Simple fractures are linear breaks of the bone and may be seen in almost any region of the body. They typically result from the direct application of force. The significance depends, of course, on the bone broken. Even simple fractures of major long bones such as the femur may be associated with significant hemorrhage, as well as bone marrow or fat emboli, all of which may cause or contribute to death.

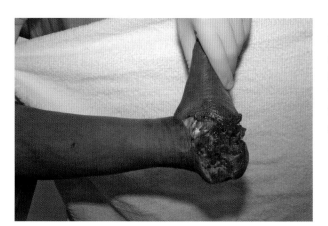

◄ Figure 10.12 Compound fractures
Compound fractures are fractures that breach the skin. The ends of fractured bones tend to be sharp and readily cut through skin and muscle. Such "open" fractures are a potential source of infection. The fractured ends are usually readily apparent on external examination. (Image courtesy of Dr. A. Jeffrey.)

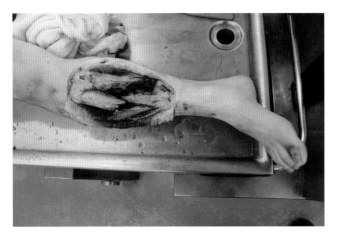

◀ **Figure 10.13a** Comminuted fracture
Comminuted fractures are fractures in which the bone is splintered into fragments. These fractures are usually associated with high-energy impacts. The shards of bone may penetrate adjacent tissue. In the limbs, this may cause damage to muscle, nerves, or blood vessels, but a comminuted skull fracture may force bone fragments into the brain, with severe consequences. In comminuted fractures, the bone may splinter into three (a) or more (b) fragments. ((b) Courtesy of Dr. A. Jeffrey.)

◀ **Figure 10.13b** Comminuted fracture

198

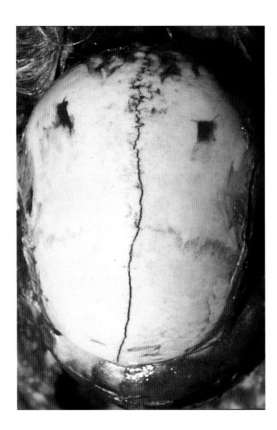

◀ **Figure 10.14** Linear fracture of the skull vault
Linear skull fractures result from blunt force trauma. They are not associated with significant bone displacement. In this example, the fracture runs parallel to the sagittal suture. Fractures that lie close to or transverse skull sutures may be complicated by intracranial hemorrhage or venous sinus thrombosis. (Image courtesy of Dr. A. Jeffrey.)

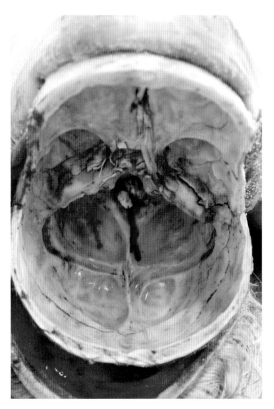

◄ **Figure 10.15a** Base of skull fracture
Basal skull fractures are common, particularly in falls
onto the back of the head. Unlike the smooth, regular
vault of the skull, the base is irregular, relatively weak,
and prone to fractures. These fractures may be seen
in any of the cranial fossae and often involve the sella
turcica. So-called contrecoup fractures of the very thin
orbital plates may be seen in impacts to the rear of
the head. Basal skull fractures are frequently associated
with subdural bleeding and brain injury.

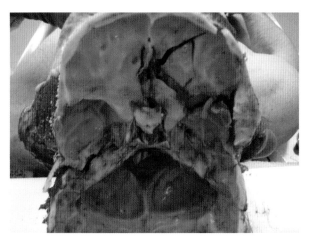

◄ **Figure 10.15b** Comminuted base of skull fracture

◄ **Figure 10.16** Neck fractures
Fractures of the cervical spine may be seen in situations
causing hyperflexion, hyperextension, compression,
or distraction. The actual bony fractures are of limited
relevance, but any injury that causes bone to impinge
on the spinal cord may result in sudden death or
may interfere with motor and sensory functions, thus
leading to long-term disability and immobility. These
fractures may lead to death months or even years
after the incident causing the injury, and the pathologist
should be careful to ensure that the circumstances
of this incident are known because criminal or civil
proceedings may still be possible.

◀ **Figure 10.17** Odontoid peg fracture
The odontoid peg of the second cervical vertebra is prone to fracture in cervical hyperflexion and extension injuries. In older persons, these fractures may occur as a result of simple falls. They are also seen in deaths from judicial hanging, but not typically in suicidal hanging unless there has been a long drop. Such fractures are unstable and life-threatening because there may be associated cervical spinal cord compression or transection.

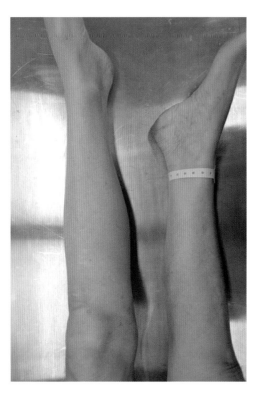

◀ **Figure 10.18** Hip fractures: external
Fractures of the femoral neck are rare in young people but are commonly seen in the aging population. The fracture, combined with the contraction of muscles, leads to the classical clinical finding of the shortened and externally rotated limb. As the femoral head is at risk of avascular necrosis, joint replacement (arthroplasy or hemiarthroplasty) is commonly undertaken.

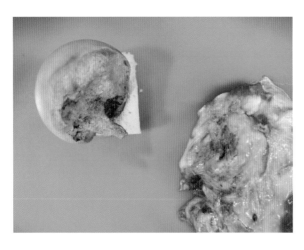

◀ **Figure 10.19** Hip fractures: internal
The site of hip fractures should be examined at autopsy in order to confirm the diagnosis. Examination of the site of a recent arthroplasty is of equal or greater importance to identify hemorrhage or infection. Reaming of the femur during surgery may lead to fat embolism which should be diligently sought, particularly in individuals dying several days after surgery. As hip replacement is a very common surgical procedure, a careful examination for the typical scars on the lateral aspects of the hips should form part of any autopsy examination.

◄ Figure 10.20a Rib fractures

The ribs are relatively fragile bones and are prone to trauma in compression or impacts to the chest. Cardiopulmonary resuscitation (CPR) is often carried out in cases of sudden collapse and is often associated with rib fractures, particularly in persons with osteoporosis. Fractures from correctly administered CPR are typically anterior or parasternal, involve the second to sixth ribs bilaterally, and may be associated with transverse sternal fractures. These are usually associated with limited or absent hemorrhage. Fractures elsewhere in the ribs are most likely as the result of "true" trauma and may lead to significant hemorrhage from intercostal vessels, penetration of the parietal pleura from fractured rib ends with hemothorax, or, in severe cases, laceration of the lungs with pneumothorax or hemopneumothorax.

◄ Figure 10.20b Rib fractures

201

Malignant Disease and the Skeleton

◄ Figure 10.21a Bony metastases

Many malignant tumors including breast, lung, thyroid, kidney, and prostate may metastasize to bone. Most cause osteolytic lesions, but prostate tumors in particular cause osteosclerotic deposits. Metastases may be seen in any bone and, as with any lesion that interferes with the integrity of bone structure, lead to a propensity to fractures with only a history of minor trauma, or indeed no evidence of trauma.

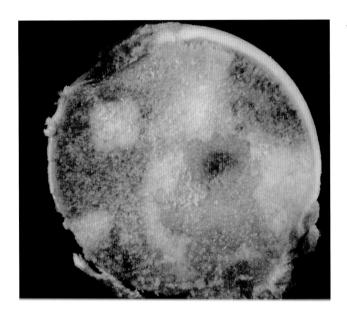

◀ **Figure 10.21b** Bony metastases

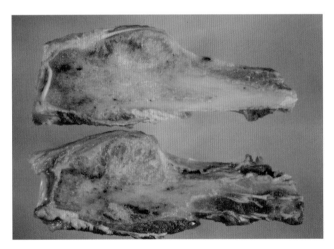

◀ **Figure 10.22** Osteosarcoma

Osteosarcoma is a primary malignant disease of bone, most commonly seen in teenagers. These tumors are typically seen in the long bones of the lower limbs or in the humerus, near the shoulder. Macroscopically, they are seen as fungating exophytic lesions on the cortex of the affected bone. They are readily identifiable on radiology. Most tumors will be diagnosed in life, but if the lesion has not been suspected clinically, then histological examination should be performed to confirm the diagnosis. Osteosarcomas may metastasize, particularly to the lung.

Chapter 11

The Central Nervous System

Introduction

The central nervous system is composed of the brain and the spinal cord. The brain plays a central role in the control of most bodily functions, including movement, sensations, and breathing. The range of pathological processes that can affect the brain is vast and varied. The brain can be the cause of death in many cases, both natural and unnatural, such as head injury, stroke, space-occupying lesions, epilepsy, cerebral hypoxia, dementias, and movement disorders. Furthermore, compromise of the brain may lead to reduced mobility or immobility, causing potentially fatal complications such as bronchopneumonia or pressure sores (see relevant chapters). A detailed examination of the central nervous system, or at the very least the brain, is essential during an autopsy and is often overlooked if an apparent cause of death is identified elsewhere.

If disease or injury in the brain is considered to be the cause of the death, for example, epilepsy or dementia, then the brain may require examination by a specialist neuropathologist and in such cases should be retained and fixed complete. Even if the brain is not submitted for such examination, it may also be reasonable to retain the brain for a few days of fixation to allow more accurate dissection by the pathologist. It is important that the brain is removed very carefully in an appropriate manner. This should be either done by the pathologist or by an experienced technician with the pathologist present during the removal.

The skull should be examined for the presence of trauma, namely fractures, and any disease process, such as Paget disease. The skull cap is then removed, and the meninges are examined for the presence of blood, infection, previous surgery, and/or trauma. The dura mater is then stripped away to examine the cerebral hemispheres. The brain is carefully removed and examined for general features, such as the presence of swelling, contusions, infarcts, and areas of necrosis associated with raised intracranial pressure. The brain is then serially sliced to look for areas of focal disease. The vault, base of the skull, and the cranial fossae are also examined after removal of the dura mater for fractures, hemorrhage within the mastoid air sinuses, hyperostosis frontalis interna, and other disorders.

Examination of a fresh brain is at best a very crude assessment because of the softness of the tissue. The ideal is to fix the brain and cut into 1-cm sections or to undertake a "landmark-based dissection." However, current coronial legislation makes this impossible as a routine practice. Where permission for retention of the whole brain is refused, it may be possible to retain a smaller amount of brain tissue for histological examination. Guidelines for histological sampling of the brain are available on the Royal College of Pathologists website and in standard texts. If in doubt, refer to a local neuropathologist for advice.[1]

For a more detailed description of how to remove and examine the brain, please refer to Chapter 12, "Dissection of the Central Nervous System," in *The Hospital Autopsy*.[2]

Meninges

The meninges are the membranes that cover the brain and the spinal cord. The meninges consist of three layers: the dura mater, the arachnoid mater, and the pia mater. The arachnoid and pia are collectively referred to as the leptomeninges. The primary function of the meninges and of the cerebrospinal fluid is to protect the central nervous system.

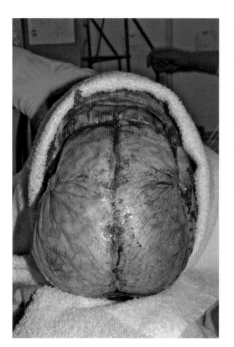

◀ **Figure 11.1** Normal dura mater
The dura (dura mater) is the outermost layer of the meninges. The dura has two distinct layers. The outer layer is fused to the periosteum and lines the inner surface of the skull. The inner layer is fibrous and is in contact with cerebrospinal fluid surrounding the brain. The dura undergoes a number of infolds or fibrous extensions around the brain that hold the brain firmly in position. These are the falx cerebri, falx cerebelli, and tentorium cerebelli.

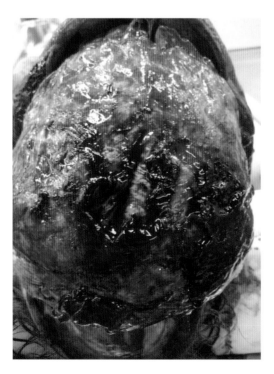

◀ **Figure 11.2** Extradural hematoma
Extradural hemorrhage is a pathological collection of blood in the potential space between the skull and the dura. The expanding mass forms a convex, lens-shaped mass pushing into the brain. The source of the bleeding is usually from tearing of the middle meningeal artery and associated with a fracture of the temporal bone. Extradural hemorrhages take a period of time to accumulate. The typical history is a head injury, often to the temple region, followed by a "lucid period," after which the signs of raised intracranial pressure are seen.

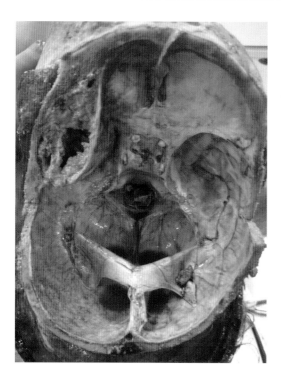

◀ **Figure 11.3** Chronic extradural hematoma
Chronic extradural hematomas are rare. Over time, the hematoma transforms into a mass of yellow grumous material, and the dura over this becomes thickened and may calcify. Typical symptoms include headache, nausea, vomiting, cognitive impairment, and unconsciousness. In this patient, the hematoma was a coincidental finding and there was no known history of falls, head injury, or neurological deficit.

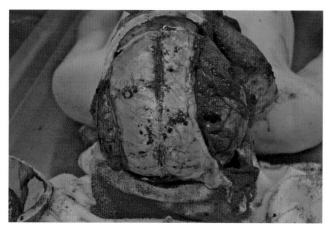

◀ **Figure 11.4a** Subdural hematoma
A subdural hematoma or hemorrhage is a pathological collection of blood between the dura and the arachnoid mater. These lesions result from trauma, which may be minimal. Subdural hemorrhages can be classified as acute, chronic, or acute-on-chronic. Acute subdural hemorrhages may accompany any head trauma. The most common causes are movement of the brain within the skull and tearing of the delicate bridging brains. Therefore, individuals whose brain has shrunk (older persons) and where the dura is mobile (infants) are more likely to have a fatal outcome. Acute subdural hemorrhages have a high mortality rate.

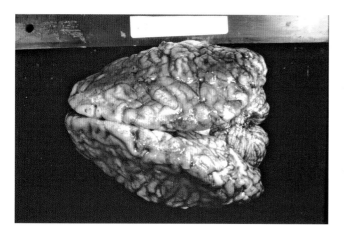

◀ **Figure 11.4b** Subdural hematoma
Chronic subdural hematomas develop over a period of days to weeks and can result from minor trauma. The bleeding is slower than in acute hematomas. If left to resolve, the hematoma becomes encapsulated by a pseudomembrane and can often appeared layered. Chronic subdural hematomas are more common in older persons, and death usually results from a final major hemorrhage, so-called acute-on-chronic bleeding. The age of a chronic hematoma can be estimated from macroscopic and histological features.[3]

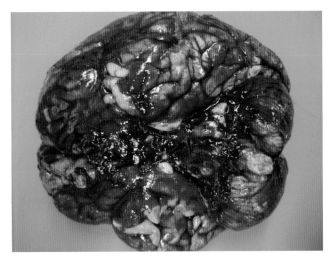

◀ **Figure 11.5** Subarachnoid hemorrhage

A subarachnoid hemorrhage is pathological bleeding in the potential space between the arachnoid and the pia mater surrounding the brain. These hemorrhages can occur spontaneously, most commonly from a ruptured cerebral aneurysm arising from the circle of Willis at the base of the brain (often called a "berry aneurysm"). Rarer causes are arteriovenous malformations, tumors, and disorders of blood vessel walls.[4] Traumatic subarachnoid hemorrhages can be seen in association with head injuries in isolation or occurring with other disorders such as extradural hematomas and contusions. These are typically patchy areas of hemorrhage over the hemispheres and lobes. Hemorrhage can also result from tearing of the vertebral arteries. This occurs with blows to the neck and face that cause hyperextension and rotation. This is most commonly seen in assaults, often in intoxicated individuals who are unprepared for a blow. The hemorrhage is seen around the base of the brain and posterior fossa and is referred to as a "traumatic basal subarachnoid hemorrhage."

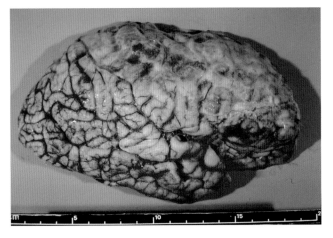

◀ **Figure 11.6** Meningitis

Bacterial meningitis is the most common form of meningitis seen at autopsy. The gross appearance of purulent meningitis is of an opaque, creamy exudate over the sulci of the cerebellum. In adults, it is usually secondary to septicemia, although previous neurosurgery and skull fracture are other risk factors. The most common bacterial agents responsible for meningitis vary according to the age of the patient and the clinical setting. In adults, *Streptococcus pneumoniae* and *Neisseria meningitidis* are the likely causative organisms. Microbial swabs of the brain surface and inside the ventricles, along with blood cultures, will help identify the organism.[5]

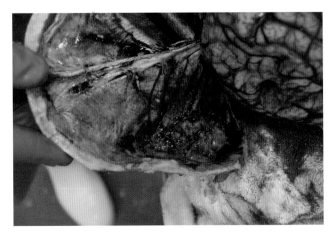

◀ **Figure 11.7a** Meningioma

Meningiomas are the most common benign tumors found in the cranium. They arise from the dura mater and are usually slow growing. They are seldom associated with herniation, but they do frequently compress the underlying brain tissue. These well-circumscribed lesions are most often seen in the skull vault, skull base, at the choroid plexus, and at sites of dural infolding. They are often an incidental finding at autopsy. The incidence increases with age, especially after 50 years.

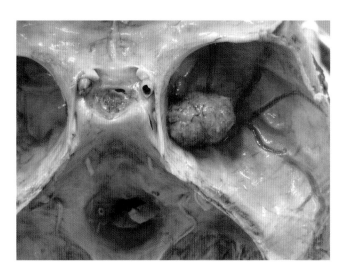

◀ **Figure 11.7b** Meningioma

Cerebral Vasculature

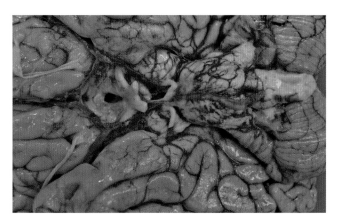

◀ **Figure 11.8a** Normal circle of Willis
The circle of Willis is the circle of connecting arteries that supply the brain. The circle is found on the base of the brain, and it is composed of the following arteries: left and right anterior cerebral artery, anterior communicating artery, left and right internal carotid artery, left and right posterior cerebral artery, basilar artery, and posterior communicating artery. There can be significant anatomical variation in the circle of Willis.

207

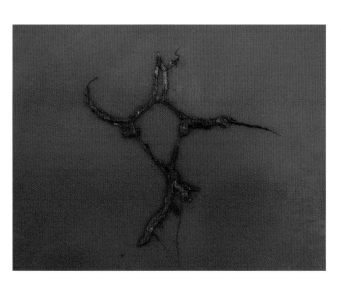

◀ **Figure 11.8b** Normal circle of Willis

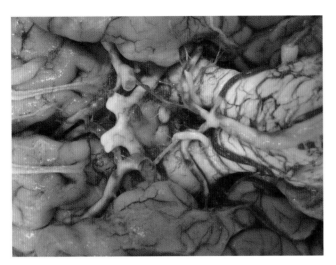

◄ **Figure 11.9** Atheroma
As with other arteries within the body, the arteries in the circle of Willis are affected by atherosclerosis. The atheroma can be complicated by thrombosis and reduced flow secondary to stenosis. This can lead to cerebral ischemia and infarction.

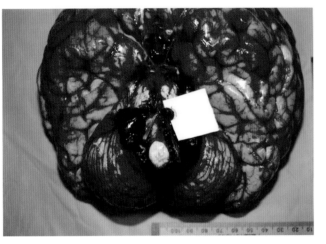

◄ **Figure 11.10a** Berry aneurysms
Berry aneurysms (or saccular aneurysms) are sac-like out-pouches of the cerebral vessels that are said to look like berries. They tend to occur at the bifurcations of arteries. Most aneurysms occur singly, with the most frequent sites being the circle of Willis and the bifurcation of the middle cerebral artery. However, they can be multiple. They can cause subarachnoid hemorrhage. These aneurysms can occur sporadically or be associated with diseases such as polycystic kidney disease, Ehlers-Danlos syndrome, Marfan syndrome, and neurofibromatosis.[5]

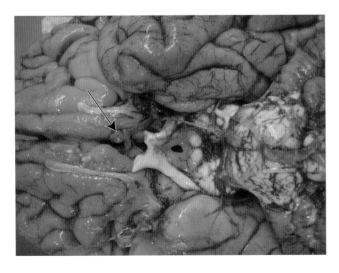

◄ **Figure 11.10b** Berry aneurysms

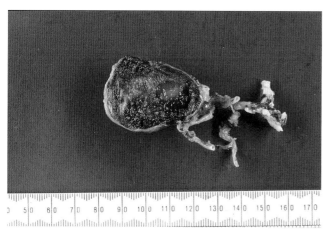

◀ **Figure 11.11** Large berry aneurysm with thrombus

As with aneurysms at other sites, berry aneurysms may spontaneously become partially or completely filled with thrombus. In this example, the aneurysm is very large and full of thrombus.

Brain

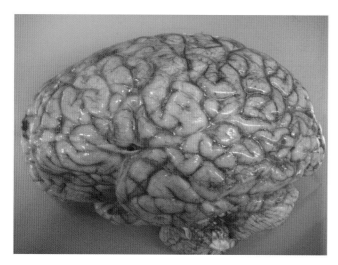

◀ **Figure 11.12** Normal brain

The normal brain weight is 1290 to 1440 g for men and 1230 to 1390 g for women.[6] The normal brain is composed of two cerebral hemispheres with a visible pattern of gyri and sulci. The cerebral hemispheres are divided into several lobes, namely the frontal, parietal, temporal, and occipital lobes. The cerebellum and brainstem are found on the inferior aspect of the cerebral hemispheres. The brain is protected by the cranial bones, the meninges, and the circulation of cerebrospinal fluid.

209

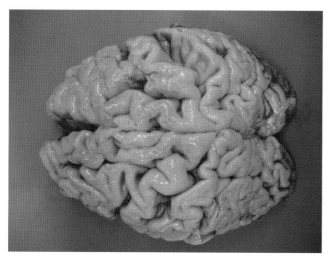

◀ **Figure 11.13** Cerebral atrophy

Cerebral atrophy is the loss of neurons and neural connections in the brain. It is a common feature associated with aging. It can be generalized or focal, depending on the cause. Diseases that cause cerebral atrophy include stroke, traumatic brain injury, cerebral palsy, Alzheimer disease, Pick disease, and many other forms of dementia.

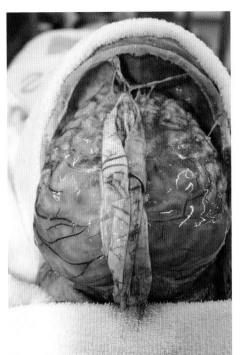

◀ **Figure 11.14** Cerebral edema
True cerebral edema (as opposed to congestive swelling) is a microscopic diagnosis best addressed by a neuropathologist. When the brain becomes swollen, the gyri appear flattened and widened, with narrowed sulci. On slicing, the lateral ventricles are compressed. The brain will weigh more than expected for the age and sex of the individual. The consequences of cerebral edema include disruption of the blood-brain barrier, direct physical injury from compression of the brain (e.g., uncal grooving or tentorial herniation), and global hypoxia (primarily from compression of small blood vessels within the brain) if severe.

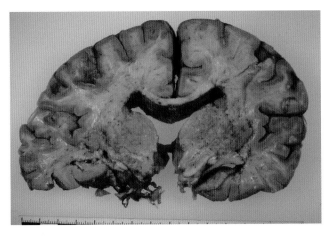

◀ **Figure 11.15** Viral encephalitis
In viral encephalitis, the brain is edematous, and there is widespread necrosis, either patchy, as in this example, or diffuse. Various viruses cause encephalitis, of which the most common are herpes simplex virus and varicella-zoster virus. Rabies is a rare but important cause. Cytomegalovirus, influenza virus, measles virus, mumps virus, Epstein-Barr virus, and human immunodeficiency virus can cause postinfectious encephalitis. Samples of the brain and cerebrospinal fluid should be retained for virology and histopathological examination to confirm the diagnosis.

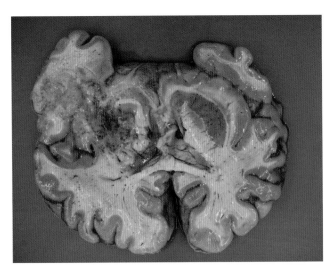

◀ **Figure 11.16** Acute cerebral infarct
Acute infarcts in the first 24 hours appear as poorly demarcated areas of softening, and they can be difficult to determine at autopsy. After 48 hours, they appear as more demarcated areas of dark discoloration. Cerebral infarction occurs most often because of embolic occlusion of a cerebral arterial branch. Thrombotic occlusion can also occur when there is cerebral atherosclerosis. Reperfusion of the damaged vessels and tissue from collateral circulation or after dissolution of an embolus can lead to the hemorrhagic appearance in the tissue.[5]

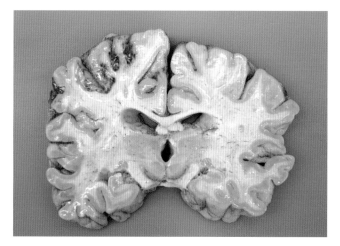

◀ Figure 11.17a Watershed infarcts

Those parts of the brain that lie at the ends of the territories of the main cerebral arteries are at risk of ischemic infarction should an individual suffer a period of prolonged hypotension or hypoxia. Such infarcts are known as watershed infarcts, and they may affect the cortex or deeper brain structures.

Cortical watershed infarcts are located between the cortical territories of the anterior, middle, and posterior cerebral arteries. In this example, the patient had a period of profound hypotension, which resulted in an extensive watershed infarct between the territories of the anterior and middle cerebral arteries. There is blurring of the gray-white matter junction and secondary hemorrhage in the affected cortex of the left parietal lobe.

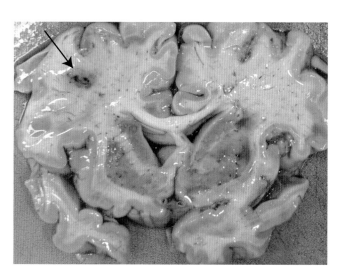

◀ Figure 11.17b Watershed infarcts

Internal watershed infarcts typically affect the white matter of the centrum semiovale and the tissue between the territories of the anterior and middle cerebral arteries. In this example from the same patient as in (a), there is a focus of infarction with secondary hemorrhage in the centrum semiovale of the left parietal lobe. Note also the cortical watershed infarct in the right parietal lobe.

211

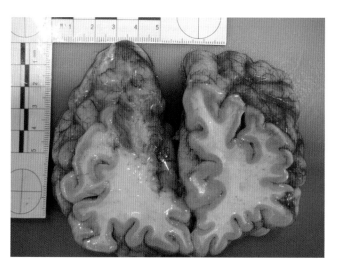

◀ Figure 11.18a Old cerebral infarct

Older infarcts undergo liquefactive necrosis, which then progresses to cystic space formation. This occurs in the first 2 weeks following infarction and proceeds for months. Older areas of infarction can be seen as dark yellow or tan cystic areas. The size and location of infarcts follow the anatomy of the vascular territories.

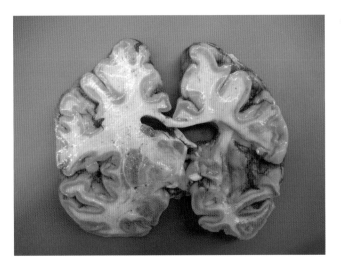

◀ **Figure 11.18b** Old cerebral infarct

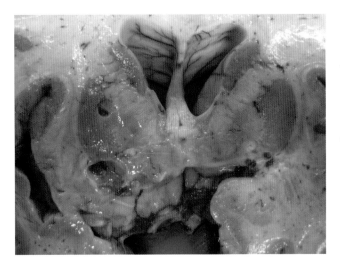

◀ **Figure 11.19** Lacunar infarcts
Lacunar infarcts are small infarcts that result from arterial sclerosis secondary to chronic hypertension. They are seen in the thalamus, internal capsule, caudate, pons, and deep white matter. They are smaller than 5 mm in diameter. They can be clinically insignificant or cause stroke-like symptoms. If many infarcts occur, then the cumulative effects can cause multi-infarct dementia.

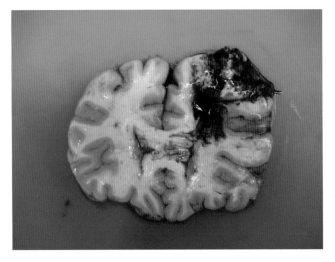

◀ **Figure 11.20** Hemorrhagic stroke
Intraparenchymal hemorrhages can occur as a result of a wide number of causes, including tumors, infections, vasculitis, amyloid angiopathy, and coagulopathies. They are seen as well-defined areas of hemorrhage with the brain tissue. A mass effect from the blood can cause a midline shift, often with secondary edema. This can lead to herniation. One of the most common causes of hemorrhagic strokes is hypertension. The hemorrhage results from rupture of small penetrating arteries arising from the lenticulostriate branches of the middle cerebral artery. Hypertension stiffens the vessel wall and thereby increases its fragility, and this along with increased pressure can cause rupture. The most frequent sites are the internal capsule, the basal ganglia, and the thalamus. Cerebral hemorrhages occurring close to the surface may rupture and extend into the subdural space, the so-called "burst lobe."

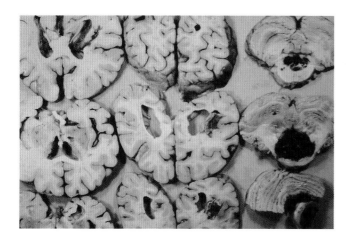

◀ **Figure 11.21** Pontine hemorrhage
The pons is an uncommon but important site of hemorrhagic stroke. In this example, one sees evidence of previous strokes within the cerebral hemispheres and a large fresh hemorrhage within the pons (on the right of the image). Sudden massive hemorrhage into the brainstem may cause sudden death.

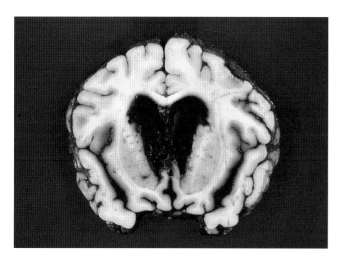

◀ **Figure 11.22** Intraventricular hemorrhage
In adults, intraventricular hemorrhage typically occurs as a consequence of head trauma or hemorrhagic stroke.

213

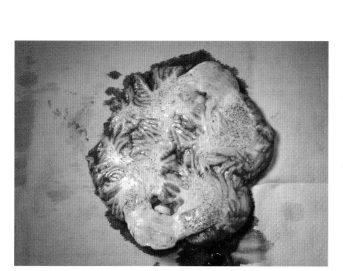

◀ **Figure 11.23** Fat emboli
Fat emboli are known complications of trauma, particularly fractures, crush injuries, and blunt force trauma to adipose tissues. Most typically, fat emboli lodge within the pulmonary vasculature and cause sudden death. Where survival is prolonged, embolic fat may be found in the brain, kidneys, and skin. In the brain, fat emboli result in numerous white matter petechiae within the cerebrum and (as shown here) the cerebellum. Histological examination of frozen tissue sections stained with Oil Red O confirms the diagnosis.

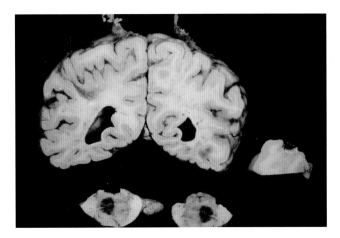

◀ **Figure 11.24** Duret hemorrhages

Duret hemorrhages are flame-shaped areas of bleeding in the paramedian areas of the midbrain or pons. They result from raised intracranial pressure that causes descending transtentorial herniation in conditions such as stroke, tumors, or trauma. This forces the brainstem downward, thus tearing the perforating vessels supplying the midbrain and resulting in hemorrhage.[4]

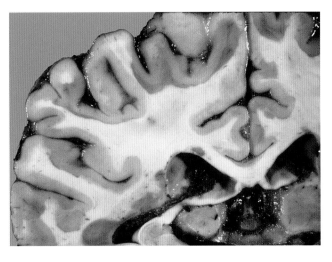

◀ **Figure 11.25** Multiple sclerosis

Multiple sclerosis is an autoimmune condition characterized by repeated episodes of inflammation of the nervous tissue in the brain and spinal cord that cause demyelination of the myelin sheath. At autopsy, there may be gray-tan plaques of demyelination with sharp borders with the adjacent normal white matter. However, there may be no autopsy findings. Plaques can be multifocal and can be seen anywhere in the white matter. If the death is expected to have resulted from the multiple sclerosis, then the brain and spinal cord should be retained and examined by a neuropathologist. (From *Forensic Neuropathology*. 3rd ed. Figure 3.83.)

◀ **Figure 11.26** Parkinson disease

Parkinson disease is a movement disorder characterized by tremor at rest, rigidity, and bradykinesia (slow initiation of movement). It is caused by degeneration of the dopaminergic in the substantia nigra affecting the nigrostriatal pathway in the brain. At autopsy, there is a loss of the dark pigmentation in the substantia nigra of the midbrain. Certain age-related conditions can cause this finding. Parkinson-like symptoms ("parkinsonism") may occur in a number of conditions, notably chronic drug abuse. (From *Forensic Neuropathology*. 3rd ed.)

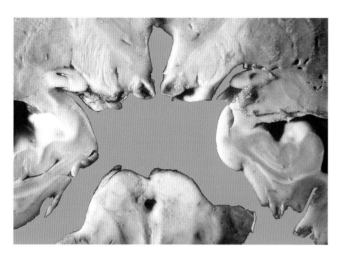

◀ Figure 11.27 Wernicke-Korsakoff syndrome

Wernicke-Korsakoff syndrome is a complication of thiamine (vitamin B1) deficiency. It is most often associated with chronic alcohol abuse. The classic clinical triad of symptoms is confusion, ataxia, and ophthalmoplegia. Korsakoff psychosis is the late manifestation of the condition, where Wernicke encephalopathy has not been adequately treated. At autopsy, bilateral small mammillary bodies can be seen.[7] Rarely, there may be petechial hemorrhages in the mammillary bodies and, less frequently, the brainstem. (From *Forensic Neuropathology*. 3rd ed.)

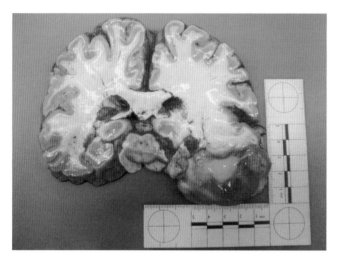

◀ Figure 11.28 Cerebral abscess

Cerebral abscesses can act as space-occupying lesions and give rise to increased intracranial pressure. They can be single or multiple, depending on the cause. Direct infection such as through the middle ear produce a single lesion, whereas spread from the blood causes multifocal lesions. Other causes are skull fractures, dental and sinus infections, foreign bodies (e.g., bullets), septic emboli from valvular heart disease, and chronic lung infections. Abscesses can be bacterial, fungal, or protozoal in origin, and the latter two are often related to impaired immune function. Microbial samples along with histological examination will help identify the causative organism.[4]

215

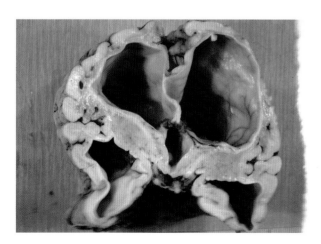

◀ Figure 11.29 Hydrocephalus

Hydrocephalus is an increase in the volume of cerebrospinal fluid (CSF) occupying the cerebral ventricles. The condition results most commonly from impaired absorption of CSF and less commonly from excessive secretion. The increased pressure causes dilatation of the ventricles and, if left untreated, damages the white matter and leads to scarring. Hydrocephalus can occur following infection or hemorrhage or as a result of tumors. It may also be congenital or idiopathic. Untreated hydrocephalus may result in death. If there is atrophy of the brain, then the CSF-containing spaces such as the ventricles may enlarge, leading to a compensatory increase in CSF (hydrocephalus *ex vacuo*). There may be symptoms from the underlying disorder.

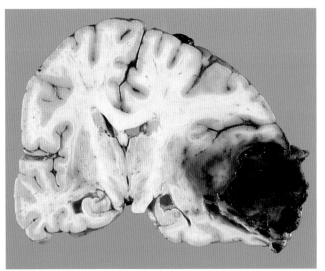

◀ **Figure 11.30** Glioblastoma multiforme
Glioblastoma (previously known as glioblastoma multiforme) is the most malignant form of astrocytoma (World Health Organization grade 4). These tumors most commonly occur in the sixth and seventh decades. Macroscopically, they resemble other astrocytomas, with the exception of the presence of necrosis and endothelial hyperplasia. There are several different variants of glioblastoma, but all carry an extremely poor prognosis. (From *Forensic Neuropathology*. 3rd ed. Permission given by Dr. Shaku Teas.)

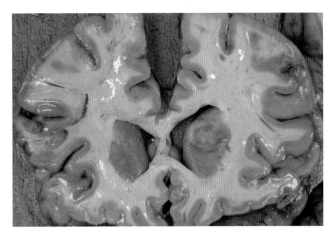

◀ **Figure 11.31a** Cerebral metastasis
Metastatic tumors are among the most common mass lesions in the brain, and they are seen at autopsy in about 20% to 35% of patients with systemic malignant disease. Metastases from systemic cancer can affect the brain parenchyma, dura, skull, and leptomeninges. Tumors that commonly metastasize to the central nervous system (making up 80%) are carcinomas of the bronchus, breast, gastrointestinal tract, and kidney and melanoma. Hematological malignant diseases also frequently spread to the brain. Metastasis can be solitary or multiple. These tumors tend to be red brown and have more discrete borders than those of primary glioma. Metastasis from malignant melanoma can appear dark brown or black.

◀ **Figure 11.31b** Cerebral metastasis

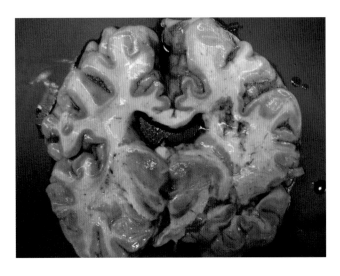

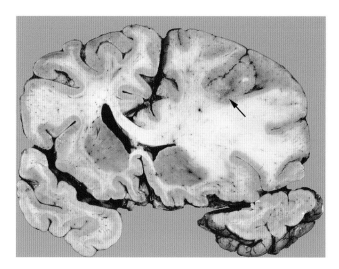

◀ **Figure 11.32** Cerebral herniation

Cerebral herniation results from raised intracranial pressure and causes the brain to shift across structures within the skull. The degree and progression of the herniation depend on the etiology and location of the insult. Herniation can be caused by a number of factors such as traumatic brain injury, stroke, or tumor. Commonly, the first sign of herniation occurs when the medial temporal lobe is pushed underneath the falx cerebri and then beneath the tentorium (often seen as uncal grooving) and down into the posterior fossa. Eventually, the brain matter is pushed down through the foramen magnum, with resulting coning. (From *Forensic Neuropathology.* 3rd ed.)

◀ **Figure 11.33** Cerebellar tonsillar hernia

Acute cerebral edema above the tentorium or in the posterior fossa can force the cerebellum into the foramen magnum, a process known as "coning." This herniation eventually leads to necrosis of the cerebellar tonsils, occlusion of the posterior cerebral artery, and compression of the brainstem that result in death. In the early stages, molding of the tonsils can be seen. As the pressure increases, focal necrosis of the tonsils occurs. (From *Forensic Neuropathology.* 3rd ed.)

217

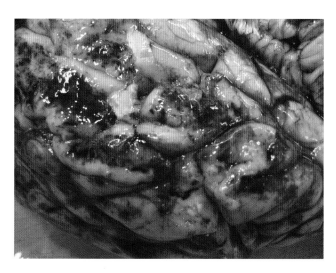

◀ **Figure 11.34** Cerebral contusion

Cerebral contusions or *coup* contusions are seen with a direct force to the head. The impact causes damage to the brain matter in the region of the impact. These contusions typically occur over the crests of the gyri. Contusions can be surrounded by areas of edema, which can cause a mass effect.[4]

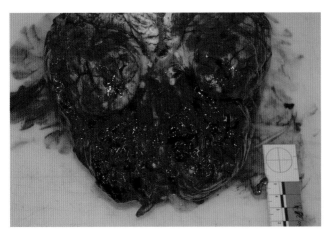

◀ **Figure 11.35** Contrecoup injury

A contrecoup injury occurs with head injuries where the force is transmitted across the brain to produce contusions to the brain matter opposite the site of impact. Commonly, this occurs with a fall backward in which the occiput is struck, and contusions are seen in the frontal lobes and temporal poles. When a moving object impacts the stationary head, coup injuries are typical, whereas contrecoup injuries are produced when the moving head strikes a stationary object, although these injuries may also be seen with a blow to a fixed head.

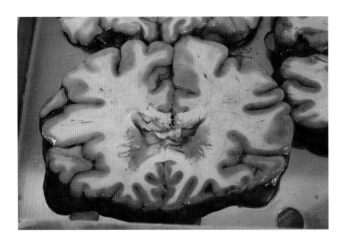

◀ **Figure 11.36** Torn corpus callosum

Severe head injuries in which there is a rotational component can apply shearing forces that tear the corpus callosum. This injury is commonly seen in motorcyclists.

References

1. Royal College of Pathologists. Neuropathology autopsy practice: post mortem examination in patients with traumatic brain injury. April 2010. Available at: http://www.rcpath.org/NR/rdonlyres/B00CE53A-4F48-40B1-9CA0-89FA2F8BC938/0/g097neuropathologyautopsypracticefinal.pdf. Accessed January 14, 2015.

2. Burton JL, Rutty GN, editors. *The hospital autopsy: a manual of fundamental autopsy practice*. 3rd ed. London: Hodder Arnold; 2010.

3. Esiri MM. *Oppenheimer's diagnostic neuropathology: a practice manual*. 3rd ed. London: Hodder Arnold; 2006.

4. Whitwell HL, editor. *Forensic neuropathology*. London: Arnold; 2005.

5. Klatt EC. *Robbins and Cotran atlas of pathology*. 2nd ed. London: Saunders; 2010.

6. Tadrous PJ. *Diagnostic criteria handbook in histopathology: a surgical pathology vade mecum*. Chichester, UK: John Wiley; 2007.

7. Finkbeiner WE. *Autopsy pathology: a manual and atlas*. 2nd ed. London: Saunders; 2009.

▌ Chapter 12
Decomposed Bodies

Introduction

Although the processes of decomposition begin at the moment of death, when considering the autopsy of the decomposed body one is generally referring to the body in which there are external and/or internal manifestations of putrefaction, adipocere formation, or mummification. Putrefaction is the breakdown of tissues in response to the action of digestive enzymes and microorganisms. Adipocere, also known as grave wax, is most often seen when bodies are immersed in water and is caused by the hydrolysis of fat. Mummification is the desiccation of tissues, typically seen when a body has lain in a dry environment. Any or all of these decompositional processes may be present in the same body. Mummification and adipocere formation retard putrefaction, but ultimately the body will proceed to skeletonization.[1] These forms of decomposition are not mutually exclusive, and different parts of the body may show different forms of decomposition.

The careful examination of a decomposing body often provides the pathologist with a cause of death. Nonetheless, these bodies pose their own specific challenges:

1. Examination of the body is physically unpleasant. Most pathologists are relieved to encounter such bodies only infrequently. Such bodies are most commonly encountered by pathologists examining the bodies of those who have died in the community. The odors produced during putrefaction, the presence of maggot infestation, and the degradation of the body render the examination unpleasant, but one should resist the temptation to perform only a cursory examination. The same principles of careful external examination followed by careful evisceration and thorough dissection of the organs that apply for nondecomposed bodies still apply to the decomposed, and although interpretation may be hindered by the process, this should never be considered a reason to perform a substandard examination.

2. Decomposition destroys the cause of death. As decomposition progresses, it inevitably destroys the body and, with it, ultimately the cause of death. With the exception of the lungs, which initially become heavier, the internal organs become lighter as decomposition progresses. Care must therefore be taken when comparing organ weights with standard tables. Nonetheless, with careful examination, a cause of death can be identified in many decomposed bodies. The discoloration of the skin that results from putrefaction can mask or mimic bruising, and a careful external examination is crucial, with particular attention paid to the neck.[1,2] Decomposition and insect predation may make it particularly difficult to identify wounds, and a careful external examination seeking trauma is essential. The pathologist who, for example, elects not to examine the back of the decomposed body risks not finding the fatal knife wound, with potentially serious medicolegal ramifications, not least for the pathologist.

Surprisingly, many natural diseases can be identified in a decomposing body. Coronary artery atherosclerosis, gastrointestinal tract hemorrhage in the form of blood or altered blood in the stomach and intestines, malignant disease, and cirrhosis may all remain identifiable macroscopically even when putrefaction is pronounced. The prostate and uterus are the internal organs most resistant to decomposition. These organs are rarely the seat of the cause of death, but their presence does assist the pathologist in determining the gender of bodies that are severely decomposed. Toxicological and histological examinations may also prove fruitful.

3. The processes of decomposition are confused with disease. Care must be taken not to confuse the appearances of decomposed but otherwise normal organs with those of disease.

4. Determining the time of death is challenging. The speed at which decomposition progresses is variable, but it depends on the ambient temperature and humidity of the environment in which the body lay and on the extent of any insect or animal predation. As decomposition progresses, it becomes more difficult to determine the date of death accurately, and it is advisable to be cautious.

This chapter presents the external and internal manifestations of decomposition, with a primary focus on putrefaction.

External Examination

The pathologist performing an autopsy on a decomposed body can expect to be asked the thorny question "When did death occur?" Various methods exist to assist the pathologist in the determination of the date and time of death. Consideration of these methods is beyond the scope of this book, and they are described in detail in other sources.[2-5] In bodies that have been refrigerated before examination, and as decomposition progresses, it becomes ever more difficult to determine the date of death. It may be possible to attain no greater degree of accuracy than a statement that death occurred sometime between when the deceased was last seen alive and the discovery of the body.

The speed at which putrefactive decomposition progresses is variable. Bodies lying in warm conditions putrefy more quickly than those in cold conditions. High humidity, insect activity, and animal predation accelerate putrefaction. Nonetheless, putrefaction progresses in a predictable fashion in temperate climes, as shown in Table 12.1.[1] The times given in Table 12.1 should be used only as an approximate guide. The author has seen

Table 12.1 Dating death from putrefactive decompositional changes

Days since death	Changes observed
0–1	Dependent postmortem hypostasis occurs. Rigor mortis develops.
1–2	Green discoloration of the anterior abdominal wall is noted, beginning in the right iliac fossa.
2–3	Bloating of the abdomen begins.
3–4	Venous marbling begins from bacterial decomposition of blood.
5–6	Abdominal bloating is established. Skin slippage and blister formation occur.
14	Marked bloating of the abdomen and scrotum is noted.
21	General softening of the tissues occurs. Eyes bulge.
28	Generalized blackening of the skin occurs. Skin liquefaction occurs.

bodies with marked bloating of the abdomen and scrotum, as well as extensive marbling, blistering, and skin slippage, for whom there were reliable witness statements that the deceased had been alive 24 hours before the autopsy. Why some bodies undergo such accelerated decomposition is not known, although antemortem septicemia has been suggested as an underlying cause.

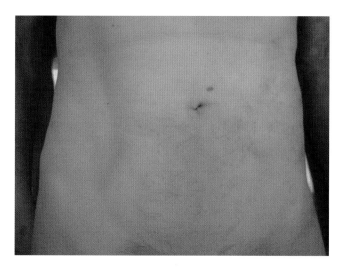

◀ **Figure 12.1a** Early skin discoloration
The earliest manifestation of putrefaction is green discoloration of the skin, caused by the bacterial conversion of hemoglobin to sulfhemoglobin.[6] This is typically seen in the lower right quadrant of the anterior abdominal wall first. This location is the result of the action of bacteria originating in the cecum, which is the portion of the large intestine that lies closest to the anterior abdominal wall.

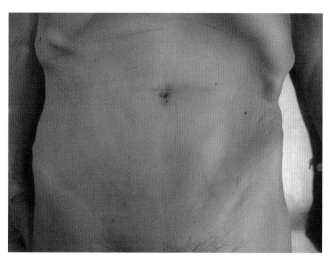

◀ **Figure 12.1b** Early skin discoloration

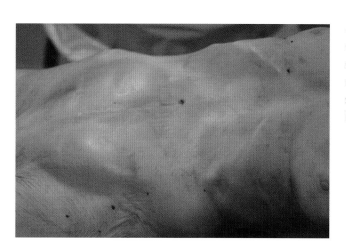

◀ **Figure 12.2** Skin discoloration
Green discoloration of the anterior abdominal wall spreads from the lower right quadrant to become more generalized. This green discoloration can render scars difficult to see, and therefore the skin should be inspected carefully.

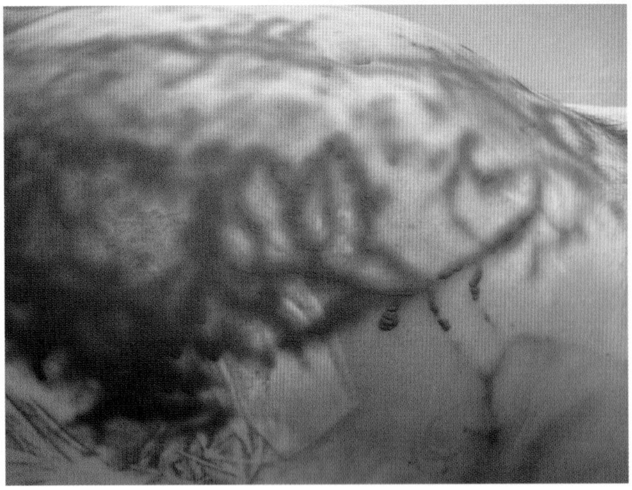

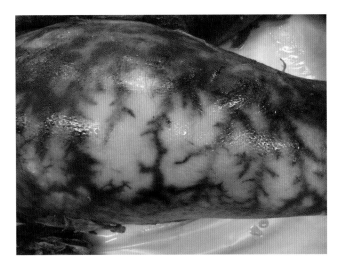

◀ Figure 12.3a Marbling

As putrefaction advances, and typically once the entire anterior abdominal wall has turned green, bacteria spread from the abdomen through the rest of the body through the vasculature. As they do so, they convert hemoglobin to sulfhemoglobin, resulting in a characteristic appearance of the skin that resembles marble.

◀ Figure 12.3b Marbling

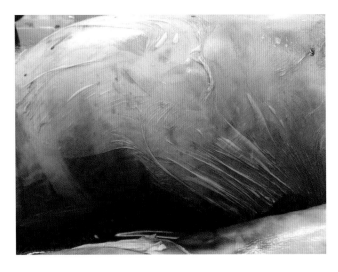

◀ Figure 12.4a Skin slippage

Putrefaction causes the epidermal layers of the skin to separate from the dermis, with a resulting appearance known as skin slippage. Five to 6 days after death, the epidermis can be wiped from the dermis with a sponge. This can aid identification of the body because tattoos appear more vivid when they are no longer masked by the epidermis (Figure 12.4b). Melanin resides within the epidermis, and so removal of this layer causes the skin of an individual belonging to a dark-skinned ethnic group to appear white. This artifact of decomposition should not be confused with vitiligo.

◀ **Figure 12.4b** Skin slippage

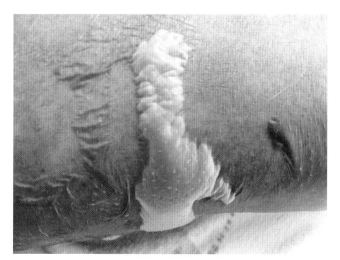

◀ **Figure 12.5** Skin blisters
The formation of blisters in putrefaction is usually associated with skin slippage. Fluid from the underlying decomposing tissue accumulates in large blisters on dependent parts of the body. Similar blisters are reported as being present in those who have taken a significant barbiturate overdose,[7] and so the initiate should be wary of using this feature in abstraction to verify that death has occurred.

223

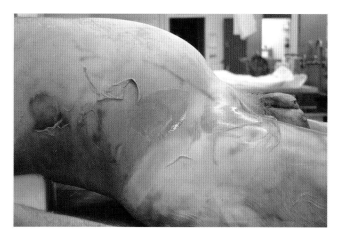

◀ **Figure 12.6** Bloating
The action of the microorganisms responsible for putrefaction results in fermentation and gas formation. As in life, the abdomen of the decomposed body may be distended by fat, feces, fluid, fetus, or gas. Gaseous distention of the abdomen begins some 2 to 3 days after death and is usually established 2 weeks after death. The anterior abdominal wall, and in men the scrotum, becomes obviously distended, taut, and resonant to percussion. The pathologist opening the peritoneal cavity in such circumstances is well advised to either hold his or her breath or open the cavity at arm's length. The sudden release of gases of putrefaction is not pleasant.

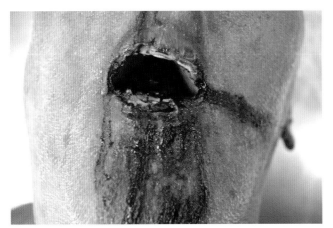

◀ **Figure 12.7** Purging

Putrefaction of the internal organs, coupled with raised intrathoracic and intra-abdominal pressure secondary to gas formation, results in the expression of blood-stained fluid from the nose and mouth. This process, known as purging, is frequently mistaken as a sign of trauma or hematemesis. Feces and urine may also be purged.

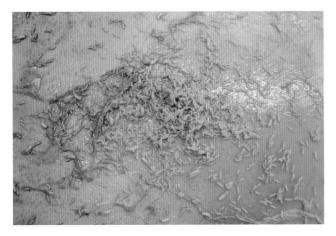

◀ **Figure 12.8** Insect predation

Insect predation is most commonly caused by maggots, the larval stages of bluebottles *(Calliphora vomitoria)* and houseflies *(Musca domestica)*. It is most commonly seen in the summer months and is least frequently seen in winter. Adult flies lay eggs in moist but not wet sites such as the eyes, nose, and mouth of the newly dead body and anywhere they can gain access once skin putrefaction begins.[2] Maggots secrete proteolytic digestive enzymes and may cause extensive tissue destruction.[2] It is not uncommon, when maggots are present, to discover that they have destroyed the eyes and tongue. Given enough time, the brain, neck structures, and organs of the chest and abdomen are similarly destroyed.

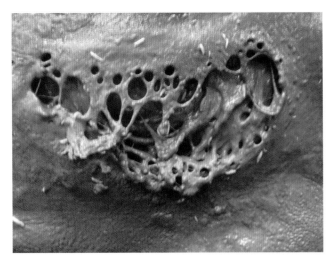

◀ **Figure 12.9** Insect predation

As maggots burrow into tissues, they leave small holes, usually 5 to 6 mm in diameter, in the skin. These should not be confused with gunshot wounds. Skin targeted by maggot predation should be inspected carefully: the adult flies will preferentially lay their eggs in open wounds. Examination of insects, larvae, and pupae may assist in determining the postmortem interval, but this is a highly specialized process that requires a forensic entomologist.

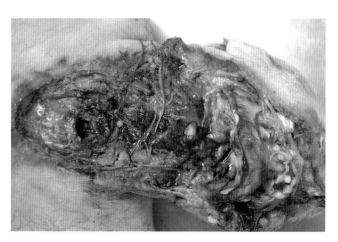

◀ **Figure 12.10a** Animal predation
Animal predation is less commonly seen than insect predation. Because most putrefied bodies are recovered from a home environment, the most common animal predators are domestic cats and dogs and rodents. Bodies found outdoors may have been predated by wild birds and animals. In this example, tissue destruction was caused by the deceased's pet dog.

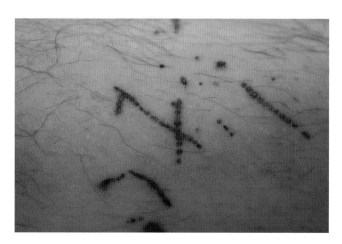

◀ **Figure 12.10b** Animal predation
Bodies recovered from water may have been predated by marine life.

225

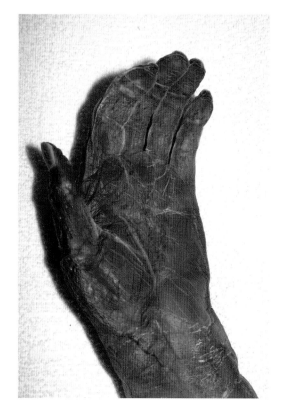

◀ **Figure 12.11** Mummification
Mummification occurs when the tissues of the deceased desiccate. All or only part of the body may be affected. The skin becomes dry, brown, and leathery. In a body that has widespread mummification, the internal organs appear dry and leathery and are much lighter than normal. The author has performed autopsies on mummified bodies in which the lungs weighed less than 20 g each.

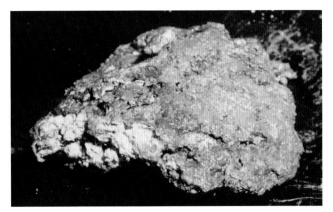

◀ **Figure 12.12** Adipocere
The bacterial hydrolysis of body fats in a cold, moist anaerobic environment leads to the formation of adipocere, also known as grave, mortuary, or corpse wax. Typically, the body or body part has been submerged in water or exhumed from a moist grave. This is a crumbly, waxy, gray-white substance with an offensive odor that replaces and forms a firm cast of subcutaneous and intra-abdominal fat. In appropriate conditions, adipocere formation begins within a month of death. The speed of adipocere formation increases as the temperature rises, although its formation is inhibited by extremes of temperature.[8]

◀ **Figure 12.13** Skeletonization
Skeletonization is rarely seen at autopsy by nonforensic pathologists, but it ultimately occurs as a result of putrefaction and the action of insect and animal predation. As with putrefaction, cold climates slow skeletonization, whereas animal predation and warm climates accelerate it.[2]

Internal Examination

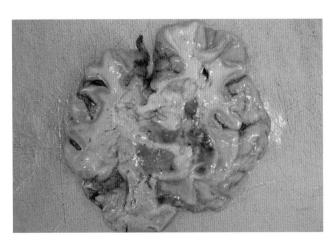

◀ **Figure 12.14** Early putrefaction of the brain
In the early stages of putrefaction, the brain takes on a green hue and becomes abnormally soft. With care, it can be removed intact from the skull, and slicing permits an assessment of its internal anatomy.

◀ **Figure 12.15** Advanced putrefaction of the brain
Advanced putrefaction turns the brain into a gray-green sludge with a foul odor that can be poured from the skull when the calvaria are removed. Clearly, in this condition, the internal anatomy of the brain cannot be assessed, but it is possible to confirm or refute the presence of intracranial hemorrhage. Ultimately, the brain is destroyed or consumed by insects and their larvae, and the cranial cavity may be found to be empty.

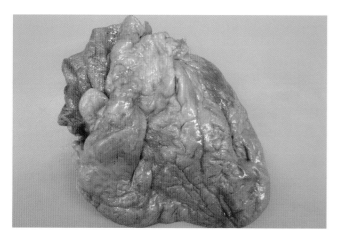

◀ **Figure 12.16a** Putrefaction of the heart
The putrefying heart is soft and flabby and becomes lighter as decomposition progresses. Coronary arteries, particularly when stenosed by calcified atheroma, resist putrefaction, and a diagnosis of significant ischemic heart disease may be possible even when the remainder of the body is markedly decomposed. The epicardial fat becomes greasy and liquefies, and holding the heart on a sponge makes it easier to manipulate. There may be gas formation in the epicardial tissues.

227

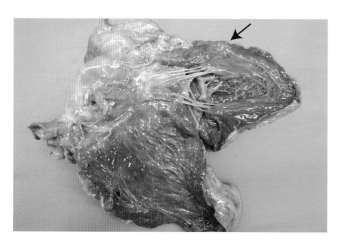

◀ **Figure 12.16b** Putrefaction of the heart
The myocardium appears abnormally soft and pale, features that should not be mistaken for myocardial infarction. Fibrosis (arrowed) and infarcts may still be visible.

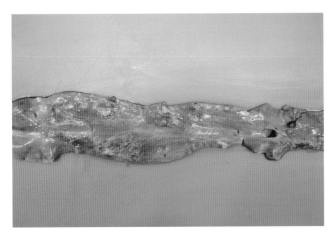

◀ **Figure 12.17** Putrefaction of the aorta
Putrefaction rapidly removes blood from the body, and the major vessels typically appear empty in the decomposed body. Decomposition results in a red discoloration of the vascular intima that, curiously, can make atherosclerotic plaques more readily apparent. On those occasions when an autopsy is performed within 24 hours of death, such red discoloration has been attributed to antemortem septicemia. The same inference cannot be drawn in the putrefying body.

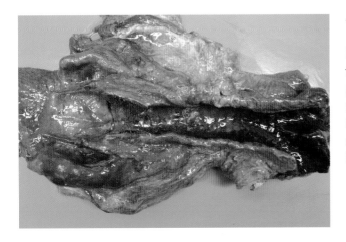

◀ **Figure 12.18** Putrefaction of the trachea and bronchi
It is common to find a slurry of gastric contents within the large airways at autopsy. This is the result of postmortem movement of gastric contents caused by moving and handling of the body, and it should not be interpreted as indicative of aspiration unless there is an accompanying inflammatory bronchoalveolar response histologically.

◀ **Figure 12.19** Putrefied lungs
In early decomposition, the lungs become heavy as fluids of putrefaction pool within them. This makes interpretation of their weight difficult and assessment for the presence or absence of pulmonary edema and congestion difficult. The cut surface appears black and increasingly jelly-like as putrefaction progresses.

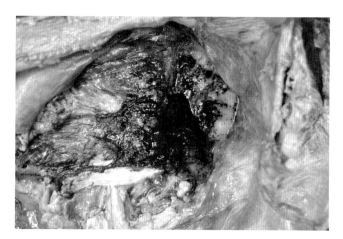

◀ **Figure 12.20** Putrefied spleen
The spleen rapidly undergoes putrefactive decomposition. Initially, the capsule and pulp appear black. As putrefaction progresses. the splenic pulp softens, often to the extent that when sliced, the substance of the spleen runs over the dissection board. This should not be confused with the diffluence seen in the septic spleen. Ultimately, little may remain of the spleen but a black sludge in the left upper quadrant of the abdomen.

◀ **Figure 12.21** Putrefied liver
As with other organs, the liver becomes lighter as it decomposes. Mold may be evident on the capsule, and the hepatic parenchyma becomes darker. Gas formation, results in the formation of innumerable bubbles within the substance of the liver and beneath its capsule. This should not be confused with gas gangrene of the liver caused by antemortem infection by organisms such as *Clostridium perfringens*.

229

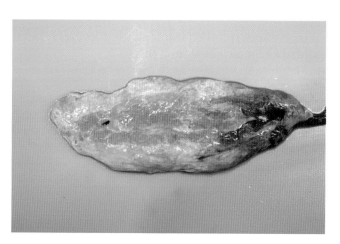

◀ **Figure 12.22** Putrefied pancreas
The pancreas is rich in proteases and lipases and very rapidly decomposes after death. As it does so, it appears gray, and there may be saponification of the surrounding fat. This should not be confused with pancreatitis.

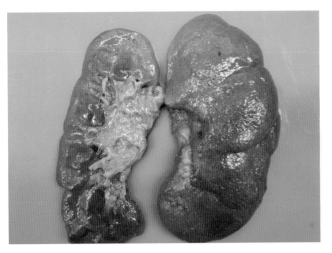

◀ **Figure 12.23** Putrefied kidney
The decomposing kidney is soft and pale. The capsule typically strips easily from the cortical surface, and any granularity of this may be lost. On slicing, the cortex appears pale brown, and the corticomedullary junction becomes increasingly indistinct.

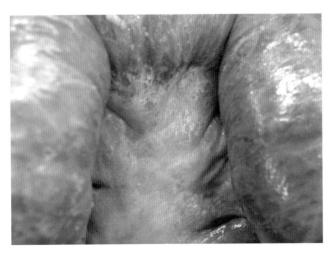

◀ **Figure 12.24** Gas formation in the mesenteries
Putrefactive decomposition results in gas formation in the mesenteries, which should not be mistaken for air emboli.

References

1. Burton JL. The decomposing body and the unascertained autopsy. In: Burton JL, Rutty GN, editors. *The hospital autopsy: a manual of fundamental autopsy practice.* 3rd ed. London: Hodder Arnold; 2010:292–307.
2. Saukko P, Knight B. The pathophysiology of death. In: Suakko P, Knight B. *Knight's forensic pathology.* 3rd ed. London, Arnold, 2004:52–97.
3. Henssge C, Knight B, Krompecher T, Madea B, Nokes L. *The estimation of the time since death in the early postmortem period.* London: Arnold; 2002.
4. Rutty GN. The estimation of the time since death using temperatures recorded from the external auditory canal. Part 1. Can a temperature be recorded and interpreted from this site? *Forensic Science, Medicine and Pathology* 2005;**1**:41–51.
5. Rutty GN. The estimation of the time since death using temperatures recorded from the external auditory canal. Part 2. Can a single temperature from this site be used to estimate the time since death? *Forensic Science, Medicine and Pathology* 2005;**2**;113–124.
6. Adachi J, Tatsuno Y, Fukunaga T, Ueno Y, Kogame M, Mizoi Y. Formation of sulfhemoglobin in the blood and skin caused by hydrogen sulfide poisoning and putrefaction of the cadaver [in Japanese]. *Nihon Hoigaku Zasshi* 1986;**40**:316–322.
7. Saukko P, Knight B. Poisoning by medicines. In: Suakko P, Knight B. *Knight's forensic pathology.* 3rd ed. London: Arnold; 2004:570–576.
8. Forbes SL, Wilson ME, Stuart BH. Examination of adipocere formation in a cold water environment. *International Journal of Legal Medicine* 2011;**125**(5):643–650.

Chapter 13
Histology of the Autopsy

Introduction

Long gone are the days when a full set of organ histological samples could be freely taken in every coronial autopsy case. Nowadays, the restrictions of the Human Tissue Act in the United Kingdom and the cost pressure on the coronial service have seen the taking of histological samples become much less common. This change, in addition to the diminishing number of hospital postmortem examinations requested, means that the exposure of the general pathologist to postmortem histology is limited. This is especially true of the histology of normal postmortem tissue.

This chapter introduces the reader to the normal appearance of tissues at differing postmortem intervals. The condition of postmortem tissue is determined by many factors. Most coronial cases are examined by autopsy within a few days of death. The postmortem interval and the environment in which the body subsequently lay affect the histological appearance of the tissues. The presence of antemortem disease such as fever and sepsis and certain drugs can accelerate decomposition. As putrefactive decomposition progresses, the histological appearance of tissues degrades, with loss of nuclear and then cellular detail. Eventually, architectural detail is lost, and the tissue becomes unrecognizable. The mucosa of the gut and the glandular epithelium of the exocrine pancreas are particularly prone to these changes.

This chapter also demonstrates a number of common disorders that have bearing on causes of death. Within the limits imposed by postmortem degradation, the histopathological features of disease are identical to those seen in surgical histopathology. Consequently, this chapter focuses on those conditions rarely encountered in specimens received from living patients. As with all autopsy observations, histological findings should be considered in the context of macroscopic findings and relevant clinical details.

231

Normal Autopsy Appearances

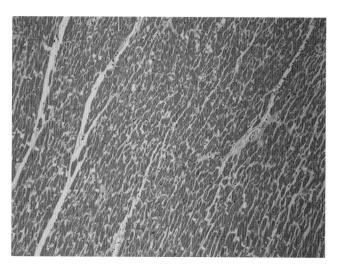

◀ **Figure 13.1** Normal myocardium
In the early postmortem interval, myocytes appear paler and more glassy. The nuclei appear to fade away. Contraction band necrosis associated with perimortem ischemia can be seen in patients who died of shock and in those who received cardiac defibrillation. These postmortem changes tend to occur uniformly throughout the myocardium and should not be mistaken for acute myocardial infarction.

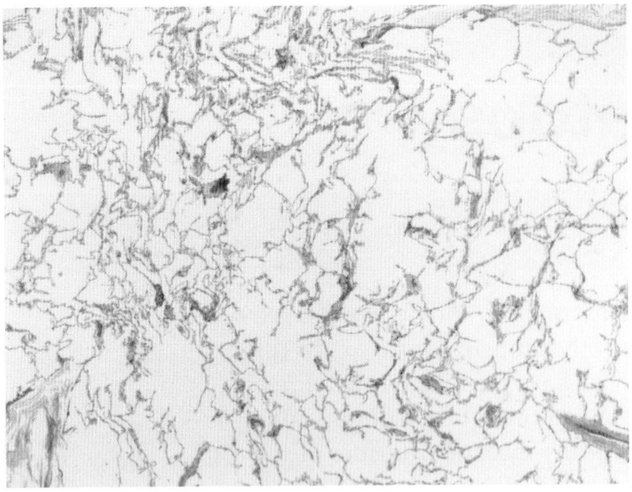

◀ **Figure 13.2** Normal lung

In the early postmortem interval lung, there is widespread desquamation of the bronchial and alveolar epithelium. The septa, however, remain intact, allowing architectural assessment. Alveolar macrophages remain visible. Postmortem lung can sometimes appear collapsed, and care must be taken not to overinterpret these findings as consolidation or atelectasis. Pulmonary edema, recognizable by the presence of a pale, eosinophilic glassy material within the alveolar airspaces, and pulmonary congestion are autopsy findings common to many modes of death.

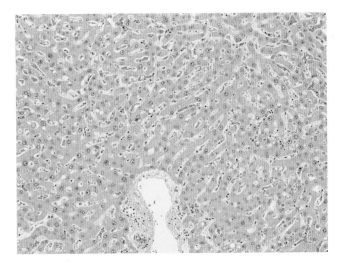

◀ **Figure 13.3** Normal liver

In the early postmortem interval, the hepatocytes lose definition of both their cell borders and nuclei. The nuclei appear to be "fading away." The cells appear more eosinophilic, granular, and vacuolated. Fibrous septa still remain, and the overall architecture can be easily appreciated including steatosis. Histochemical stains such Perls, Masson Trichrome, Reticulin, Periodic acid–Schiff diastase (PAS-D), and Orcein remain highly valuable. Small aggregates of lymphocytes are commonly seen within the portal tracts in postmortem liver, and these fragment readily. Caution must be exercised in interpreting this finding as hepatitis. Gas bubbles from putrefaction in the liver become more prominent as decomposition increases.

232

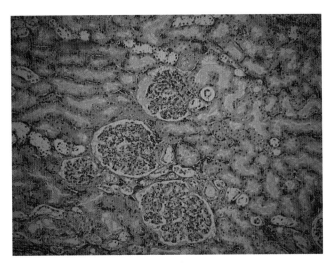

◀ **Figure 13.4** Normal kidney

Postmortem autolysis in the kidney results in diffuse pallor of the parenchyma and loss of nuclear definition. The outline of the tubules and collecting ducts can be seen in the early postmortem interval. Tubular epithelial cells detach from their basement membrane, and this should not be confused with acute tubular necrosis. Glomerulosclerosis and interstitial fibrosis can still be easily appreciated even with increasing postmortem intervals.

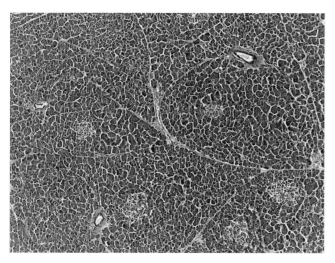

◀ **Figure 13.5** Normal pancreas
The pancreas undergoes rapid autolysis after death, and typically nuclear, cellular, and architectural details are quickly lost. Nonetheless, the presence or absence of fibrosis, hemorrhage, calcification, and fat necrosis can usually be determined.

Effects of Decomposition

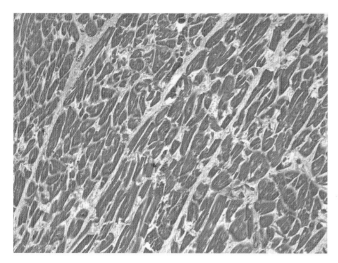

◀ **Figure 13.6** Decomposing myocardium
In the decomposed heart, the outline of the myocytes may still remain, but nuclear features are absent, giving the tissue a ghosted appearance. Such an appearance precludes the diagnosis of an early acute myocardial infarct. Ultimately, all architectural detail is lost. It is still possible in the decomposed heart to see fibrosis, and a full assessment of this should be made.

233

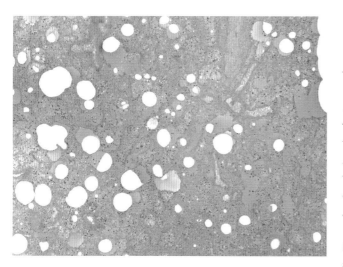

◀ **Figure 13.7** Decomposing lung
In early putrefactive decomposition, the epithelial layer is the first feature to be lost, but the outline of the alveolar septa can still be seen and emphysema can still therefore be appreciated. The respiratory epithelium in the distal airway can slough off and fill the airspaces. This artifact should not be mistaken for true disease. As decomposition progresses, the alveolar airspaces become distended with putrefactive fluids; this should not be confused with pulmonary edema or hemorrhage. Bacterial overgrowth in the airways, typically appearing as large basophilic colonies, is a common postmortem artifact and should not be mistaken for antemortem infection. The lack of associated inflammation is key.

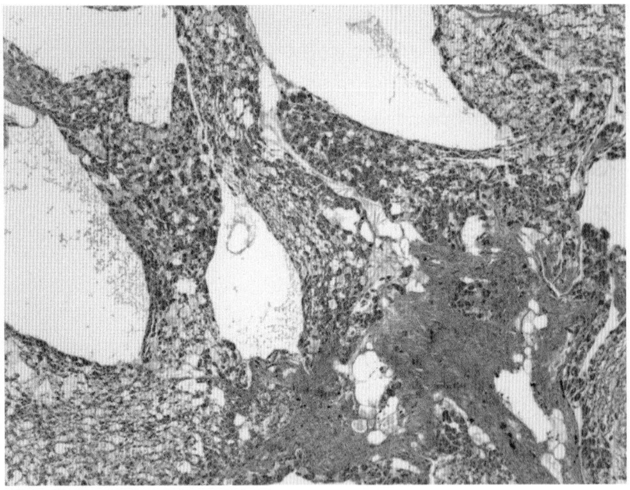

◀ **Figure 13.8** Decomposing liver

In the longer postmortem interval, the hepatocytes appear "ghosted," and the borders are only just visible. However, the overall architecture of the liver and the presence of steatosis, fibrosis, and cirrhosis can still be appreciated even in the more decomposed liver. The presence of inflammation or necrosis in such cases is difficult to determine and should not be overinterpreted. The portal tract structures are the most resistant to the effects of putrefaction.

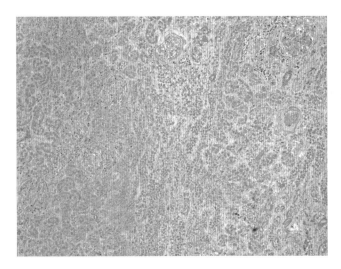

◀ **Figure 13.9** Decomposing kidney

With advancing putrefactive decomposition, there is total loss of the epithelium, but the connective tissue skeleton remains. Interstitial fibrosis and glomerulosclerosis are still detectable.

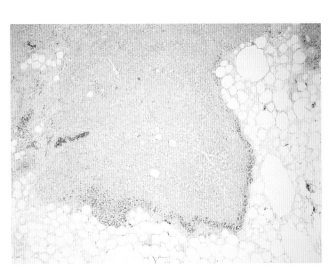

◀ **Figure 13.10** Decomposing pancreas

The pancreas can become grossly hemorrhagic as autolysis continues, and this can lead to incorrect diagnosis of acute pancreatitis by the unwary pathologist. As in many other conditions, the presence or absence of inflammation is of great assistance.

Pathological Features in the Cardiovascular System

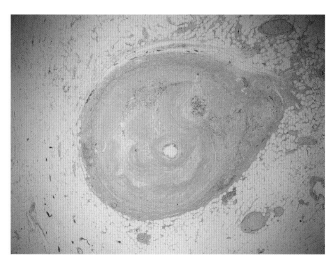

◀ **Figure 13.11a** Complicated coronary artery atheromatous plaque

Atheroma is composed of extensive lipid deposition in lipophages and cholesterol clefts that result from lipophage rupture. Atheroma becomes complicated or complex with the presence of calcification, thrombosis, or hemorrhage. These all serve to reduce the lumen of the vessel further. When the degree of stenosis is severe (>75 per cent, luminal diameter <1 mm), clinical symptoms of angina and sudden death are very likely.

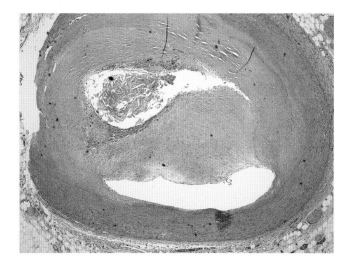

◀ **Figure 13.11b** Complicated coronary artery atheromatous plaque

235

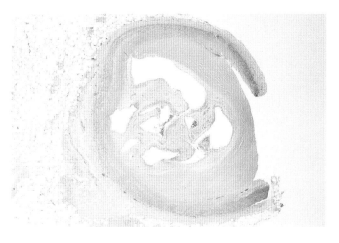

◀ **Figure 13.12** Recanalized coronary artery thrombosis

If a patient survives acute thrombotic occlusion of a coronary artery, the thrombus will gradually remodel and recannulate. This is best seen histologically because the remodeled lumens may be small.

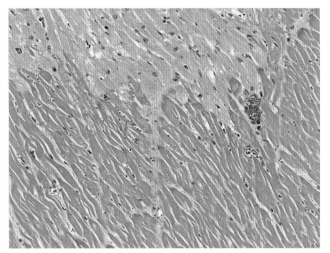

◀ **Figure 13.13** Acute myocardial infarct

If death occurs in the first 6 to 12 hours following acute occlusion of a coronary artery, the myocardium will have a normal histological appearance. Within 12 to 24 hours, the infarcted muscle fibers lose their cross-striations, their cytoplasm becomes more eosinophilic and irregular, and dark-pink wavy contraction bands appear. The contraction bands can be enhanced using a trichrome stain. At 24 to 48 hours following an infarct, the myocytes nuclei are lost, and there is an infiltration of neutrophils, initially at the periphery of the infarction. Reperfusion can cause focal interstitial hemorrhage. By day 3 to 4 following the insult, there is a heavier infiltration of neutrophils and macrophages into the infarcted tissue. The myocytes have undergone necrosis, and only the cell outlines are barely visible. It is at this point that the infarcted tissue is at its weakest and when myocardial rupture is most likely. After 7 days, healing of the infarct has begun. There is an infiltration of plump fibroblasts and hemosiderin-laden macrophages. New vessels are appearing. After 2 to 3 weeks, granulation tissue is prominent with collagen deposition and new vessel formation. The acute inflammatory infiltrate has resolved. By 2 months, a dense collagenous scar replaces the area of infarction.

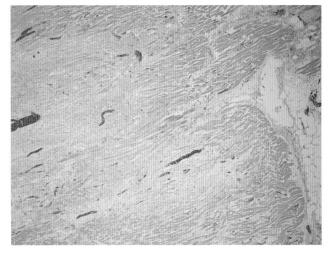

◀ **Figure 13.14a** Myocardial fibrosis

Myocardial fibrosis or scarring is the end result of myocardial injury. The interstitium is expanded by dense fibrosis that is partially revascularized. The muscle can also be replaced by adipose tissue, so-called "fatty metamorphosis." These areas are essentially nonfunctional. The architecture of fibrosis remains even with advancing decomposition. Patchy myocardial fibrosis is a common finding in those with coronary artery atherosclerosis. In the absence of coronary artery disease, its presence should alert the pathologist to the possibility of recurrent cocaine use.

◀ **Figure 13.14b** Myocardial fibrosis

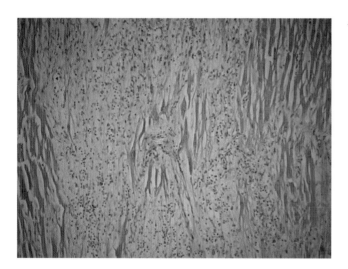

◀ **Figure 13.14c** Myocardial fibrosis

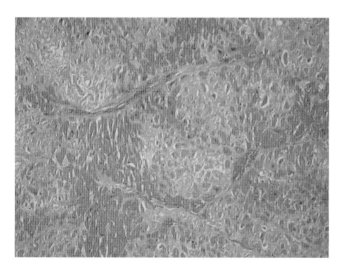

◀ **Figure 13.15** Cardiac amyloidosis
Myocardial histology showing widespread amorphous
pink matrix surrounding and replacing cardiac myocytes.
The features are those of cardiac amyloid, which may
be confirmed using Sirius or Congo Red histochemistry
stains. (Image courtesy of Dr. S. K. Suvarna.)

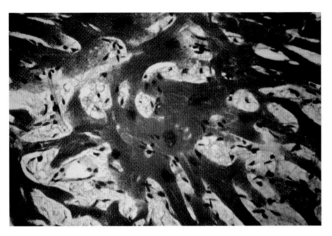

◄ Figure 13.16 Hypertrophic cardiomyopathy
Hypertrophic cardiomyopathy shows characteristic "myocyte disarray," particularly within the intraventricular septum. There is intense fibrosis surrounding the disorganized hypertrophic myocytes, which are described as having a branching or storiform appearance. This disarray leads to reduced ventricular compliance and intraventricular septal hypertrophy, eventually causing left ventricular outflow obstruction. If such a condition is suspected, either from the history or from the gross appearance, then the heart should be sent to a cardiac pathologist for assessment. Myocyte disarray is commonly found in normal hearts where the septum joins the free ventricular walls, and its presence at these sites should not be overinterpreted.

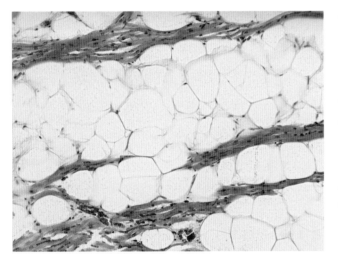

◄ Figure 13.17a Arrhythmogenic right ventricular cardiomyopathy
In arrhythmogenic right ventricular cardiomyopathy (ARVC), the wall of the right ventricle is thin and infiltrated by adipose and fibrous tissue. This gives the appearance of islands of myocytes trapped within adipose and fibrous connective tissue. The condition is linked with sudden death in young people. The amount of adipose tissue with the right ventricular myocardium normally increases with age, but the distinguishing feature of ARVC is the presence of increased fibrosis and dysplastic myocytes within the islands of myocardium.

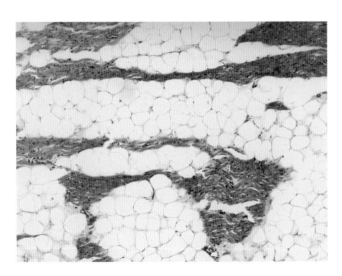

◄ Figure 13.17b Arrhythmogenic right ventricular cardiomyopathy

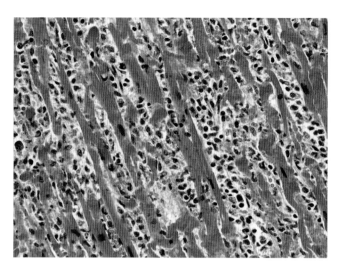

◀ **Figure 13.18** Viral myocarditis
Viral myocarditis is identified by the presence of an interstitial lymphocytic infiltrate with a few neutrophils and minimal myocyte necrosis. Because the inflammation can be both mild and very focal, numerous samples of the myocardium should be examined if the condition is to be confirmed or excluded. Early myocyte damage is indicated by increased eosinophilia and nuclear condensation. The most common agents are Coxsackieviruses.

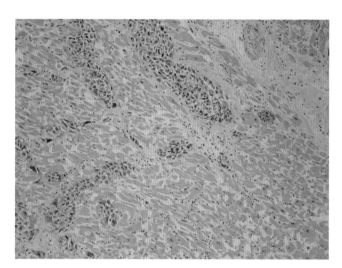

◀ **Figure 13.19** Adenocarcinoma of the lung metastatic to the myocardium
Cancers may involve the myocardium either through direct invasion or, as in this patient with adenocarcinoma of the lung, via hematogenous spread. (Same patient as Figure 13.34.) Metastasis to the heart is uncommon, and it is most frequently seen in patients with carcinomas of the lung and breast, melanoma, leukemia, and lymphoma. Diffuse myocardial thickening may result. Myocardial metastases predispose to sudden fatal cardiac arrhythmias.

239

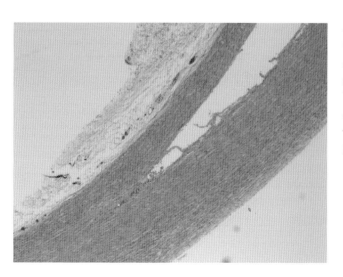

◀ **Figure 13.20** Aortic dissection
Cross-section of the aorta demonstrates the separation of the media with blood dissecting through it. The separation can create an apparent double lumen. The blood within the tear can be fresh and acute or organized from an older dissection. It is important to determine whether the dissection is new or old because this may have a bearing on the cause of death.

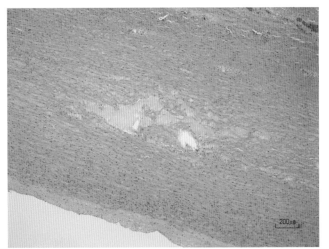

◀ **Figure 13.21** Cystic medial degeneration of the aorta

One of the causes of aortic dissection is cystic medial degeneration. This is seen in connective tissue disorders, most commonly in Marfan syndrome. The elastic fibers are disrupted by pools of mucinous ground substance. This is best demonstrated by a mucin stain. The mucin pools cause weakness of the vessel wall that leads to aortic dilatation and ultimately dissection.

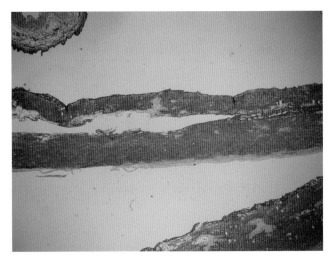

◀ **Figure 13.22** Marfan syndrome

In this photomicrograph, several pieces of aortic wall tissue are seen (hematoxylin and eosin stain) showing patchy degeneration of the medial compartment, in keeping with Marfan syndrome or connective tissue disease. A dissection plane is seen centrally within the media. (Image courtesy of Dr. S. K. Suvarna.)

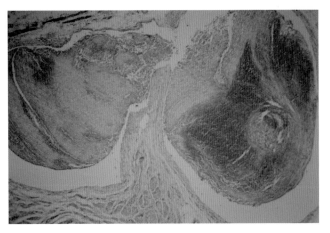

◀ **Figure 13.23** Thromboembolism

Thrombus and postmortem blood clot can be difficult to differentiate macroscopically. Antemortem thrombosis can readily be identified histopathologically by the presence of lines of Zahn. These are alternating layers of fibrin and erythrocytes within the coagulum. The periphery of thrombi becomes infiltrated with fibroblasts as organization occurs.

Pathological Features in the Respiratory System

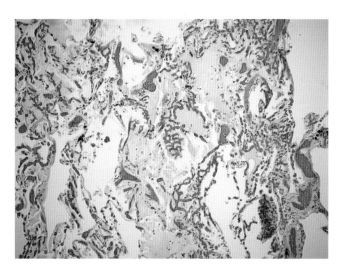

◀ **Figure 13.24** Pulmonary edema and congestion
In pulmonary edema, the alveoli become filled with an eosinophilic amorphous fluid. The background capillaries are often congested, especially where there is associated cardiac failure. Drug-induced hypoxia or apnea leads to eosinophilic protein-rich edema that fills the alveolar spaces, and this can be hemorrhagic. This fluid gives the characteristic froth in the airways in the postmortem setting.

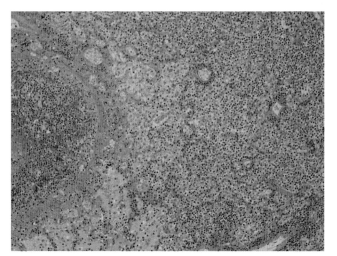

◀ **Figure 13.25** Bronchopneumonia
In bronchopneumonia, there is a heavy acute inflammatory infiltrate, mainly composed of neutrophils, that fills the alveolar spaces and causes consolidation. The inflammatory exudate is centered on bronchi and bronchioles, which themselves are filled with inflammatory cells.

241

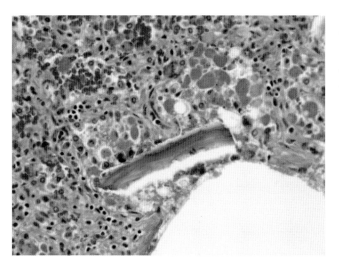

◀ **Figure 13.26** Aspiration pneumonitis
The passage of gastric contents into the airways can occur passively after death because of increased gas build-up in the gastrointestinal system and movement of the body. This is a common postmortem artifact and should not be mistaken for aspiration pneumonia or pneumonitis. If an individual has been alive at the time of inhalation of gastric contents, then a vital response develops. The diagnosis of aspiration pneumonia should be reserved for those cases in which food particles can be seen in the airways with an associated acute inflammatory cell infiltrate. Over time, a granulomatous response to foreign material may develop. Pulmonary edema and alveolar hyaline membranes may also be present.

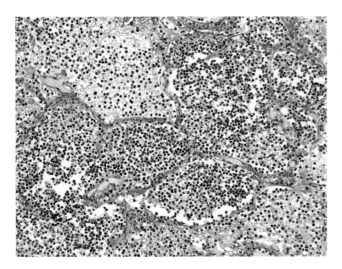

◀ **Figure 13.27** Lobar pneumonia
In lobar pneumonia, there is widespread infiltration of the alveolar airspaces by a cellular acute inflammatory cell infiltrate comprising neutrophils and macrophages. Unlike in bronchopneumonia, the infiltrate is not centered on the airways (whose lumens may remain free of inflammatory cells).

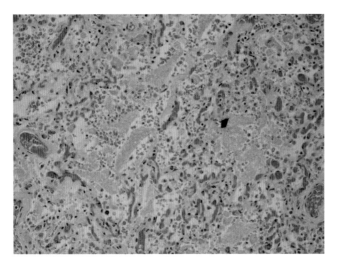

◀ **Figure 13.28a** Pneumocystis pneumonia
Infection with *Pneumocystis jiroveci* (a unicellular eukaryote) produces florid proteinaceous pulmonary edema, sometimes described as having a "frothy" appearance. Silver stains can be used to highlight the cyst walls. The infection occurs in immunocompromised individuals, and in those infected with human immunodeficiency virus, this form of pneumonia is an acquired immunodeficiency syndrome–defining illness. The causative organism may be referred to as *Pneumocystis carinii* in older texts.

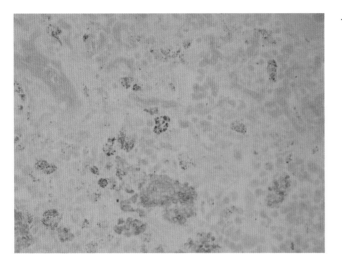

◀ **Figure 13.28b** Pneumocystis pneumonia
(Grocott stain)

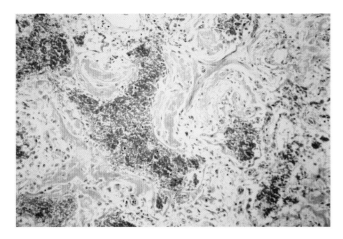

◀ Figure 13.29 Acute respiratory distress syndrome

Acute respiratory distress syndrome (ARDS) or "shock lung" is a nonspecific reaction to injurious insult on the lung tissue from a variety of conditions such as burns, infections, and trauma. The histological appearances are termed diffuse alveolar disease. In the initial phase, there is capillary injury with leakage of interstitial fluid into the alveolar space. The leaked proteins then form hyaline membranes. This membrane is gradually reabsorbed, and interstitial inflammation and fibrosis follow, if the patient survives, although mortality is high.

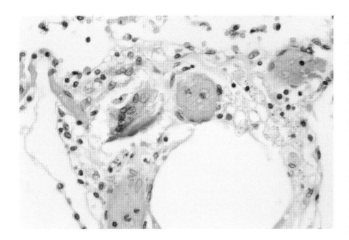

◀ Figure 13.30 Bone marrow emboli

Bone marrow emboli are commonly seen within the lungs at autopsy. They may occur because of trauma with the release of marrow from fractures, commonly ribs or long bones. In more severe trauma (e.g., explosions and gunshots), it is possible to see skeletal muscle. Commonly, however, there is no history of trauma or fracture and no evidence of such injuries at autopsy. In such cases, the pathogenesis of such emboli and their significance are unknown.

243

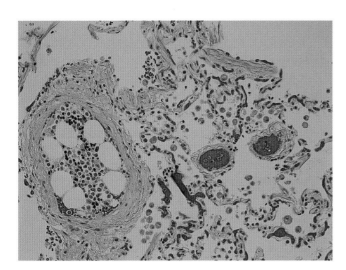

◀ Figure 13.31a Refractile emboli

So-called "intravenous drug user lung" describes a granulomatous pattern of lung fibrosis that occurs after years of intravenous drug use. The granulomas contain birefringent foreign material, often silica or talc, that has embolized to the lung following peripheral venous injection of impure "street" drugs. The fibrosis can be so extensive as to cause right ventricular hypertrophy. It is also common in the background lung tissue of long-term drug users to see microfoci of macrophages loaded with hemosiderin. This is thought to result from recurrent transient microhemorrhage and hemorrhage in pulmonary edema that occurs in intravenous drug users.

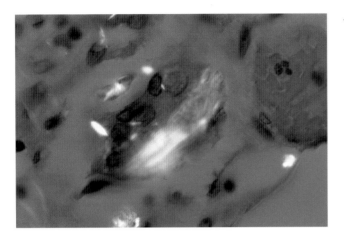

◀ **Figure 13.31b** Refractile emboli (polarized light)

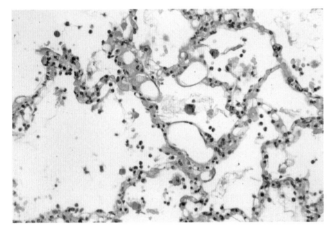

◀ **Figure 13.32a** Fat embolus

Fat emboli appear as cleared-out spaces within blood vessels; this appearance results from removal of the fat during tissue processing. As with bone marrow emboli, fat emboli occur because of trauma with the release of fat from fractures, commonly ribs or long bones. In deaths where fat embolus is suspected, samples of fresh lung tissue should be collected for frozen section and stained with Oil Red O. Formalin-fixed tissue that has not been processed to wax blocks can also be stained in this way, although it is more difficult to cut than fresh tissue.

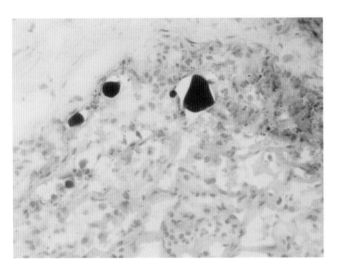

◀ **Figure 13.32b** Fat embolus (Oil Red O stain)

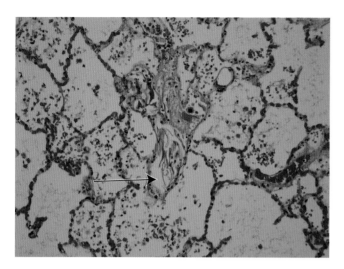

◄ Figure 13.33 Amniotic fluid embolus
Amniotic fluid emboli are rarely seen, but one should have a high index of suspicion in intrapartum deaths. The emboli are composed of hair, keratinous debris, and fetal squames, accompanied by mucin. Immunohistochemistry testing for cytokeratins is useful in reaching the diagnosis. (Image courtesy of Dr. S. K. Suvarna.)

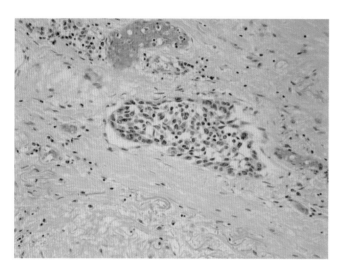

◄ Figure 13.34 Lymphangitis carcinomatosis
Lymphangitis carcinomatosis describes the spread of a carcinoma through the pulmonary lymphatic vessels. There is typically some associated chronic inflammation. It is most commonly seen in patients with carcinoma of the lung, breast, prostate, or upper gastrointestinal tract, but it may also be seen with carcinomas from other sites. This patient had adenocarcinoma of the lung. Obstruction of the pulmonary lymphatic vessels results in pulmonary edema. Symptoms may mimic those of pulmonary thromboemboli, and D-dimers may also be raised, leading to misdiagnosis in life. Consequently, in patients with a history of current or previous malignant disease and symptoms suggestive of pulmonary thromboembolus, a search for lymphangitis carcinomatosis should be made if no pulmonary thromboembolus is identified at autopsy.

245

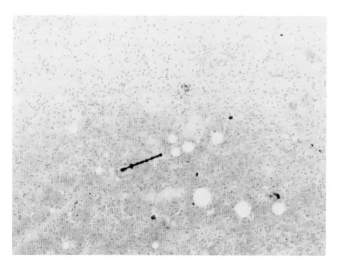

◄ Figure 13.35 Ferruginous bodies
Asbestos-related lung disease can take a number of forms. Inhaled asbestos fibers become coated with iron and calcium to form ferruginous bodies. The visualization of these features can be assisted by performing Perls Prussian Blue stain on a thick section. The inhalation of these fibers triggers a fibrogenic response mediated by macrophages and cytokines that results in asbestosis. Identifying the fibers can be laborious and time consuming, and numerous blocks from all the lobes, including peripheral lower lobe, are required.

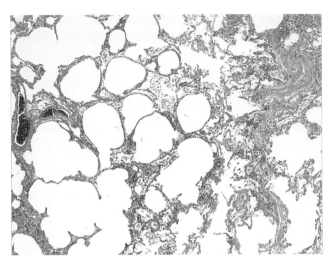

◀ **Figure 13.36** Emphysema aquosum
Emphysema aquosum is the term used to describe hyperexpanded and "waterlogged" lungs seen at autopsy as a result of drowning. Histologically, the alveoli are expanded, appearing spherical, and the interalveolar septa narrow and flatten with occasional tearing of the alveolar membranes. Elastic Van Gieson staining demonstrates tearing of the elastic fibers. There can also be rupture of capillary walls with localized hemorrhage. Foreign material within the alveolar spaces can be seen from aspiration.

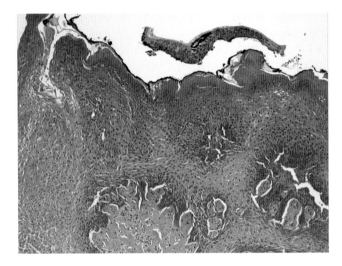

◀ **Figure 13.37** Soot in the larynx
Individuals who have died in a fire commonly have soot within the larynx. Histologically, there is deposition of carbon pigment on the surface epithelium. There may also be denaturation of the epithelium resulting from the action of hot gases. The presence of soot below the level of the vocal cords suggests that the deceased was alive when the fire started.

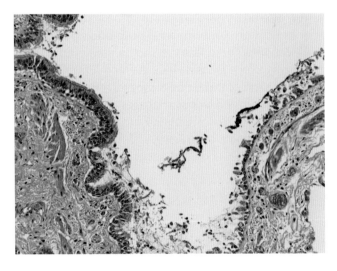

◀ **Figure 13.38** Sooted airways
Soot deposition in the airways in the absence of coagulative necrosis of the respiratory epithelium is highly suggestive of death by smoke inhalation, rather than thermal injury of the airways. This should be correlated with the levels of carbon monoxide and cyanide in the blood. Thermal injury causes coagulative necrosis with prominent nuclear streaming, and in such cases soot is often absent.

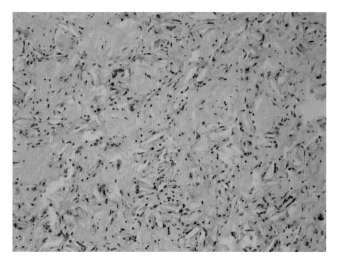

◄ **Figure 13.39a** Talc pleurodesis
Pleurodesis is a procedure performed to obliterate
the pleural space to prevent recurrent or persistent
pleural effusion or pneumothorax. This is commonly
performed by draining the pleural fluid, followed by
either a mechanical procedure (i.e., abrasion or partial
pleurectomy) or instillation of a chemical irritant into
the pleural space, which causes inflammation and
fibrosis. Talc pleurodesis is a commonly used form of
chemical pleurodesis. The talc causes an inflammatory
and fibrogenic reaction in which polarizable birefringent
crystals can be seen. These can sometimes extend into
the lung parenchyma.

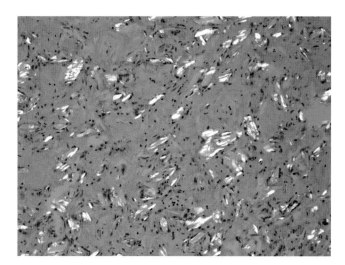

◄ **Figure 13.39b** Talc pleurodesis (polarized light)

247

◄ **Figure 13.40** Pleural plaque
Pleural plaques are common autopsy findings and
indicate significant (but not necessarily occupational)
asbestos exposure. Where asbestos-related lung
disease or mesothelioma is suspected, a sample of a
pleural plaque should be retained for histopathological
examination. Microscopically, the plaque comprises
dense hyaline fibrous connective tissue. There may be
associated chronic inflammation, and the plaque may be
focally calcified. The mechanism of formation is poorly
understood, and ferruginous bodies are rarely found
within plaques.

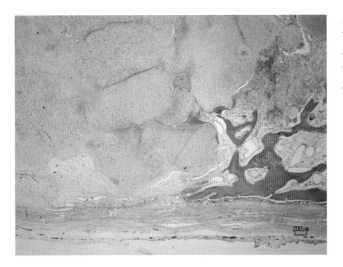

◄ Figure 13.41 Pulmonary chondroma
These chondromas are common benign solitary tumors found within the lung, typically in a subpleural location. They comprise a mass of mature hyaline cartilage. As in this example, osseous metaplasia is common.

Pathological Features In the Gastrointestinal System

◄ Figure 13.42 Infarcted intestine
Intestinal infarction can be identified by transmural necrosis with a heavy inflammatory infiltrate and severe vascular congestion. The submucosal and mesenteric vessels should be examined for the presence of thrombi and vasculitis. There may be associated mucosal perforation and serositis.

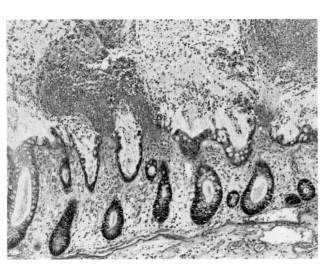

◄ Figure 13.43 Pseudomembranous colitis
Sometimes referred to as "antibiotic-related colitis," pseudomembranous colitis is the result of a toxin produced by overgrowth of *Clostridium difficile*. There is loss of the surface epithelium with a mucopurulent exudate that appears to erupt out of the crypts to form a volcanic-like cloud with a linear configuration of karyorrhectic debris and neutrophils that adheres to the surface. Superficial crypts show patchy necrosis and dilation. As the disease progresses, entire crypts become necrotic, and the picture resembles ischemic colitis.

Pathological Features in the Hepatopancreatobiliary System

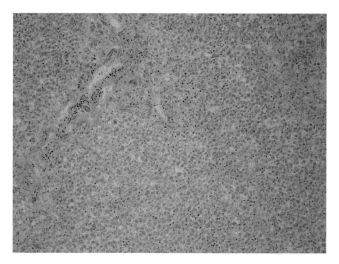

◀ **Figure 13.44a** Paracetamol (acetaminophen) poisoning

In early poisoning, the hepatocytes adjacent to the central veins become necrotic, and hepatocytes near the portal tracts remaining viable but show ballooning injury and steatosis. There is no associated inflammation. As the toxicity progresses, the liver cells undergo necrosis starting in zone 3 (centrilobular) and progressing to zone 2 and ultimately to complete fulminant liver necrosis and failure. These features, although typical of paracetamol poisoning, are not specific, and toxicology and virology tests are required to confirm the diagnosis.

◀ **Figure 13.44b** Paracetamol (acetaminophen) poisoning

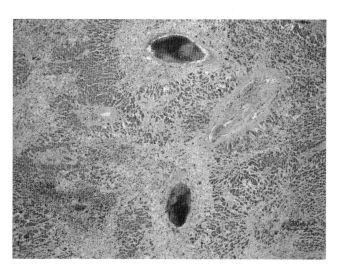

◀ **Figure 13.45** Budd-Chiari syndrome

This rare syndrome is caused by thrombotic occlusion of the venous outflow of the liver. In this example, thrombi are seen within branches of the hepatic veins, with resultant congestion and necrosis.

Pathological Features in the Lymphoreticular System

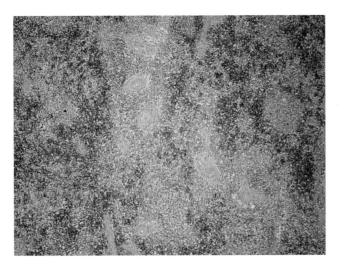

◀ **Figure 13.46** Congested spleen

Congestion is the most common cause of an enlarged spleen, and it results from both right ventricular cardiac failure and hepatic cirrhosis. The red pulp of the spleen becomes expanded, sometimes markedly.

Pathological Features in the Genitourinary System

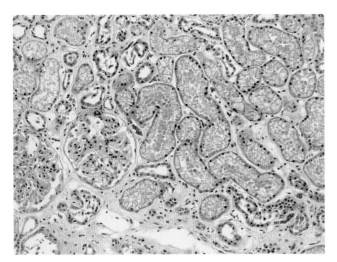

◀ **Figure 13.47** Acute tubular necrosis

Ischemia of the kidney results in acute tubular necrosis (ATN), and the tubules appear ragged. In the early stages, the proximal convoluted tubular epithelium swells and undergoes apoptosis with sloughing of cells into the lumen. The glomeruli and distal convoluted tubules are preserved. At this stage, the damage is reversible. As the condition progresses, all the tubular epithelium undergoes necrosis and sloughs into the lumen, thus causing tubular dilation and hyaline cast formation. ATN resulting from toxins (nephrotoxic ATN) usually has diffuse tubular involvement, whereas ATN resulting from ischemia (as in profound hypotension from cardiac failure) has patchy tubular involvement.

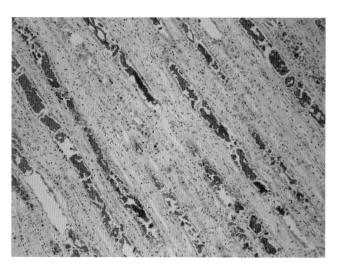

◀ Figure 13.48 Rhabdomyolysis kidney
Rhabdomyolysis is characterized by skeletal muscle cell necrosis and release of muscle cell components into the circulation, most notably creatine kinase and myoglobin. Complications include cardiac arrest and myoglobinuric acute renal failure. In the autopsy setting, the most common history is of an older person lying on the floor for a prolonged period following a fall. It is also common in cases of heroin injection. There is hypoperfusion that leads to acute tubular necrosis. Reddish-brown myoglobin casts are seen within the tubules. Intratubular casts are positive for myoglobin on immunoperoxidase staining.

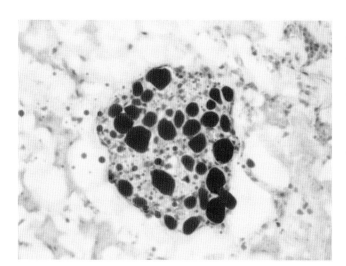

◀ Figure 13.49 Fat embolus in glomerulus
Where fat emboli are suspected, Oil Red O staining of frozen sections of the lung most commonly reveals the diagnosis. Fat emboli may pass through the lungs into the systemic circulation (see Figure 13.32) and become lodged in the microcirculation of other organs. In this patient, Oil Red O staining shows fat emboli within the glomerular capillaries.

251

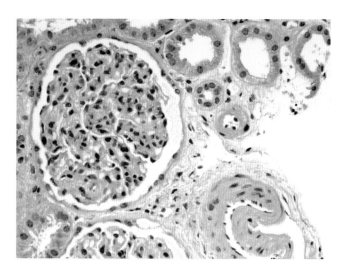

◀ Figure 13.50 Acute thrombotic microangiopathy
Acute thrombotic microangiopathy is the histologic correlate of disseminated intravascular coagulopathy. One of the common places to see the stigmata of thrombotic microangiopathy is in the kidney. Multiple small thrombi can be seen in the hilum of the glomeruli. The background vessels may show onion skinning if the process has a chronic component.

Chapter 14

Medical Procedures and Devices Encountered at Autopsy

Introduction

Medical and surgical devices and procedures are commonly encountered at autopsy. They may relate to the deceased's past medical history or be the result of recent medical and/or surgical intervention. In the latter case, the nature and position of the device may be of crucial importance in both determining the cause of death and in determining whether or not the intervention caused or contributed to death.

This chapter describes some of the commonly encountered medical devices and procedures. In all cases, careful documentation is required, and the pathologist should have a low threshold when considering whether or not photography is needed. Photographs of devices *in situ* can prove invaluable at inquest when the pathologist needs to prove that a device was correctly or incorrectly placed. Where autopsy reveals a discrepancy between the operative history and the actual placement of the device, photography should always be used.

A plethora of implantable medical devices exists, and it is not possible to consider them all in this chapter. It is helpful to keep copies of catalogues of such devices in the mortuary to aid in the correct identification of unfamiliar devices.

Certain medical devices are hazardous and pose a risk to the autopsy pathologist. Such devices include retained needles and other sharps, inferior vena caval filters, implanted defibrillators, and brachytherapy pellets. Although the presence of these devices should be known from the medical history before the autopsy examination, the medical history may be incomplete, and it is not uncommon for the pathologist to become aware that such devices are present partway through the autopsy. (The author has certainly had instances where the placement of an inferior vena caval filter became apparent only when it punctured his glove!) As a result, care is needed in every autopsy, irrespective of the history.

General Devices

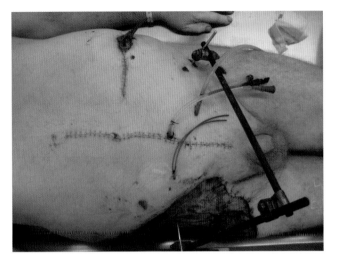

◀ **Figure 14.1a** Surgical drains

Surgical drains are commonly encountered at autopsy, and their type, site, and positioning should be recorded. Drains may take the form of corrugated rubber or plastic sheets (so-called "open" drains) or tubes (so-called "closed" drains). They may drain passively into a bag or actively under suction. Surgical drains rarely result in death, but the position of the drain tip should be recorded, as should the presence or absence of local complications such as perforation or obstruction of a viscus or vessel.

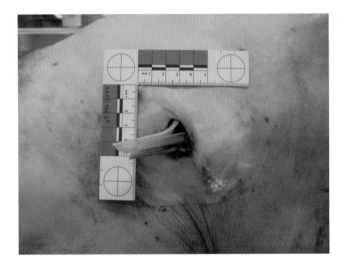

◀ **Figure 14.1b** Corrugated surgical drain

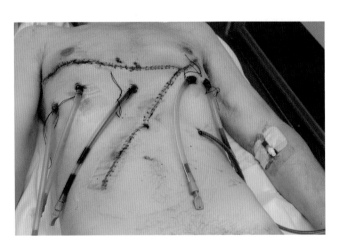

◀ **Figure 14.1c** Multiple surgical drains

Cardiovascular System

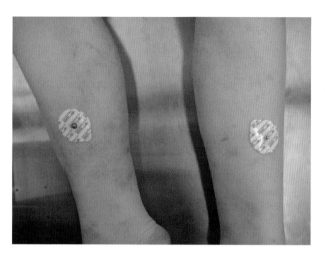

◀ **Figure 14.2** Electrocardiographic electrodes
Electrocardiographic electrodes are commonly seen at autopsy during external examination. Their placement may represent attempts to confirm life extinct or to take a 12-lead electrocardiogram, and hence their positioning can be highly variable. The position of the electrodes should be noted on external examination.

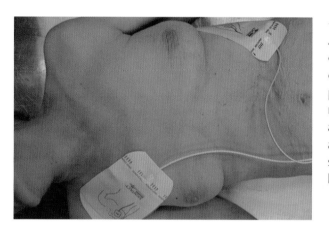

◀ **Figure 14.3** Automated defibrillator pads
Automated defibrillator pads are commonly encountered at autopsy, particularly when cardiopulmonary resuscitation has been attempted by paramedics in a community setting. The pads are large, rectangular, and self-adhesive, and each is attached to a lead. The positioning of the pads should be noted at autopsy. Typically, they are placed to the right of the sternum above the level of the nipple and on the left lateral chest wall below the level of the nipple.

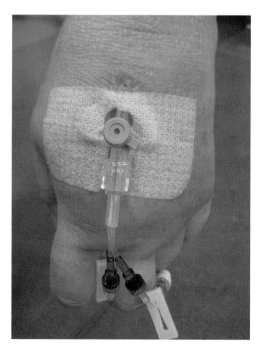

◀ **Figure 14.4** Intravenous cannula
Intravenous cannulae are commonly encountered at autopsy. These are venous cannulae used for the administration of intravenous fluids and drugs. Their location should be recorded on external examination. The port caps are color coded according to size. (For Venflon cannulae, from smallest to largest: blue, 22 gauge [G]; pink, 20 G; green, 18 G; white, 17 G; gray, 16 G; orange, 14 G.)

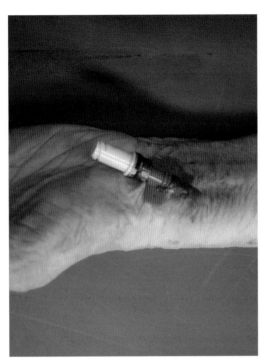

◀ **Figure 14.5** Arterial cannula
Arterial cannulae are used in the management of critically ill patients where there is a need for frequent arterial blood gas sampling and/or continuous blood pressure monitoring. They are most commonly sited in one or other of the radial arteries, but they may also be found sited in the ulnar, brachial, axillary, femoral, posterior tibial, or dorsalis pedis arteries.

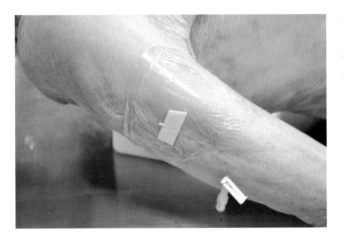

◀ **Figure 14.6** Subcutaneous butterfly needle
Butterfly needles are used for the subcutaneous administration of fluids in patients in whom intravenous access cannot be obtained. They are typically found in patients receiving end-of-life care.

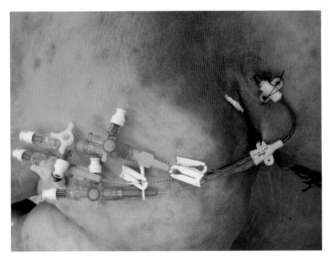

◀ **Figure 14.7** Central venous catheter
Central venous catheters ("central lines") are used to deliver large volumes of fluid and/or irritant drugs directly into the central venous circulation. They are also used to monitor central venous pressure or temporarily for hemodialysis. The lines typically have two or more channels and are located in the anterior triangle of the neck, below the clavicle, or in the groin. When placed in the neck, these lines are typically associated with hemorrhage into the strap muscles. Their position should be recorded. Where there are concerns of sepsis of uncertain origin, the tip of the catheter can be retained for microbiological examination.

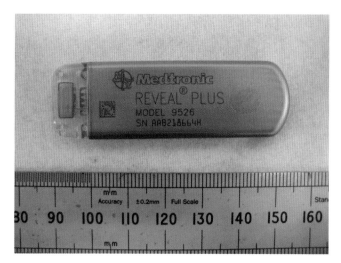

◀ **Figure 14.8** Insertable cardiac monitor
In patients with intermittent or paroxysmal dysrhythmias or arrhythmias, it is possible that investigations such as 24- or 48-hour monitoring may not detect the problem if the arrhythmia does not occur during the monitoring period. This poses a challenge to diagnosis, and so in some patients a small device is inserted under the skin in the same location as a pacemaker to sense the cardiac electrical activity continuously. Such devices can be distinguished from pacemakers or Implantable cardioverter-defibrillators because they do not have wires running into the heart. Interrogation of an insertable cardiac monitoring (Reveal, Medtronic, Minneapolis, MN) device may prove useful in identifying the rhythm at the time of death.

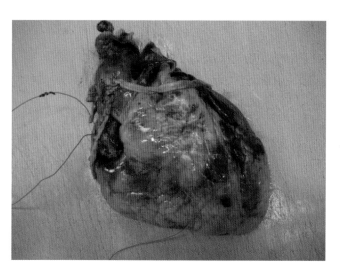

◀ **Figure 14.9** Temporary pacing wires
Temporary pacing wires may be endocardial or epicardial. Endocardial pacing wires are sited via cannulation of a central vein. Epicardial pacing wires, shown here, are sited during cardiac surgery. As the name suggests, they are embedded into the epicardial surface of the heart, and they typically emerge below the xiphisternum, alongside surgical drains.

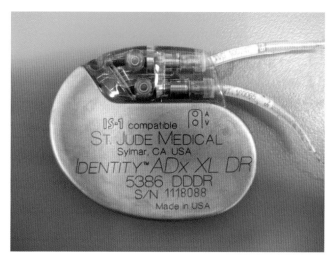

◀ **Figure 14.10a** Permanent pacemaker
Cardiac pacemakers are commonly found at autopsy. They can be palpated as a box beneath the clavicle and are associated with a subclavicular scar from insertion. There are many variants, some of which have wires that travel to only one chamber of the heart, whereas other pacemakers pace both the atrium and the ventricle.

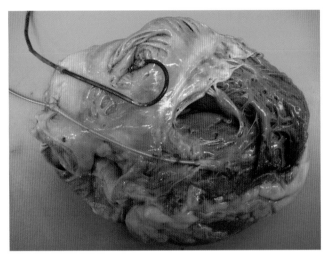

◀ **Figure 14.10b** Permanent pacemaker
The wires travel under the skin, thence to the superior vena cava and the right side of the heart. The pathologist should note whether the wires are correctly sited in the chambers and whether they have penetrated the wall of the heart.

◀ **Figure 14.11** Implantable defibrillator
Implantable defibrillators (or implantable cardioversion devices), unlike pacemakers, not only maintain cardiac rhythm but also are able to cardiovert if a potentially lethal arrhythmia occurs. Such devices are typically larger than pacemakers and pose a risk to mortuary staff because cutting the wires may cause the device to deploy a potentially fatal shock.

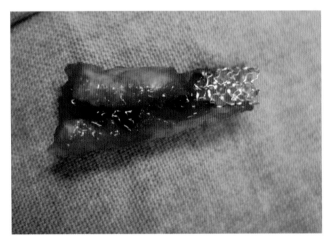

◀ **Figure 14.12** Stented coronary artery
Coronary artery stents are metal mesh stents used in the treatment of coronary artery atherosclerosis. Stent placement may be complicated by perforation, dissection, or thrombosis of the coronary artery, and the presence or absence of such complications should be noted at autopsy. The stent may be examined either by opening it longitudinally with artery scissors or by retaining the stented portion of the artery, fixing it, and then embedding it in methylmethacrylate resin and taking sections with a diamond saw. In either case, the deployment and patency of the stent and the presence or absence of complications should be recorded. (Image courtesy of Dr. S. K. Suvarna.)

◀ Figure 14.13a Artificial heart valves
A range of cardiac valves is present, comprising the moderate twin-metal prostheses, as well as more "vintage" tilting discs and ball-in-cage styles. The latter elements were more likely to be prone to thrombosis onto the grafts, cause significant hemolysis, or be associated with variable prosthesis failure. The modern twin-leaflet device and tissue prosthesis produce a functional equivalency to a normal valve with a relatively low risk of complications. A tissue valve with trileaflet architecture is also present, derived from animal tissues. (Image courtesy of Dr. S. K. Suvarna.)

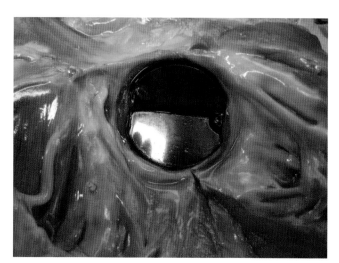

◀ Figure 14.13b Artificial heart valves
Mechanical valves have a longer life span but require life-long anticoagulation because of the significant increased risk of thrombus formation. A variety of problems can complicate prosthetic heart valves: thrombosis, infections, structural failure, and dehiscence leading to paravalvular leakage. There are many different types, but two of the most common are the hinged valves or the ball and ring values (so-called Starr-type).

259

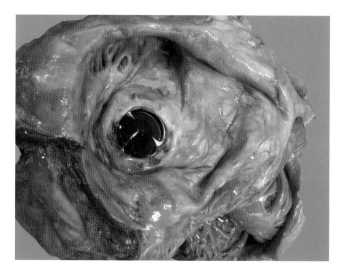

◀ Figure 14.13c Artificial heart valves
Courtesy of Dr. S. K. Suvarna.

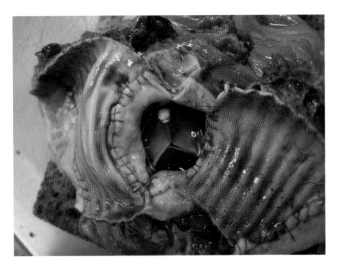

◀ **Figure 14.14a** Porcine valves
Tissue valves can be derived from either cadaveric human grafts or porcine xenografts. The valves consist of the donor valve grafted onto a metal stent. The main advantage of these bioprostheses is the lack of need for continued anticoagulation. However, the valves have a limited life span of 5 to 10 years because of wear and calcification.

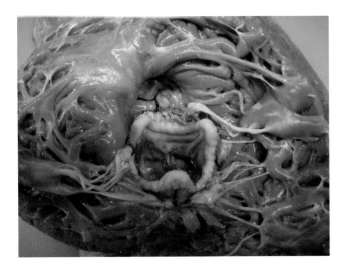

◀ **Figure 14.14b** Porcine valves

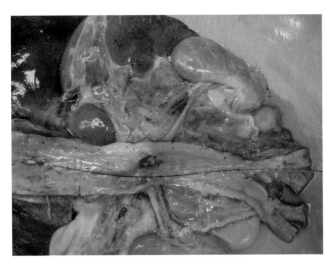

◀ **Figure 14.15** Intra-aortic balloon pump
Intra-aortic balloon pumps are used in the management of critically ill patients. They are cylindrical polyethylene balloons and are placed to lie in the descending thoracic and abdominal aorta. The pump operates via a counterpulsation mechanism, collapsing in systole (facilitating cardiac output via the creation of a vacuum) and inflating in diastole (facilitating coronary artery blood flow). The balloon is typically filled with helium.

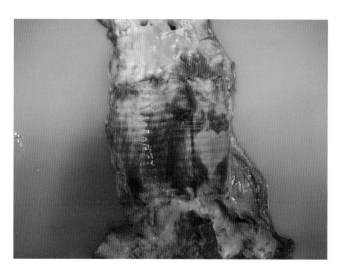

◀ **Figure 14.16** Aortic graft

Aortic grafts are commonly encountered at autopsy and are used in the repair of aortic aneurysms. In open repairs of the aorta, grafts composed of polyethylene terephthalate (Dacron) are often used, and these remain the most common form of grafts encountered at autopsy. An example of such a graft is shown here. In recent years, endovascular repair has become more frequent, and in such repairs a fabric graft supported by a metal mesh stent is used.

◀ **Figure 14.17a** Endovascular stent

Endovascular stents are increasingly used in the repair of abdominal aortic aneurysms. At autopsy, they are found within the lumen of the vessel and comprise a series of metal struts that support a fabric lining.

261

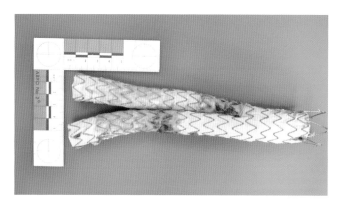

◀ **Figure 14.17b** Endovascular stent

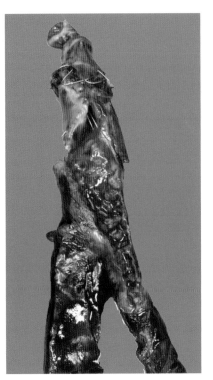

◀ **Figure 14.18** Greenfield filter

Greenfield (or inferior vena cava) filters typically comprise a conical series of wires that are anchored to the wall of the inferior vena cava by a series of sharp hooks. They are used in the management of patients with venous thromboembolus, particularly where anticoagulation is contraindicated or where there is a risk of recurrent thromboembolus. An indication of the presence of such a filter is frequently absent from the available clinical history, and these filters therefore pose a significant sharps hazard to the autopsy pathologist. The position of the filter and the presence or absence of any enmeshed thrombus should be noted. Inferior vena cava filters may be complicated by perforation of the inferior vena cava, embolization of the filter to the heart or pulmonary vasculature, and filter fracture. (Image courtesy of Dr. S. K. Suvarna.)

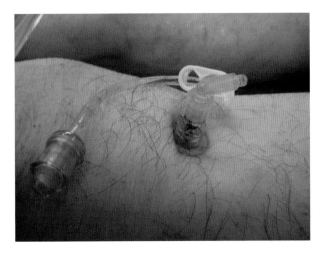

◀ **Figure 14.19a** Intraosseous needle

Intraosseous needles are used to provide immediate emergency access to the venous system for the administration of drugs and fluids, particularly when siting a peripheral intravenous cannula is difficult or impossible. Their use has become markedly more common since 2010. Typically, these needles are sited in the shin, with the needle penetrating the tibia, although other accessible bony sites (e.g., the head of the humerus) may be used.

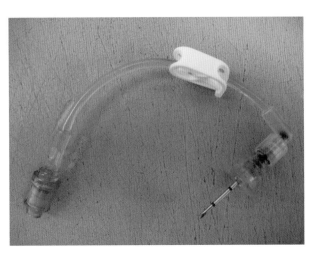

◀ **Figure 14.19b** Intraosseous needle

Respiratory System

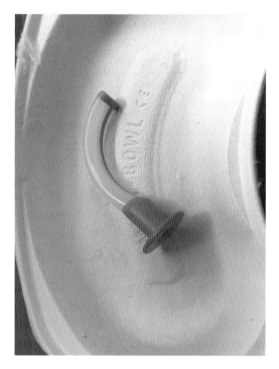

◀ **Figure 14.20** Guedel airway
Guedel (oropharyngeal) airways are used to help maintain the airway by preventing the tongue from covering the epiglottis and are commonly encountered in individuals in whom basic life support has been administered. They come in a variety of sizes. Improper sizing may result in closure of the glottis or bleeding into the airway. Oropharyngeal airways do not protect against aspiration of gastric contents.

◀ **Figure 14.21a** Nasopharyngeal airway
Nasopharyngeal airways are inserted via the nostril into the oropharynx. The flared end serves to guide insertion. Insertion of a nasopharyngeal airway into an individual with a basal skull fracture may result in direct intrusion of the device into the brain. Nasopharyngeal airways do not protect against aspiration of gastric contents.

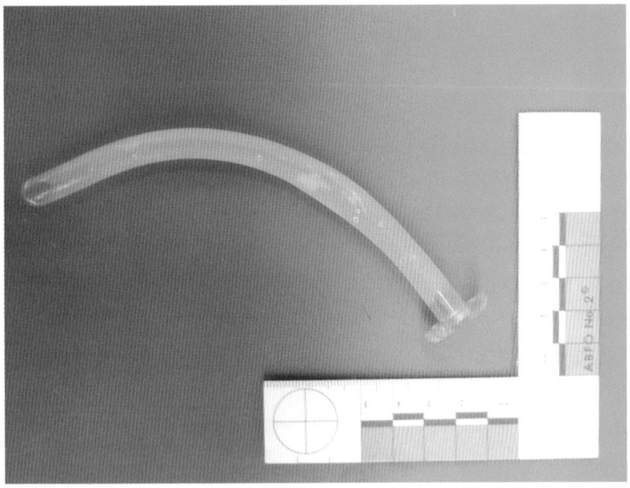

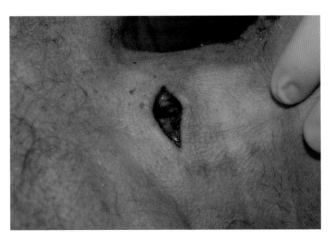

◀ **Figure 14.21b** Nasopharyngeal airway

◀ **Figure 14.22** Endotracheal tube
Endotracheal tubes are catheters that are inserted into the trachea via either the mouth (orotracheal) or nose (nasotracheal). These curved tubes come in a variety of sizes and are typically made of polyvinyl chloride. The tube may or may not have an inflatable cuff near the distal end that serves to anchor the tube in the trachea and prevent aspiration of gastric contents, blood, and other secretions. The position of the tube should be noted, to ensure that it has been correctly placed in the trachea rather than the esophagus, and the status of the cuff should also be noted.

◀ **Figure 14.23a** Tracheostomy and tracheostomy tube
Tracheostomies are performed to secure the airway in individuals with severe facial trauma, head and neck cancers, and severe acute angioedema of the larynx. A horizontal incision 20 to 30 mm in length is made over the anterior aspect of the trachea below the cricoid cartilage.

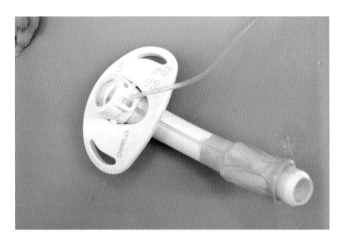

◀ **Figure 14.23b** Tracheostomy and tracheostomy tube

Tracheostomy tubes are curved plastic tubes in various sizes that can be placed through the tracheostomy to maintain the airway.

◀ **Figure 14.24** Airway stents

Stents can be placed into the airway to relieve obstruction or collapse resulting from strictures, external masses, tracheomalacia, or bronchomalacia. They come in a variety of shapes and sizes and may be made of plastic or metal mesh.

265

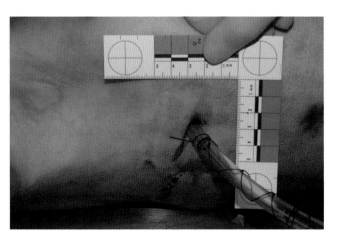

◀ **Figure 14.25** Chest drain

Chest drains are used to drain pneumothoraces and fluid collections in the pleural cavity. They consist of a plastic tube inserted between the ribs, usually in the midaxillary line. The tube is typically secured in place with the aid of a purse-string suture. At autopsy, the pathologist should note whether or not the tube has been correctly placed and look for evidence of perforation of the heart, lungs, or major vessels by the tube or the trocar used to insert the tube.

Gastrointestinal System

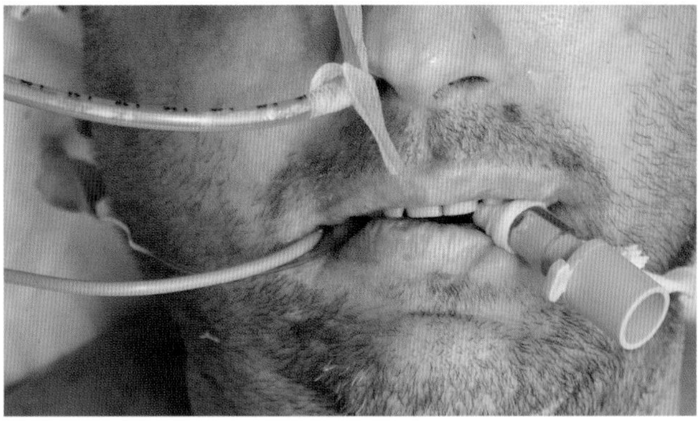

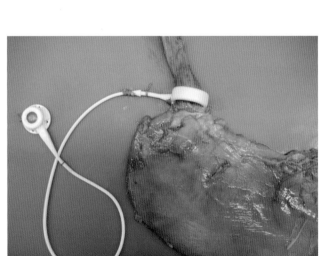

◀ Figure 14.26 Nasogastric tube

Nasogastric tubes may be placed to relieve gastrointestinal obstruction or to provide temporary enteral nutrition and drugs to patients who cannot swallow. They are narrow-bore tubes typically made of polyurethane or silicone. The tip of the tube should lie within the stomach. At autopsy, the pathologist should check that the tube has been correctly placed. Erroneous placement of the tube into the trachea with subsequent enteral feeding results in aspiration pneumonia. Placement of the tube in patients with a base of skull fracture can result in intrusion of the tube into the brain.

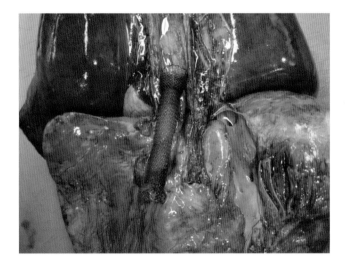

◀ Figure 14.27 Esophageal stent

Patients who have inoperable cancer of the esophagus or gastroesophageal junction may undergo the endoscopic insertion of a metal mesh stent. This is a palliative procedure intended to maintain patency of the esophagus and allow the patient to swallow. The position of the stent should be noted.

◀ Figure 14.28 Gastric band

Gastric bands are used in the surgical management of severe obesity. They comprise an inflatable balloon that is positioned around the abdominal portion of the esophagus connected to a port that is sited in the subcutaneous tissue of the anterior abdominal wall.

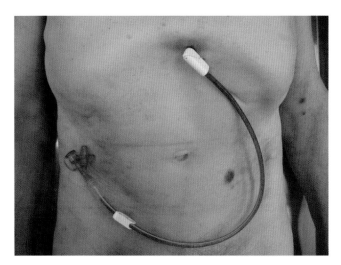

◀ **Figure 14.29** Percutaneous endoscopic gastrostomy tube

Percutaneous endoscopic gastrostomy (PEG) tubes are used to provide long-term enteral nutrition to those who cannot eat as a result of dementia, stroke, or other neurological disorder. The tube is held in place by a button, which should lie firmly against the wall of the stomach. A flange holds the tube in place and the stomach against the abdominal wall. The placement of PEG tubes can be complicated by wound infection, perforation of other organs including the esophagus and transverse colon, aspiration pneumonitis, gastrostomy leakage, peritonitis, and tube migration.[1]

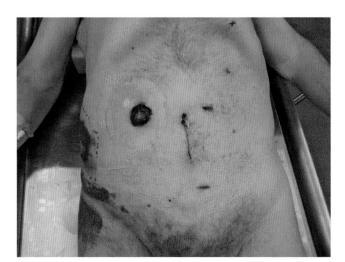

◀ **Figure 14.30** Ileostomy

An ileostomy is created when the end of the small intestine, or a small intestinal loop, is brought to the skin to allow the small intestinal contents to drain into a pouch stuck to the skin. An ileostomy is typically located in the right iliac fossa and may have a single (as shown here) or double-barrelled lumen. At autopsy, the pathologist should check that the bowel is securely attached to the skin circumferentially and that the bowel is viable.

267

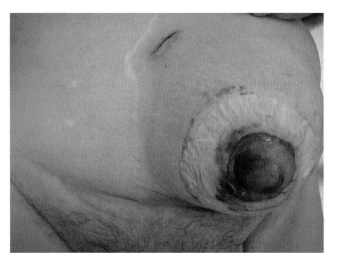

◀ **Figure 14.31** Colostomy

A colostomy is created when the end of the large intestine, or a large intestinal loop, is brought to the skin to allow feces to drain into a pouch stuck to the skin. A colostomy is typically located in the left iliac fossa and may have a single (as shown here) or double-barrelled lumen. At autopsy, the pathologist should check that the bowel is securely attached to the skin circumferentially and that the bowel is viable. In double-barrelled colostomies, only the proximal opening is functioning. The distal opening is effectively a mucous fistula.

◀ Figure 14.32 Capsule endoscope
Capsule endoscopy is used to visualize disease within the small intestine. After taking a bowel preparation solution to clear the intestine, the patient swallows the capsule endoscope, which contains a camera, battery, light, and transmitter. Data are collected by sensors attached to the abdominal wall. The capsule endoscope, shown here, is typically the size of a large vitamin pill.

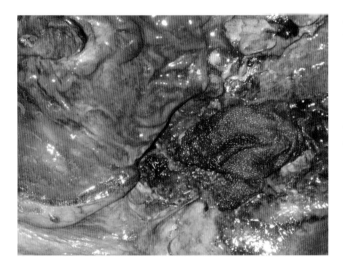

◀ Figure 14.33 Absorbable hemostat (Surgicel)
Surgicel (Ethicon, Somerville, NJ) is a hemostatic agent made from a cellulose polymer. It is used to control bleeding and may be found at several operative sites. It has the appearance of cloth or gauze and comes in a variety of sizes, but care should be taken not to confuse it with surgical swabs. If in doubt, retain and/ or photograph the material so that it may be accurately identified by the operating surgeon.

Hepatopancreatobiliary System

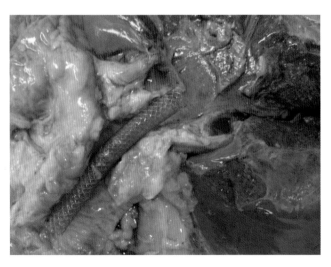

◀ Figure 14.34 Biliary stent
In patients with gallstones or tumor obstructing the common bile duct, a stent may be placed to relieve obstructive jaundice. These stents commonly have a "pig-tail" appearance, with the proximal and/or distal ends curling back in a loop like a pig's tail. The Zimmon biliary stent (Cook Medical, Bloomington, IN) is an example of such a stent. Metal mesh stents and straight, C-shaped, or V-shaped plastic stents may also be found in the common bile duct.[2]

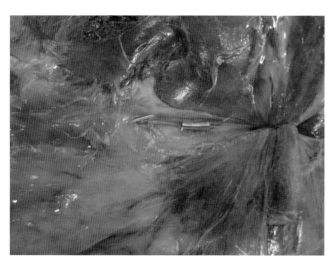

◀ **Figure 14.35** Clips after laparoscopic cholecystectomy

Laparoscopic cholecystectomy is a common surgical procedure. The surgical scars left on the anterior abdominal wall are small and easily overlooked at autopsy. The gallbladder may be absent at autopsy as a result of surgical removal, congenital absence (rare), or marked fibrosis secondary to chronic cholecystitis. The presence of metal or plastic clips on the bile ducts and vessels adjacent to the gallbladder bed allows one to identify confidently that the patient has undergone a cholecystectomy.

Genitourinary System

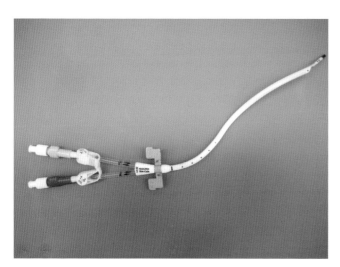

◀ **Figure 14.36** Temporary dialysis line

Although many patients in chronic renal failure are monitored over months or years and it is possible to prepare for the time when hemodialysis becomes necessary by creating arteriovenous fistulas (see the following section), other patients suffer rapid and catastrophic renal failure requiring urgent dialysis. In such cases, a temporary method of dialysis can be used. The most common is a dual-lumen dialysis catheter that is commonly inserted into the femoral vein. Such a device is readily identifiable because the two tails of the catheter are red (for the "arterial" side) and blue (for the "venous" side). Such intravenous devices are not a long-term solution but are extremely valuable in the acute situation.

269

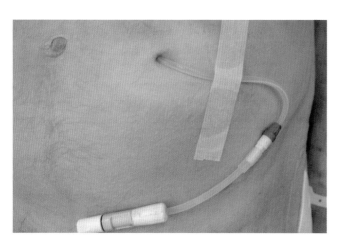

◀ **Figure 14.37a** Peritoneal dialysis catheter

Peritoneal dialysis is an alternative to traditional hemodialysis. It has the advantage of giving the patient greater freedom and independence because peritoneal dialysis can be undertaken at home rather than requiring attendance at a dialysis unit several days each week. Dialysis fluid flows into the peritoneal cavity via a surgically inserted abdominal catheter and drains in the same way.

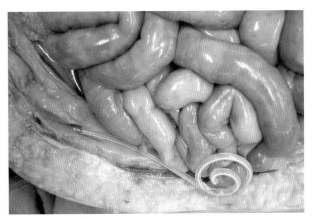

◀ Figure 14.37b Peritoneal dialysis catheter
Careful evisceration allows the pathologist to identify the location of the catheter within the peritoneum and permits it to be readily differentiated from, for example, a percutaneous endoscopic gastrostomy [PEG] tube (assuming that the dialysis catheter or PEG tube is appropriately sited). If there is doubt regarding the nature of the device, then medical records should be consulted.

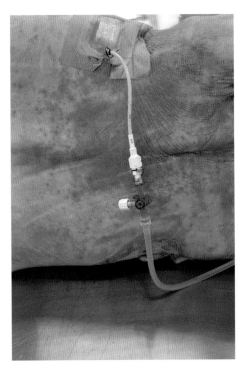

◀ Figure 14.38 Nephrostomy
Nephrostomies are formed primarily for drainage from the renal pelvis when there are obstructive lesions in the ureter such as stones. Nephrostomies usually consist of a catheter that sits within the renal pelvis and then traverses the tissue posterior to the kidney to leave the body on the back of the torso. For this reason the pathologist, having examined the back of the body carefully (as is appropriate in all autopsies), should be cautious in evisceration because rough handling of the diaphragm and upper peritoneal or retroperitoneal structures may dislodge the nephrostomy, thus rendering it impossible to identify whether it was appropriately sited or otherwise in life. This finding may be highly significant, depending on the clinical situation.

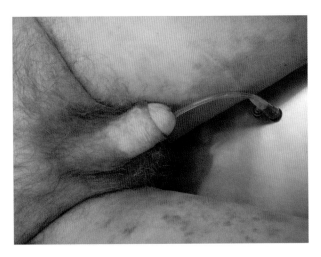

◀ Figure 14.39 Urethral urinary catheter
These catheters are commonly encountered by pathologists at autopsy. The typical latex catheter is used in the short term for drainage of the bladder or monitoring urine output. It consists of a tube for urinary drainage, often attached to a bag, and an inflatable balloon to ensure that it remains within the urinary bladder. Such catheters may cause problems if the balloon is inflated within the urethra (more commonly seen in men) or within the ureter, where inflation may lead to, in extreme circumstances, rupture of a ureter. If longer-term catheterization is required, a more robust Silastic catheter may be used, or a suprapubic catheter may be sited (see later). In addition, although urine from the bag is useless for bacteriological examination, should toxicological tests be required such a sample is perfectly acceptable.

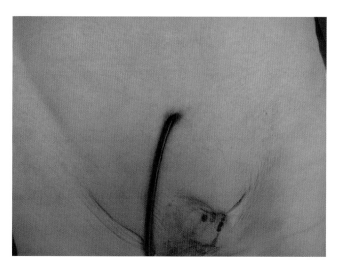

◀ Figure 14.40 Suprapubic catheter

Suprapubic catheters enter the bladder via the skin immediately above the pelvic brim. They are most commonly seen in individuals with long-term bladder dysfunction such as a "neurogenic bladder." If the case involves issues regarding the care provided to a vulnerable individual, the hygiene and care of the subrapubic catheter site on the skin would be worth noting.

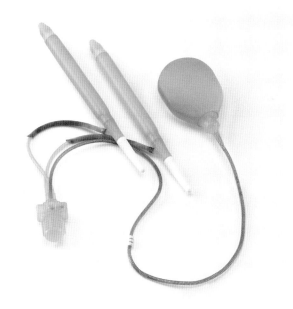

◀ Figure 14.41 Penile prostheses for erectile dysfunction

Several treatments for erectile dysfunction have been developed. The best known is sildenafil (Viagra), but direct injection of alprostadil (Caverject) can also be used. Less commonly, there can be surgical insertion of a tube or tubes into the shaft of the penis that are connected to a pump. This allows fluid to be pumped into the tubes to cause firmness of the penis and allow sexual activity. The author takes the view that unless the presence of such a device is of immediate relevance to the case, documenting it in a report that could be made public is somewhat unkind to grieving relatives. The author will write to the coroner to inform him or her that the device was present and the pathologist has not "missed" it but considers it unnecessary in many cases to highlight. (Image courtesy of American Medical Systems, Minnetonka, MN.)

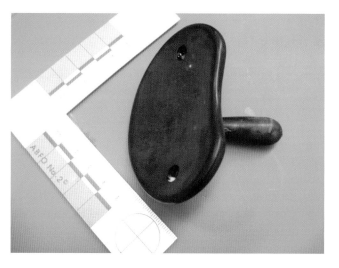

◀ Figure 14.42 Shelf pessary

Shelf pessaries are devices inserted into the vagina to support the pelvic organs, particularly the uterus and cervix, in patients who have prolapse. As the name suggests, the pessary is a shelf-like structure with a handle for insertion and removal.

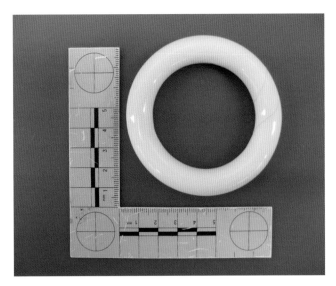

◀ **Figure 14.43** Ring pessary
Ring pessaries, again as the name suggests, are formed of a ring that is inserted into the vagina to support the cervix and uterus. Neither shelf nor ring pessaries are usually of great significance in the autopsy examination.

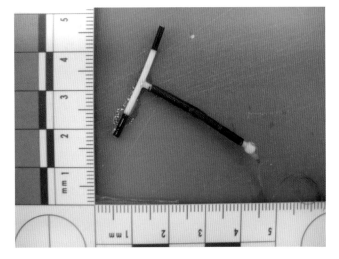

◀ **Figure 14.44** Intrauterine contraceptive device
Intrauterine contraceptive devices (IUCDs) are small, usually T-shaped devices inserted into the uterine cavity to prevent implantation of the fertilized ovum. The "simplest" form of the device is a coil of copper wire (hence the common description of an IUCD as a "coil"), although more recent variants such as the Mirena (Bayer HealthCare Pharmaceuticals, Whippany, NJ) elute hormones that act locally on the endometrium and, in addition to acting as a contraceptive, have a use in the treatment of menorrhagia. (There may be discussion within society as to whether these devices are contraceptive or abortifacient. Such discussions are beyond the scope of this book, and therefore "contraceptive" is used in the text.) The IUCD typically has a wire or wires that protrude through the cervical os to allow removal. As with all medical devices, the autopsy examination should confirm whether the IUCD is correctly sited.

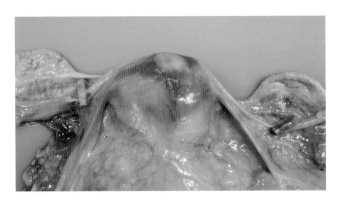

◀ **Figure 14.45** Fallopian tube sterilization clips
Clipping of the fallopian tubes to prevent ova from traveling from the ovary to the uterine cavity is used as a form of contraception, with or without surgical transection of the tube. As the pelvic organs are examined, the presence of these small clips surrounding the fallopian tubes should be readily apparent to the prosector. Fallopian tube ligation is rarely of direct pathological significance, although a malpositioned clip (e.g., a clip applied to the broad ligament rather than to the fallopian tube) may be of medicolegal importance, and the presence of such clips and their location should be noted in autopsy reports.

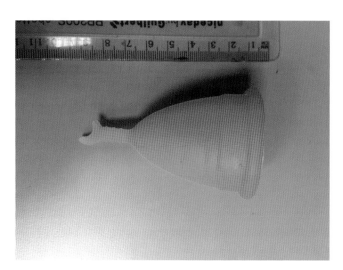

◀ **Figure 14.46** Menstrual cap

Whereas tampons are disposable devices, some women choose to use a reusable menstrual cup during the menses. This is a small plastic cup that collects the menstrual flow for disposal at a practical time. Such devices may not be immediately apparent externally and are rarely of pathological significance.

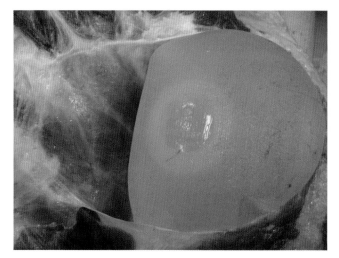

◀ **Figure 14.47a** Breast implant

Breast implants may be inserted purely for cosmetic reasons in healthy women or in reconstruction after mastectomy. Most implants are made of silicone, although some saline-based implants exist. If an implant has been inserted during reconstruction after surgery, then scars associated with that surgery are often apparent. Modern implants may produce a very natural appearance and consistency. Careful examination of the inframammary fold will reveal the surgical scars from the insertion of the prosthesis. Because the insertion of such implants is for cosmetic purposes (either purely cosmetic or in reconstruction after surgery), these scars are often very fine and easily missed in a cursory external examination.

273

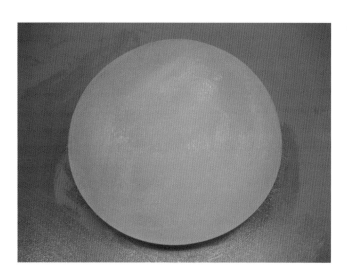

◀ **Figure 14.47b** Breast implant

Locomotor System

◀ **Figure 14.48a** Joint replacement—hip
Joint replacements are very common and most often involve the hips or knees. Surgical scars on the lateral aspects of the hips or over the anterior aspects of the knees are frequent autopsy findings. In most cases where the joint replacement surgery has healed, it is not necessary to examine the prosthesis directly (unless specifically indicated), but if death has occurred shortly after surgery, it is appropriate to incise and examine the operative site for evidence of infection or excessive hemorrhage.

◀ **Figure 14.48b** Joint replacement—knee

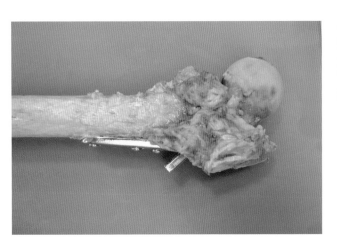

◀ **Figure 14.49a** Dynamic hip screw
Dynamic hip screws are used in the surgical management of intertrochanteric femoral fractures. The screw is inserted into the femoral neck and is held in place by a plate secured to the femoral shaft.

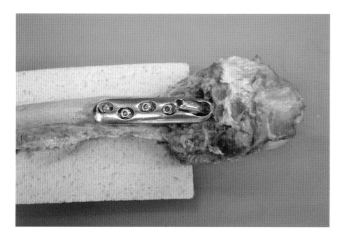

◀ **Figure 14.49b** Dynamic hip screw

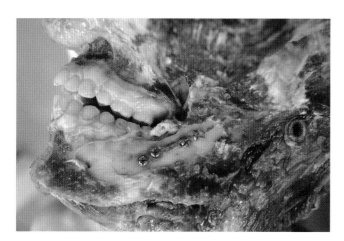

◀ **Figure 14.50** Plates
Surgical plates may be applied to any bone to stabilize fractures. They are commonly seen in the long bones or the spine. Such plates may represent a nidus for infection, in which case dissection and sampling of that region histologically and microbiologically are appropriate. If the identification of the deceased is in question, the presence of such plates (most easily visualized radiologically) may assist in the identification process, or at the very least exclude possible candidates for the body.

275

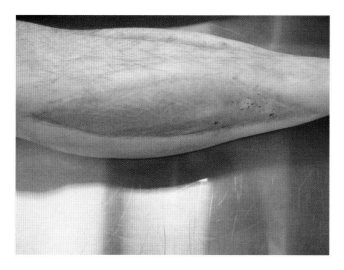

◀ **Figure 14.51** Fasciotomy scars
Patients who develop compartment syndrome are treated with fasciotomies in which deep linear longitudinal incisions are made in the skin and underlying fascia to lower the pressure within a fascial compartment of a limb. The surgical incisions are allowed to heal by secondary intention, with or without skin grafting, thus resulting in characteristic large, elliptical scars.

Nervous System

◄ **Figure 14.52** Cerebrospinal fluid shunt
Cerebrospinal fluid (CSF) shunts (also known as ventriculoperitoneal shunts or V-P shunts) are used in cases of chronic hydrocephalus where increased intracranial pressure is an issue (rather than hydrocephalus *ex vacuo*, where there is an increase in the CSF to fill dilated ventricles caused by tissue loss in cases of cerebral atrophy). Such shunts redirect CSF from the cerebral ventricles to the peritoneal cavity, where it is reabsorbed. They traverse the body under the skin and should be meticulously dissected out to identify any possible sites of occlusion or infection.

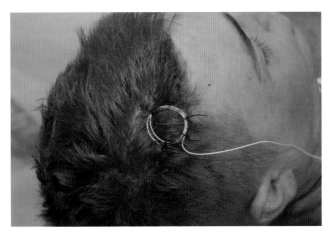

◄ **Figure 14.53** Intracranial pressure monitor
Also known as intracranial pressure (ICP) bolts, these devices are pressure transducers inserted to allow monitoring of the ICP, usually in patients who have sustained a head injury. They are inserted through the scalp and then through a narrow burr hole in the skull. At autopsy, only the transducer and associated wires are usually present. In such patients, the medical notes should be available, but if not they should be obtained and examined for evidence of the ICP of the patient before death because such evidence may assist greatly in determining the cause of death.

◄ **Figure 14.54a** Embolization coils
Coil embolization involves the endovascular insertion of stainless steel or platinum coils into an aneurysm or arteriovenous malformation. These coils were extracted from a bronchial artery aneurysm, but similar coils may be found in berry aneurysms.

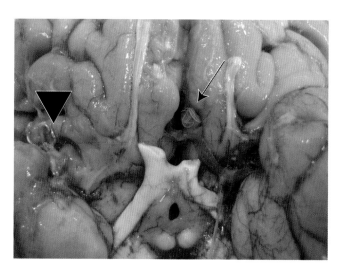

◀ **Figure 14.54b** Embolization coils
In this example, embolization coils can be seen within a berry aneurysm of the left anterior cerebral artery. Note also the surgical clip on an aneurysm of the right middle cerebral artery.

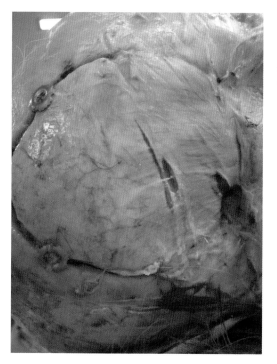

◀ **Figure 14.55a** Craniotomy
In patients who require neurosurgery, craniotomy is often performed. A flap of the calvaria is removed to permit access to the brain and is then replaced. The replaced bone flap is secured in place with metal screws, rivets, or wires.

277

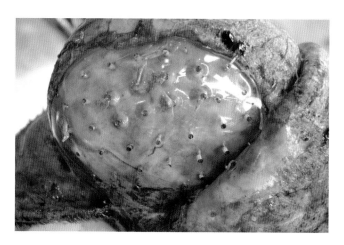

◀ **Figure 14.55b** Craniotomy
Alternatively, the removed bone may be replaced with a prosthesis.

◀ **Figure 14.56** Burr holes
Burr holes are used in the neurosurgical management of patients with extradural or subdural hematomas. A drill is used to remove a circle of bone approximately 1 cm in diameter. The smaller hole to the right of the burr hole in this image was used for the placement of an intracranial pressure monitor.

Transplantation

◀ **Figure 14.57** Torso after organ harvesting
In this patient, organ harvesting was performed following confirmation of brainstem death. The heart, liver, and kidneys have been removed. The right hemidiaphragm has been disrupted, and the small intestine lies within the right pleural cavity. The lungs are focally atelectatic. The spleen and pancreas lie free within the left upper quadrant of the abdominal cavity. There is a small volume of blood in the retroperitoneal space.

278

References

1. Burton JL. Perioperative and postoperative deaths. In: Burton JL, Rutty GN, editors. *The hospital autopsy: a manual of fundamental autopsy practice.* 3rd ed. London: Hodder Arnold; 2010:269–270.
2. Blue Neem Medical Devices. Biliary stent. Available at: http://www.indiamart.com/bnmdpvtltd/gastroenterology-products.html. Accessed January 14, 2015.

Index